010101001010111010101
101010100101001010010101
001001001010010100100 1
0000100111101111101001
0011111101111010100101 0
0101001001001010010100
101010100010101010100101
010010010010101010101000
101 01000101   010

01   01
001   010010   010
0101 1010111010 0100
110101000010101010100101
011110101011010101010010
100101001010010010100101
00101001001000010011 11
1000101011101010101111
0100101011101011010011
0101000010101010010101
1110101011010101001010
0101001010010010010100
1010010010000100100101
0010010101110101101001
1010100001010101001010
1110101011101010100101
0010100101001001001010
0101001001000010010011
1000111001001010101010
1000110101101110001010
1010101000001110101000
1000101010100100100100
1001001010010100100100

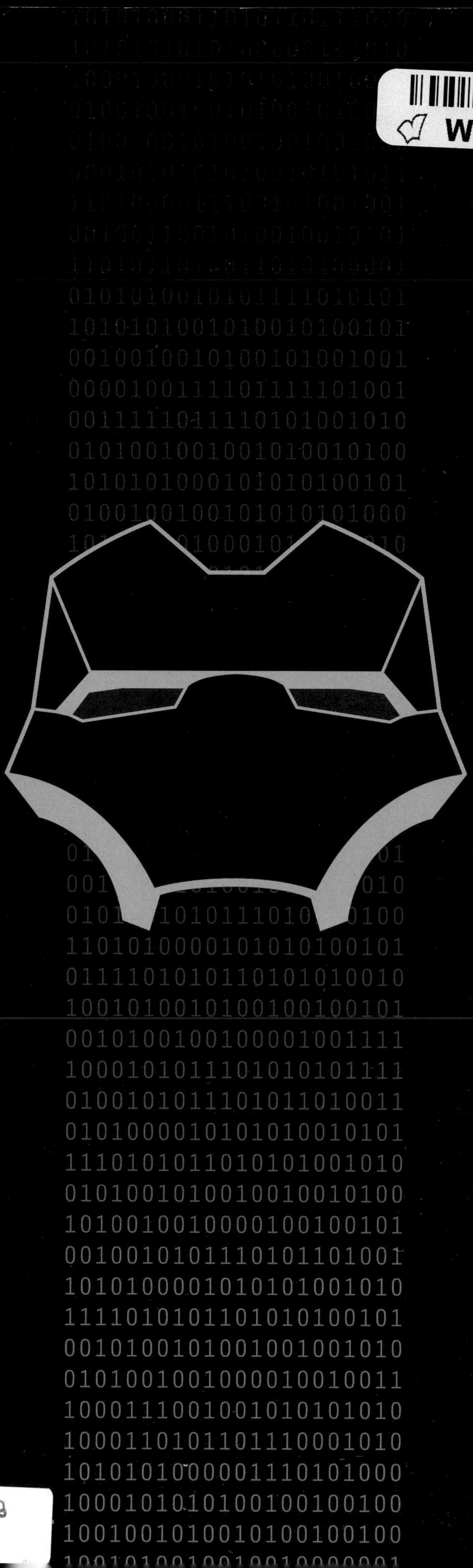

Billionaire playboy and genius industrialist Tony Stark was kidnapped during a routine weapons test. His captors attempted to force him to build a weapon of mass destruction. Instead he created a powered suit of armor that saved his life. From that day on, he used the suit to protect the world as the invincible Avenger Iron Man.

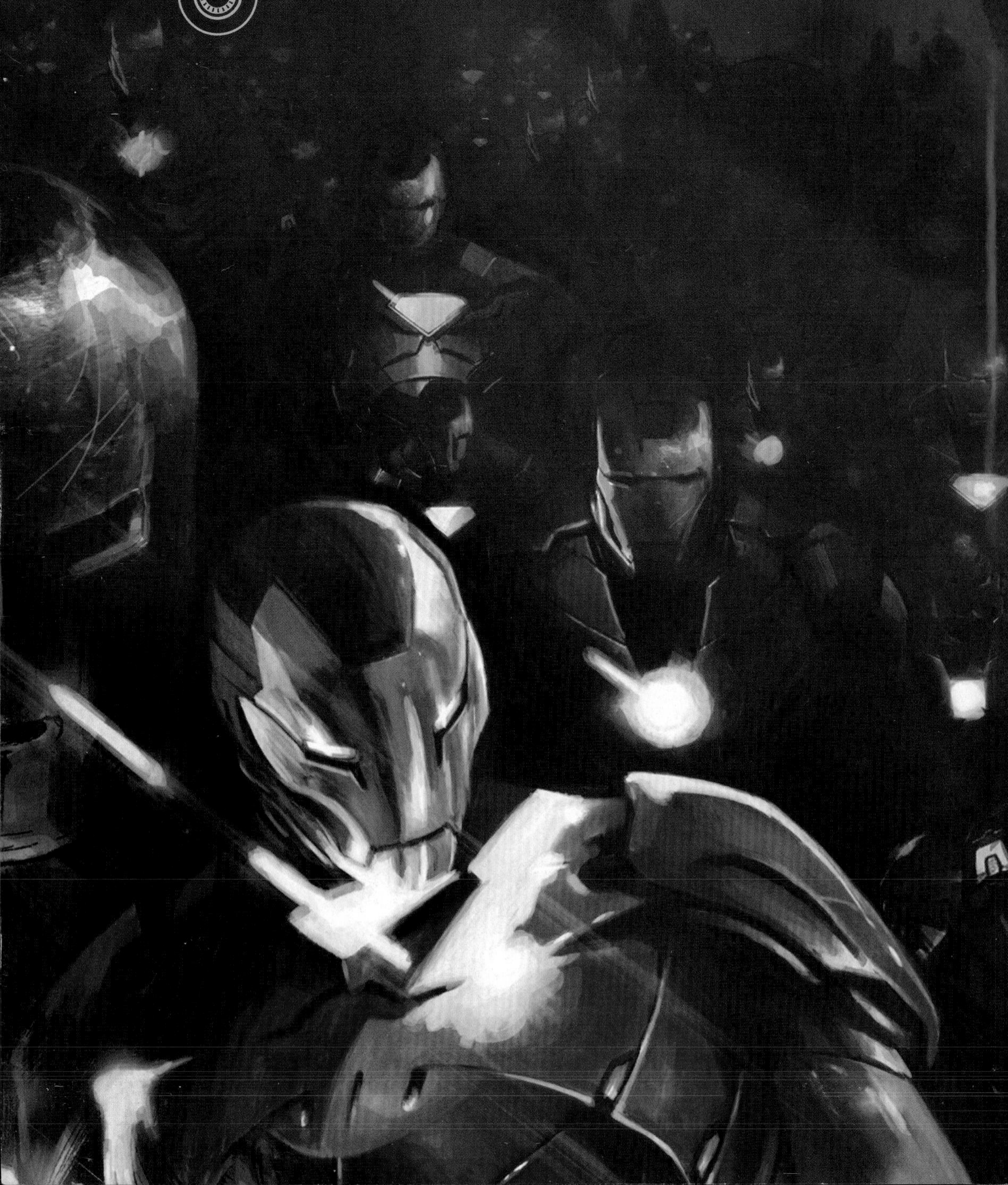

TONY STARK

IRON MAN

SELF-MADE MAN

WRITER
DAN SLOTT

ISSUES #1-4

ARTIST
VALERIO SCHITI
COLOR ARTISTS
EDGAR DELGADO WITH
RACHELLE ROSENBERG (#3)

LETTERERS
VC'S JOE CARAMAGNA (#1-2, #4-5)
& TRAVIS LANHAM (#3)

ISSUE #5

ARTISTS
**MAX DUNBAR &
GANG HYUK LIM**
COLOR ARTIST
DONO SÁNCHEZ-ALMARA

COVER ART
ALEXANDER LOZANO
ASSOCIATE EDITOR
ALANNA SMITH
EDITOR
TOM BREVOORT

IRON MAN created by STAN LEE, LARRY LIEBER, DON HECK & JACK KIRBY

TONY STARK: IRON MAN VOL. 1 — SELF-MADE MAN. Contains material originally published in magazine form as TONY STARK: IRON MAN #1-5. First printing 2018. ISBN 978-1-302-91272-7. Published by MARVEL WORLDWIDE, INC., a subsidiary of MARVEL ENTERTAINMENT, LLC. OFFICE OF PUBLICATION: 135 West 50th Street, New York, NY 10020. Copyright © 2018 MARVEL No similarity between any of the names, characters, persons, and/or institutions in this magazine with those of any living or dead person or institution is intended, and any such similarity which may exist is purely coincidental. **Printed in Canada.** DAN BUCKLEY, President, Marvel Entertainment; JOHN NEE, Publisher; JOE QUESADA, Chief Creative Officer; TOM BREVOORT, SVP of Publishing; DAVID BOGART, SVP of Business Affairs & Operations, Publishing & Partnership; DAVID GABRIEL, SVP of Sales & Marketing, Publishing; JEFF YOUNGQUIST, VP of Production & Special Projects; DAN CARR, Executive Director of Publishing Technology; ALEX MORALES, Director of Publishing Operations; DAN EDINGTON, Managing Editor; SUSAN CRESPI, Production Manager; STAN LEE, Chairman Emeritus. For information regarding advertising in Marvel Comics or on Marvel.com, please contact Vit DeBellis, Custom Solutions & Integrated Advertising Manager, at vdebellis@marvel.com. For Marvel subscription inquiries, please call 888-511-5480. **Manufactured between 11/9/2018 and 12/11/2018 by SOLISCO PRINTERS, SCOTT, QC, CANADA.**

10 9 8 7 6 5 4 3 2 1

Collection Editor: **JENNIFER GRÜNWALD**
Assistant Editor: **CAITLIN O'CONNELL**
Associate Managing Editor: **KATERI WOODY**
Editor, Special Projects: **MARK D. BEAZLEY**
VP Production & Special Projects: **JEFF YOUNGQUIST**
SVP Print, Sales & Marketing: **DAVID GABRIEL**
Book Designer: **JEFF POWELL**

Editor in Chief: **C.B. CEBULSKI**
Chief Creative Officer: **JOE QUESADA**
President: **DAN BUCKLEY**
Executive Producer: **ALAN FINE**

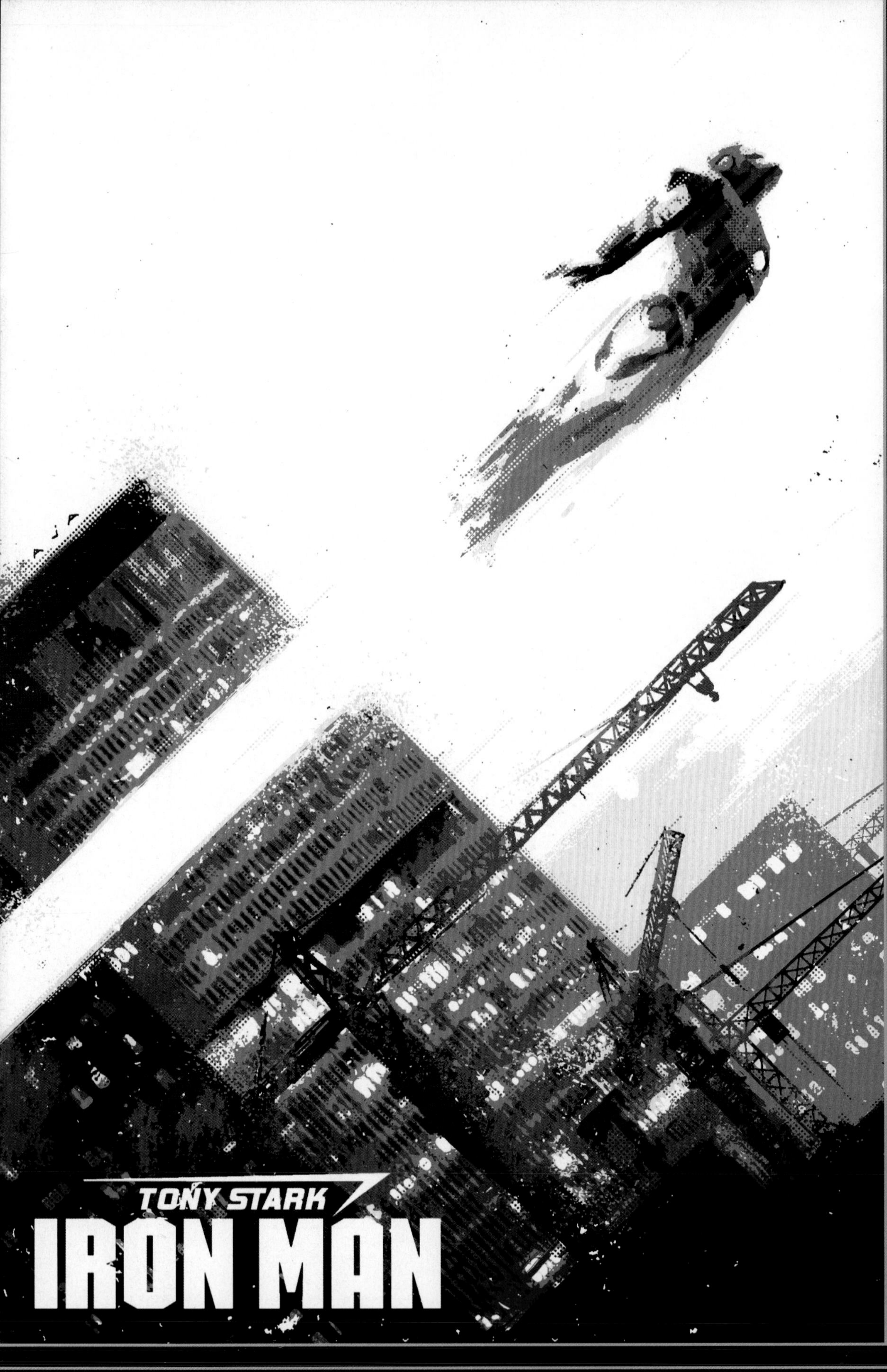
AJA
TONY STARK
IRON MAN

#1 VARIANT BY **DAVID AJA**

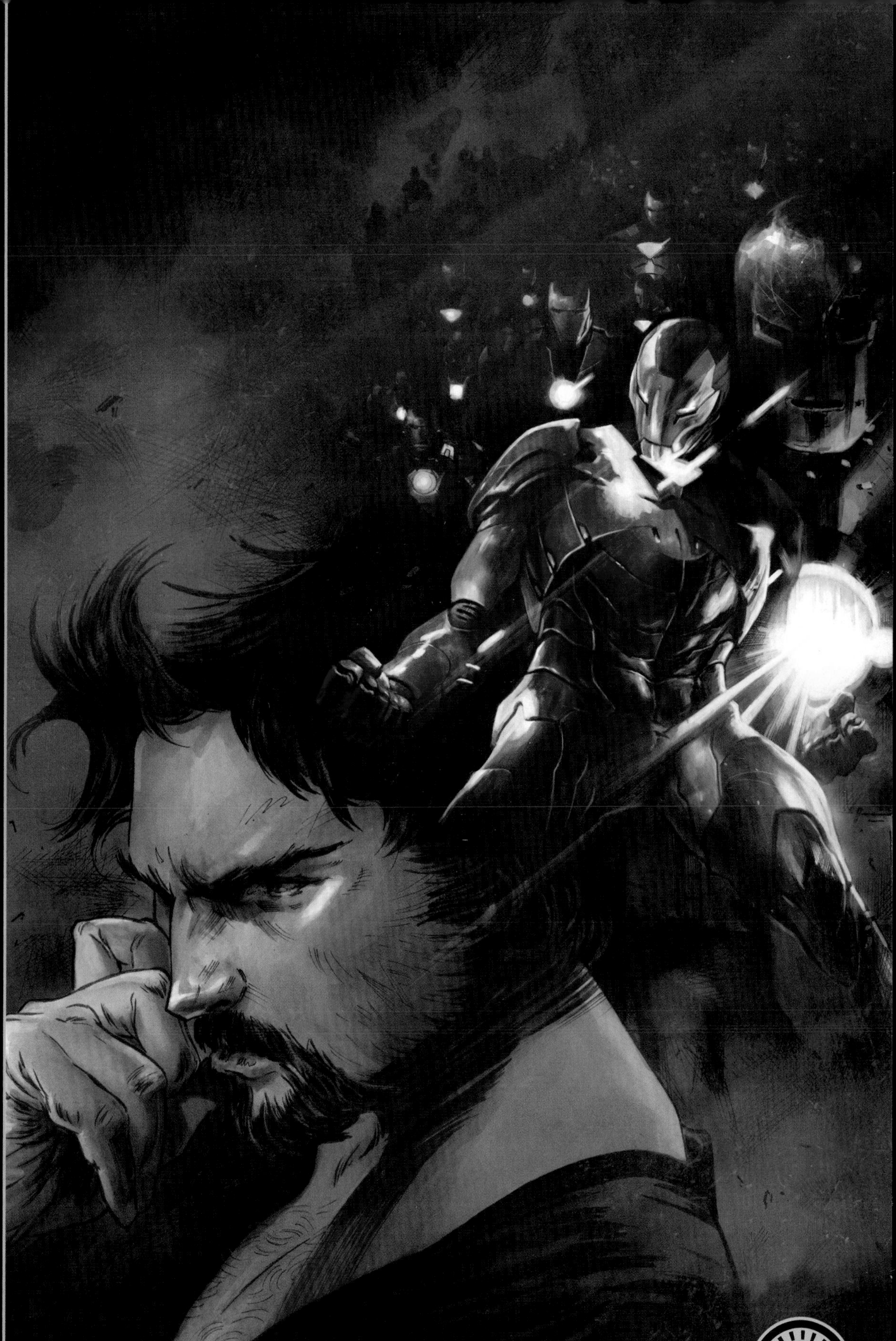

1

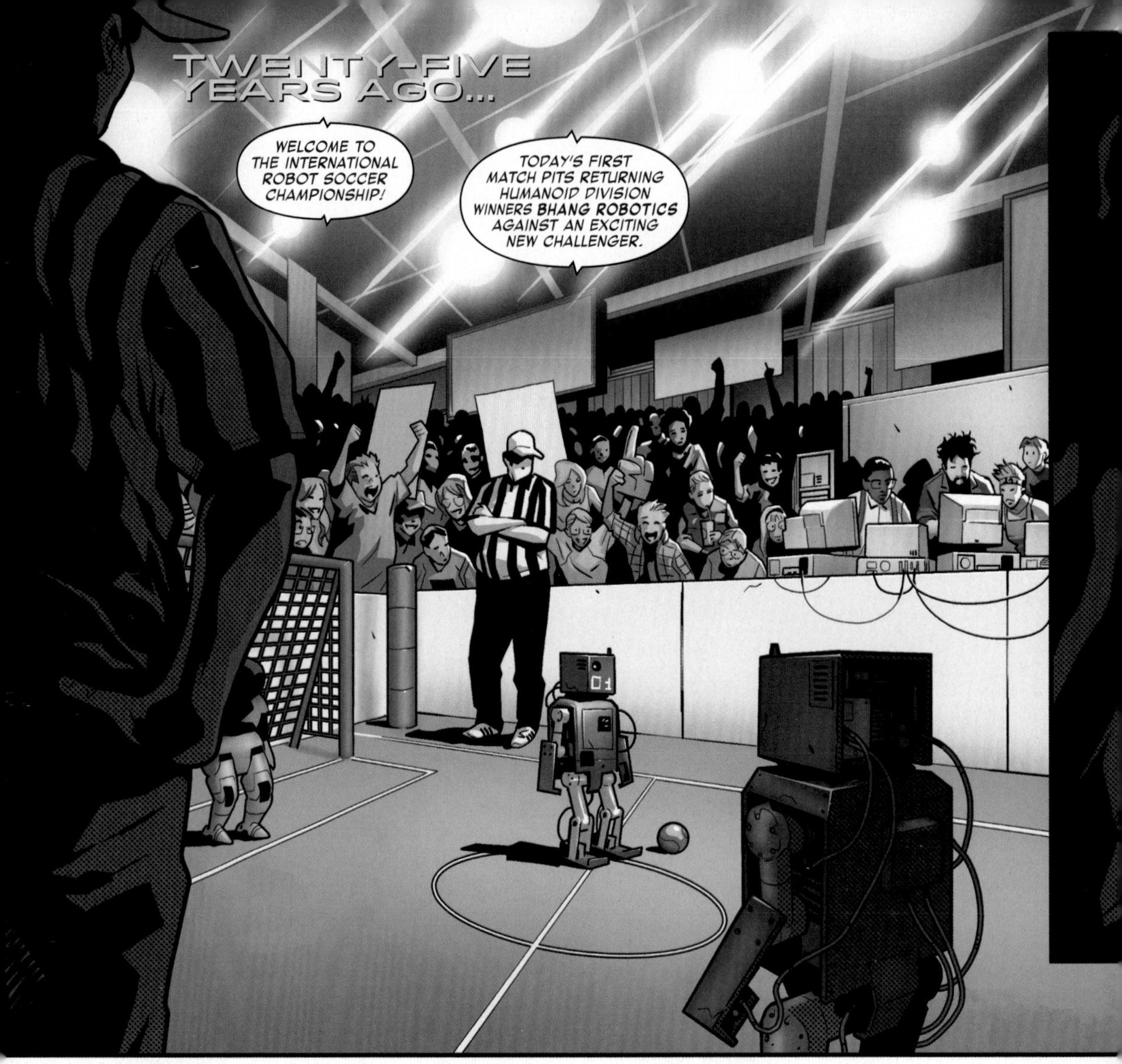
TWENTY-FIVE YEARS AGO...
WELCOME TO THE INTERNATIONAL ROBOT SOCCER CHAMPIONSHIP!
TODAY'S FIRST MATCH PITS RETURNING HUMANOID DIVISION WINNERS BHANG ROBOTICS AGAINST AN EXCITING NEW CHALLENGER.

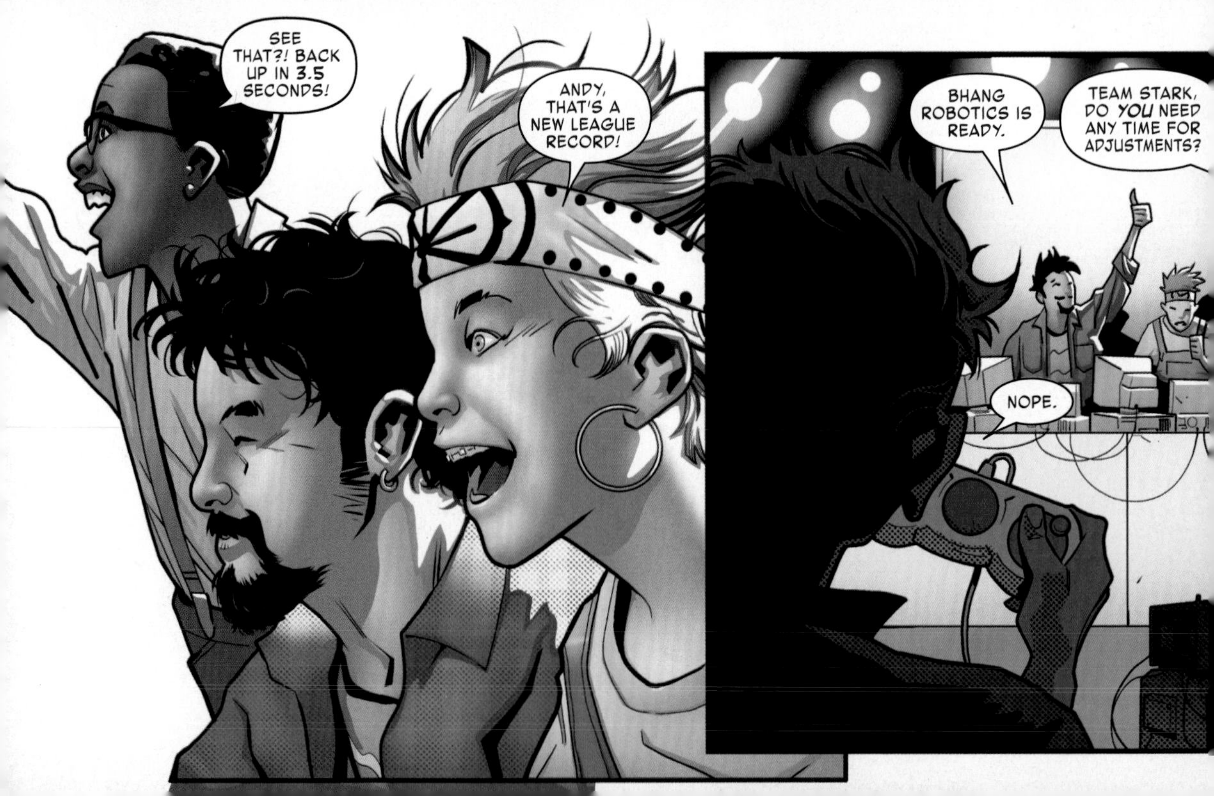
SEE THAT?! BACK UP IN 3.5 SECONDS!
ANDY, THAT'S A NEW LEAGUE RECORD!
BHANG ROBOTICS IS READY.
TEAM STARK, DO *YOU* NEED ANY TIME FOR ADJUSTMENTS?
NOPE.

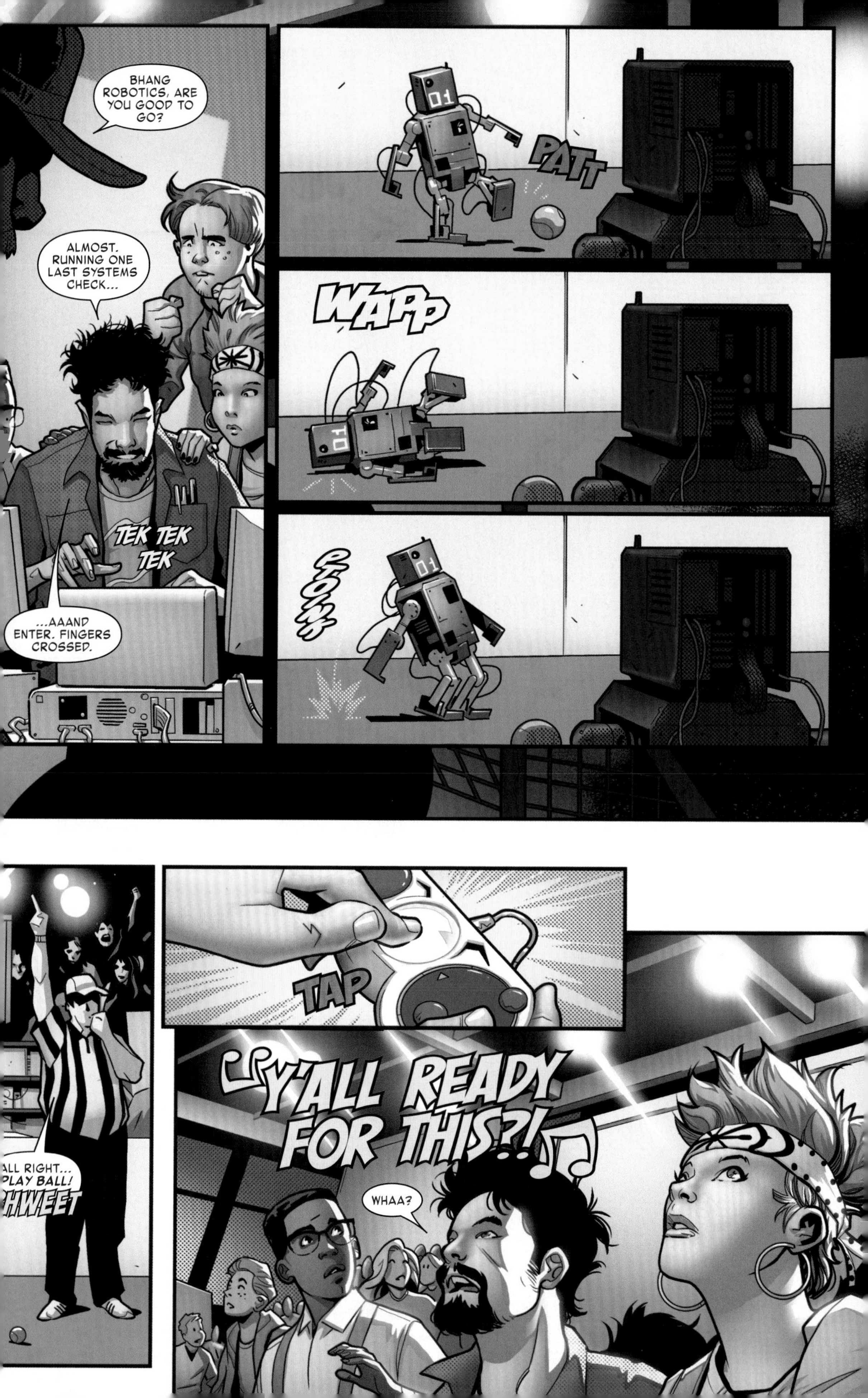
BHANG ROBOTICS, ARE YOU GOOD TO GO?
ALMOST. RUNNING ONE LAST SYSTEMS CHECK...
TEK TEK TEK
...AAAND ENTER. FINGERS CROSSED.
PATT
WARP
ALL RIGHT... PLAY BALL!
HWEET
TAP
Y'ALL READY FOR THIS?!
WHAA?

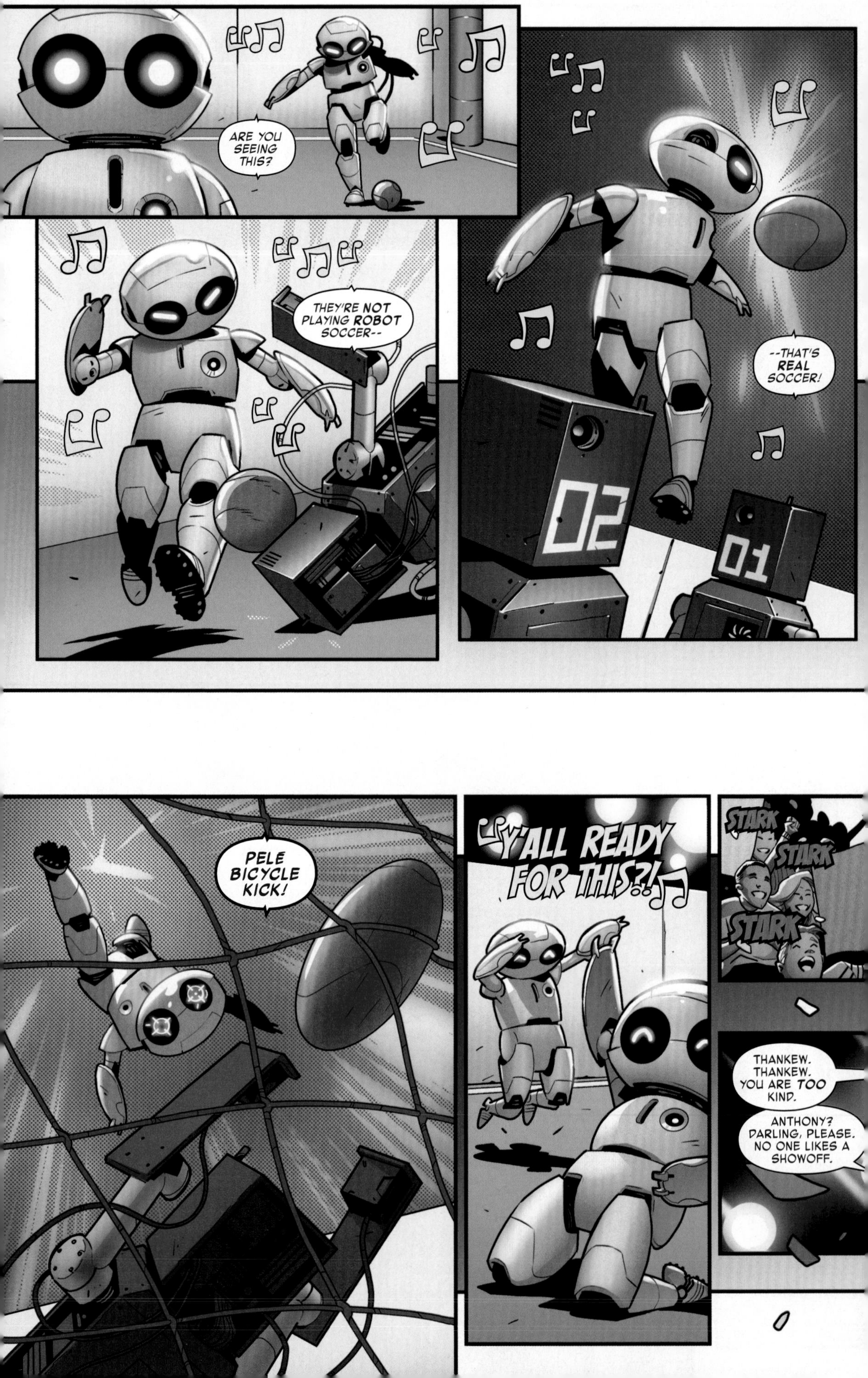
ARE YOU SEEING THIS?
THEY'RE NOT PLAYING ROBOT SOCCER--
--THAT'S REAL SOCCER!
02
01
PELE BICYCLE KICK!
Y'ALL READY FOR THIS?!
STARK
STARK
STARK
THANKEW. THANKEW. YOU ARE TOO KIND.
ANTHONY? DARLING, PLEASE. NO ONE LIKES A SHOWOFF.

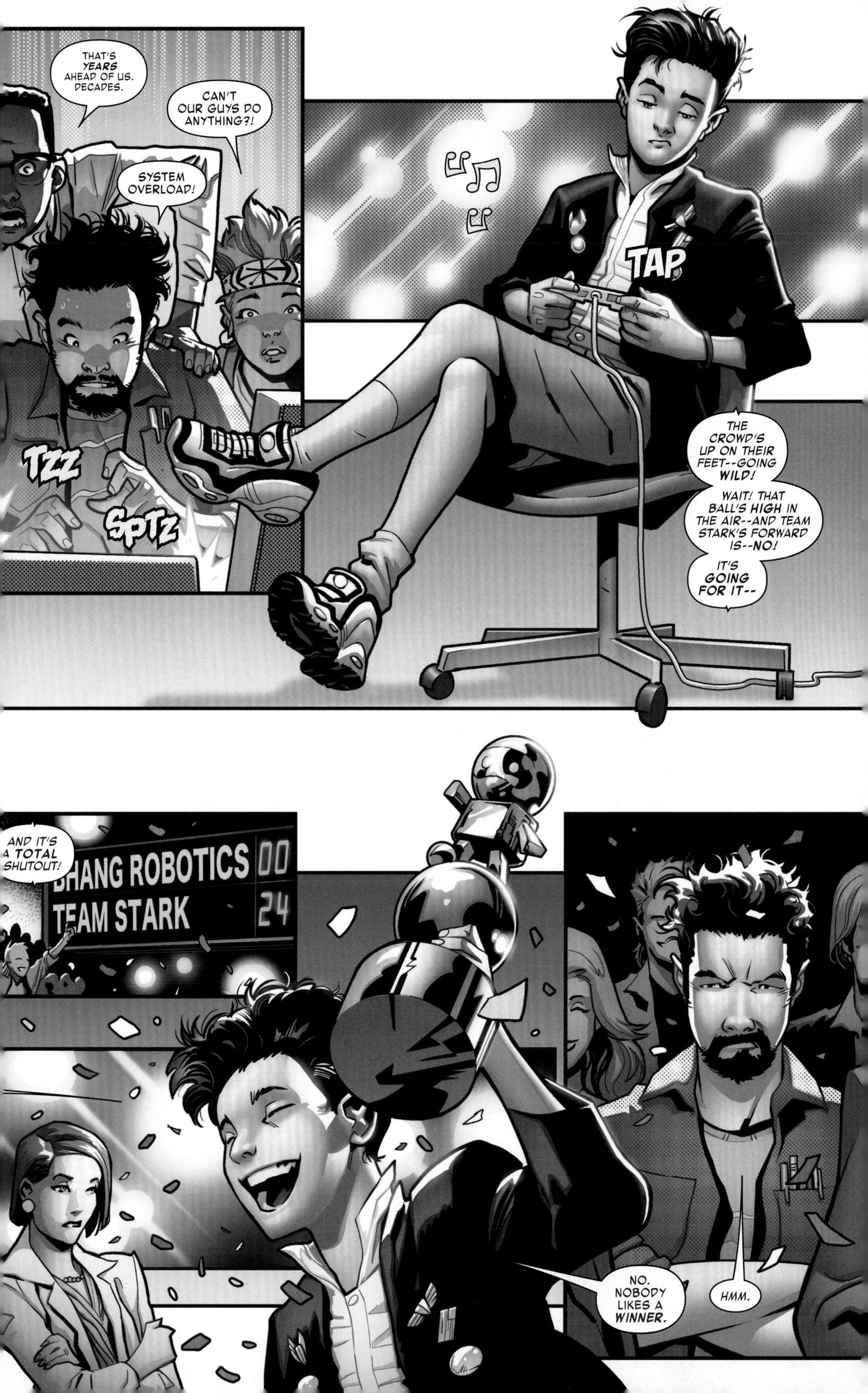
THAT'S YEARS AHEAD OF US. DECADES.
CAN'T OUR GUYS DO ANYTHING?!
SYSTEM OVERLOAD!
TZZ
SPTZ
TAP
THE CROWD'S UP ON THEIR FEET--GOING WILD!
WAIT! THAT BALL'S HIGH IN THE AIR--AND TEAM STARK'S FORWARD IS--NO!
IT'S GOING FOR IT--
AND IT'S A TOTAL SHUTOUT!
BHANG ROBOTICS 00
TEAM STARK 24
NO. NOBODY LIKES A WINNER.
HMM.

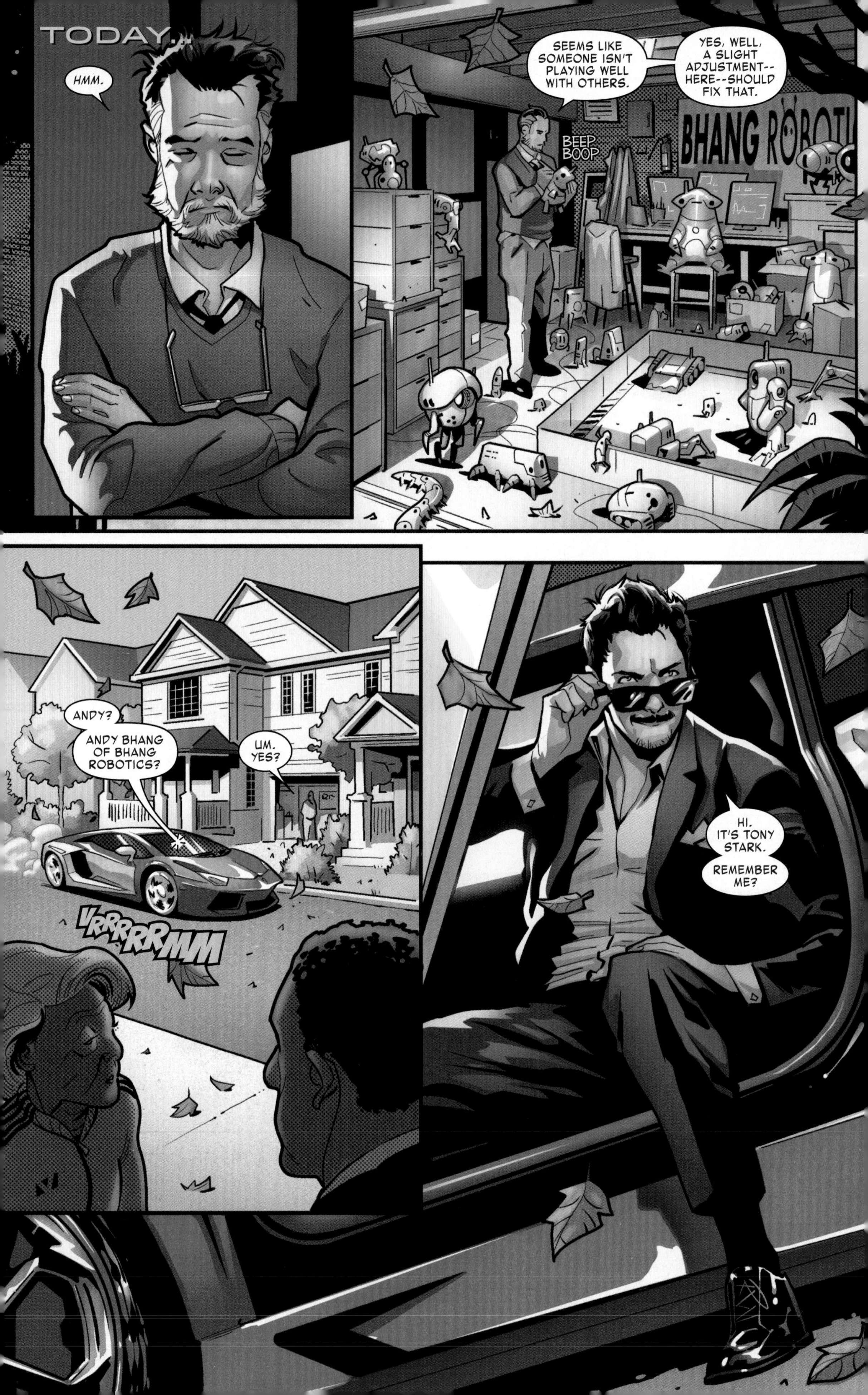
TODAY...
HMM.
SEEMS LIKE SOMEONE ISN'T PLAYING WELL WITH OTHERS.
YES, WELL, A SLIGHT ADJUSTMENT--HERE--SHOULD FIX THAT.
BEEP BOOP
BHANG ROBOTI
ANDY?
ANDY BHANG OF BHANG ROBOTICS?
UM. YES?
VRRRRRMM
HI. IT'S TONY STARK.
REMEMBER ME?

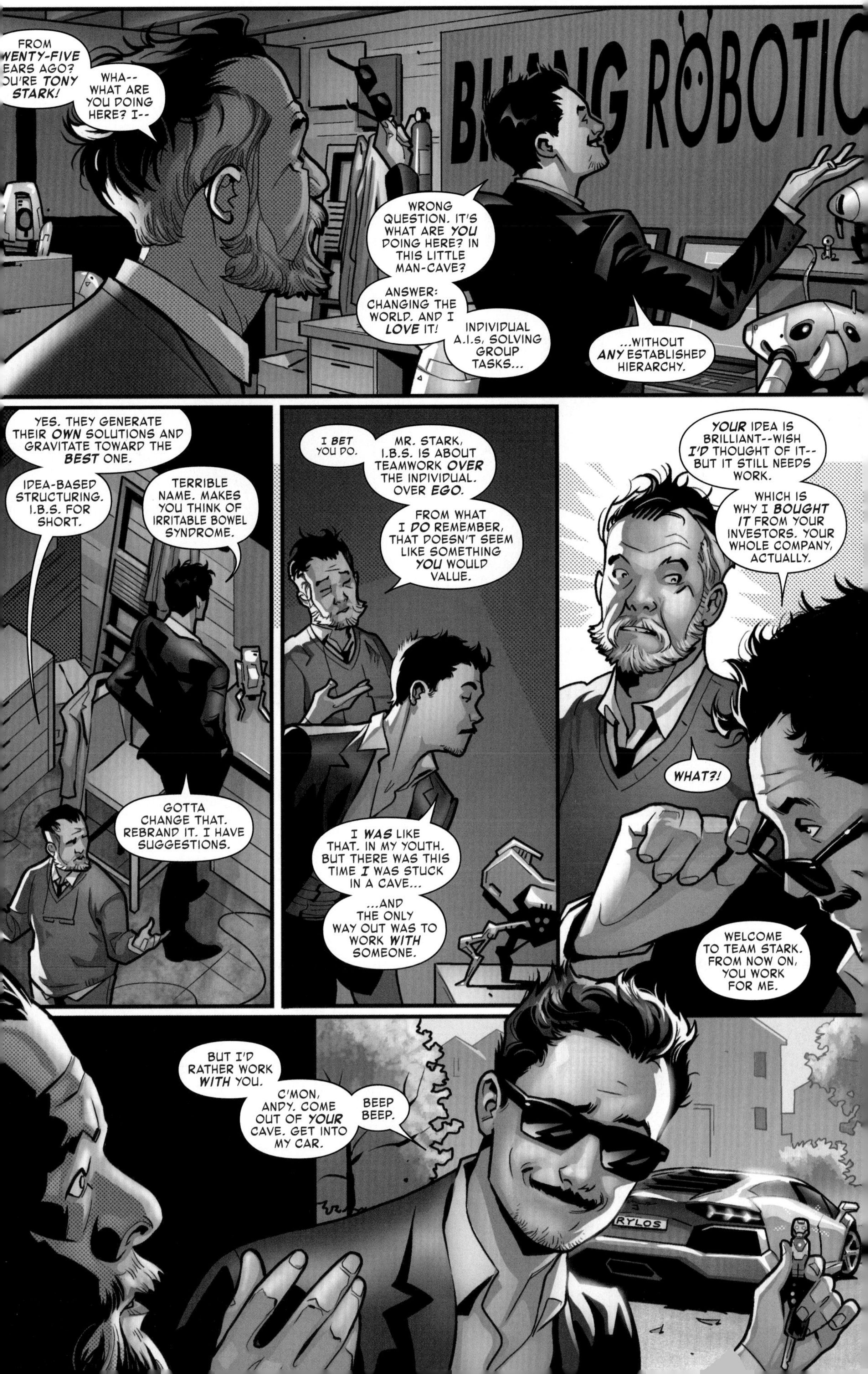
FROM WENTY-FIVE EARS AGO? OU'RE TONY STARK!
WHA-- WHAT ARE YOU DOING HERE? I--
BHANG ROBOTIC
WRONG QUESTION. IT'S WHAT ARE YOU DOING HERE? IN THIS LITTLE MAN-CAVE?
ANSWER: CHANGING THE WORLD. AND I LOVE IT!
INDIVIDUAL A.I.s, SOLVING GROUP TASKS...
...WITHOUT ANY ESTABLISHED HIERARCHY.
YES. THEY GENERATE THEIR OWN SOLUTIONS AND GRAVITATE TOWARD THE BEST ONE.
IDEA-BASED STRUCTURING. I.B.S. FOR SHORT.
TERRIBLE NAME. MAKES YOU THINK OF IRRITABLE BOWEL SYNDROME.
GOTTA CHANGE THAT. REBRAND IT. I HAVE SUGGESTIONS.
I BET YOU DO.
MR. STARK, I.B.S. IS ABOUT TEAMWORK OVER THE INDIVIDUAL. OVER EGO.
FROM WHAT I DO REMEMBER, THAT DOESN'T SEEM LIKE SOMETHING YOU WOULD VALUE.
I WAS LIKE THAT. IN MY YOUTH. BUT THERE WAS THIS TIME I WAS STUCK IN A CAVE...
...AND THE ONLY WAY OUT WAS TO WORK WITH SOMEONE.
YOUR IDEA IS BRILLIANT--WISH I'D THOUGHT OF IT--BUT IT STILL NEEDS WORK.
WHICH IS WHY I BOUGHT IT FROM YOUR INVESTORS. YOUR WHOLE COMPANY, ACTUALLY.
WHAT?!
WELCOME TO TEAM STARK. FROM NOW ON, YOU WORK FOR ME.
BUT I'D RATHER WORK WITH YOU.
C'MON, ANDY. COME OUT OF YOUR CAVE. GET INTO MY CAR.
BEEP BEEP.
RYLOS

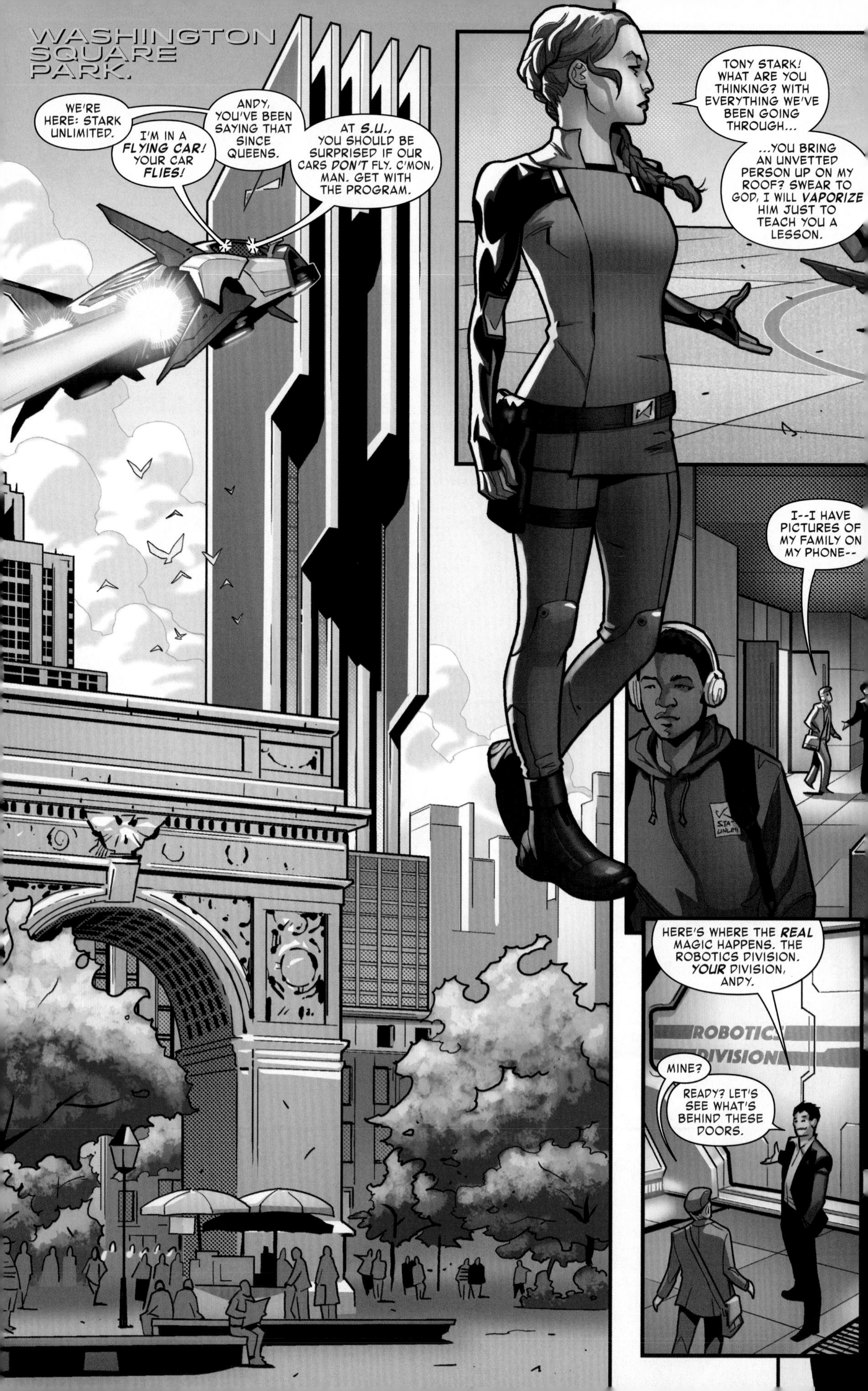
WASHINGTON SQUARE PARK.
WE'RE HERE: STARK UNLIMITED.
I'M IN A FLYING CAR! YOUR CAR FLIES!
ANDY, YOU'VE BEEN SAYING THAT SINCE QUEENS.
AT S.U., YOU SHOULD BE SURPRISED IF OUR CARS DON'T FLY. C'MON, MAN. GET WITH THE PROGRAM.
TONY STARK! WHAT ARE YOU THINKING? WITH EVERYTHING WE'VE BEEN GOING THROUGH...
...YOU BRING AN UNVETTED PERSON UP ON MY ROOF? SWEAR TO GOD, I WILL VAPORIZE HIM JUST TO TEACH YOU A LESSON.
I--I HAVE PICTURES OF MY FAMILY ON MY PHONE--
HERE'S WHERE THE REAL MAGIC HAPPENS. THE ROBOTICS DIVISION. YOUR DIVISION, ANDY.
ROBOTICS DIVISION
MINE?
READY? LET'S SEE WHAT'S BEHIND THESE DOORS.

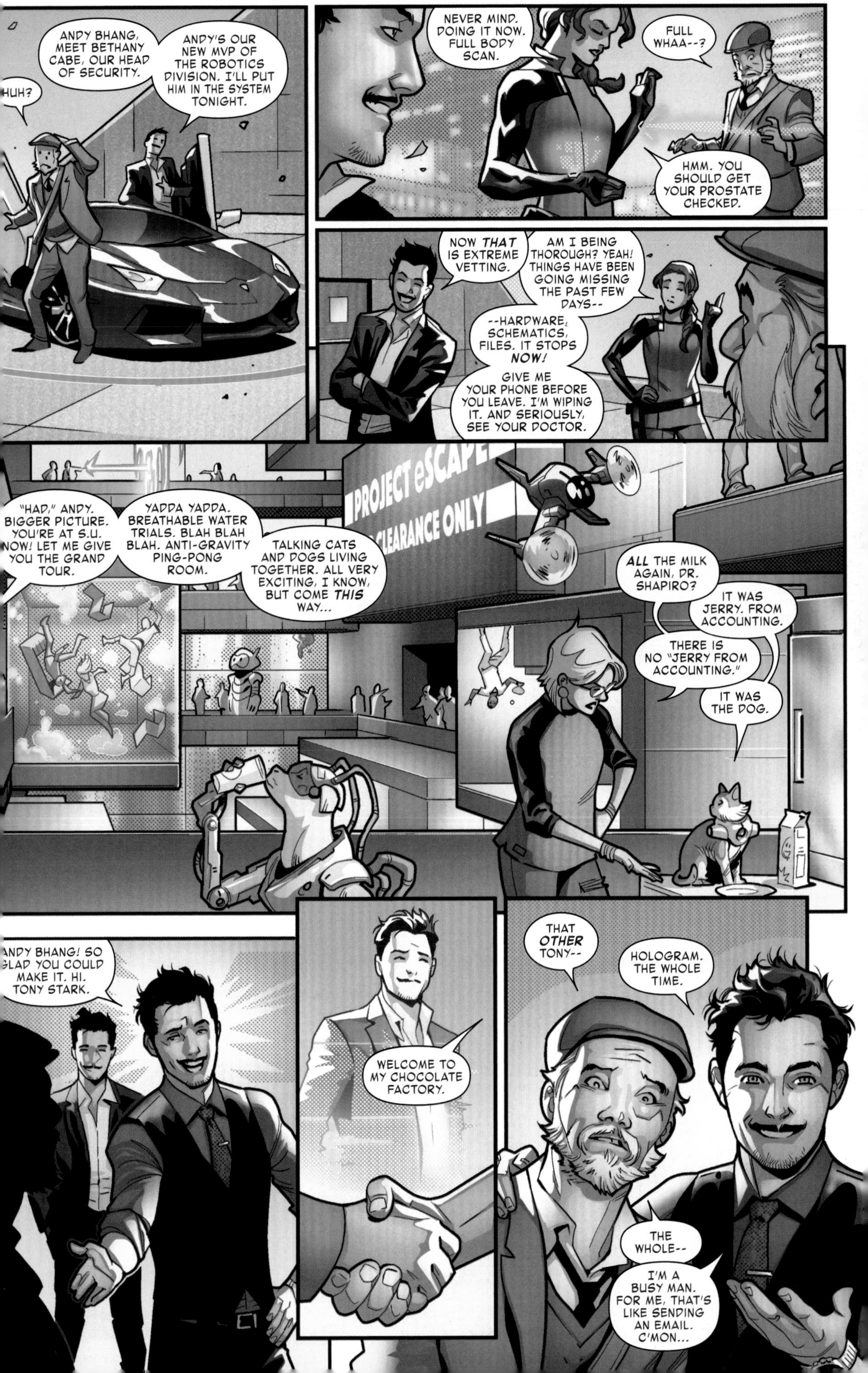

ANDY BHANG, MEET BETHANY CABE, OUR HEAD OF SECURITY.
HUH?
ANDY'S OUR NEW MVP OF THE ROBOTICS DIVISION. I'LL PUT HIM IN THE SYSTEM TONIGHT.
NEVER MIND. DOING IT NOW. FULL BODY SCAN.
FULL WHAA--?
HMM. YOU SHOULD GET YOUR PROSTATE CHECKED.
NOW *THAT* IS EXTREME VETTING.
AM I BEING THOROUGH? YEAH! THINGS HAVE BEEN GOING MISSING THE PAST FEW DAYS--
--HARDWARE, SCHEMATICS, FILES. IT STOPS *NOW!*
GIVE ME YOUR PHONE BEFORE YOU LEAVE. I'M WIPING IT. AND SERIOUSLY, SEE YOUR DOCTOR.
PROJECT eSCAPE
CLEARANCE ONLY
"HAD," ANDY. BIGGER PICTURE. YOU'RE AT S.U. NOW! LET ME GIVE YOU THE GRAND TOUR.
YADDA YADDA. BREATHABLE WATER TRIALS. BLAH BLAH BLAH. ANTI-GRAVITY PING-PONG ROOM.
TALKING CATS AND DOGS LIVING TOGETHER. ALL VERY EXCITING, I KNOW, BUT COME *THIS* WAY...
ALL THE MILK AGAIN, DR. SHAPIRO?
IT WAS JERRY. FROM ACCOUNTING.
THERE IS NO "JERRY FROM ACCOUNTING."
IT WAS THE DOG.
ANDY BHANG! SO GLAD YOU COULD MAKE IT. HI. TONY STARK.
WELCOME TO MY CHOCOLATE FACTORY.
THAT *OTHER* TONY--
HOLOGRAM. THE WHOLE TIME.
THE WHOLE--
I'M A BUSY MAN. FOR ME, THAT'S LIKE SENDING AN EMAIL. C'MON...

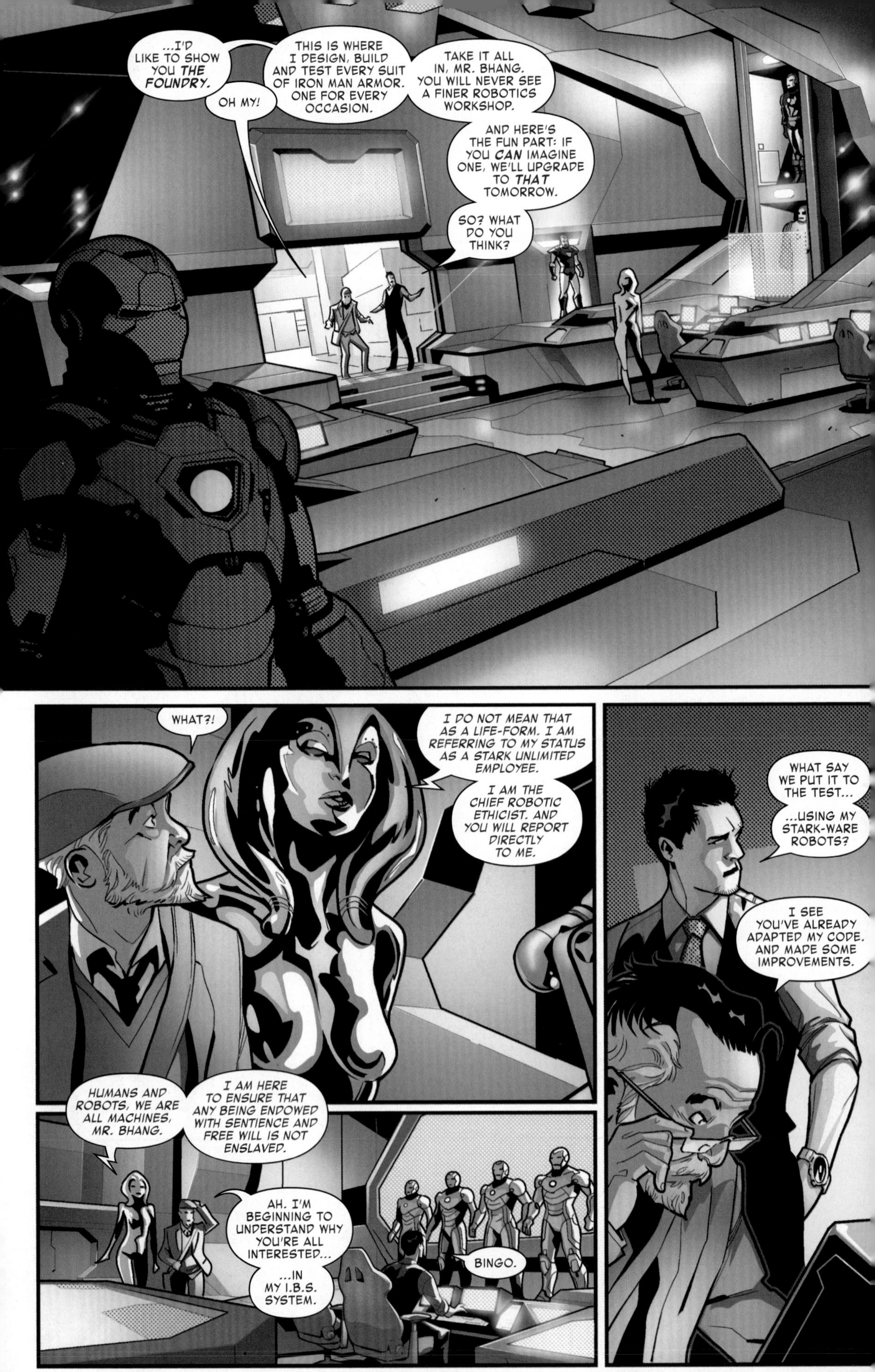
...I'D LIKE TO SHOW YOU THE FOUNDRY.
OH MY!
THIS IS WHERE I DESIGN, BUILD AND TEST EVERY SUIT OF IRON MAN ARMOR. ONE FOR EVERY OCCASION.
TAKE IT ALL IN, MR. BHANG. YOU WILL NEVER SEE A FINER ROBOTICS WORKSHOP.
AND HERE'S THE FUN PART: IF YOU CAN IMAGINE ONE, WE'LL UPGRADE TO THAT TOMORROW.
SO? WHAT DO YOU THINK?
WHAT?!
I DO NOT MEAN THAT AS A LIFE-FORM. I AM REFERRING TO MY STATUS AS A STARK UNLIMITED EMPLOYEE.
I AM THE CHIEF ROBOTIC ETHICIST. AND YOU WILL REPORT DIRECTLY TO ME.
HUMANS AND ROBOTS, WE ARE ALL MACHINES, MR. BHANG.
I AM HERE TO ENSURE THAT ANY BEING ENDOWED WITH SENTIENCE AND FREE WILL IS NOT ENSLAVED.
AH. I'M BEGINNING TO UNDERSTAND WHY YOU'RE ALL INTERESTED...
...IN MY I.B.S. SYSTEM.
BINGO.
WHAT SAY WE PUT IT TO THE TEST...
...USING MY STARK-WARE ROBOTS?
I SEE YOU'VE ALREADY ADAPTED MY CODE. AND MADE SOME IMPROVEMENTS.

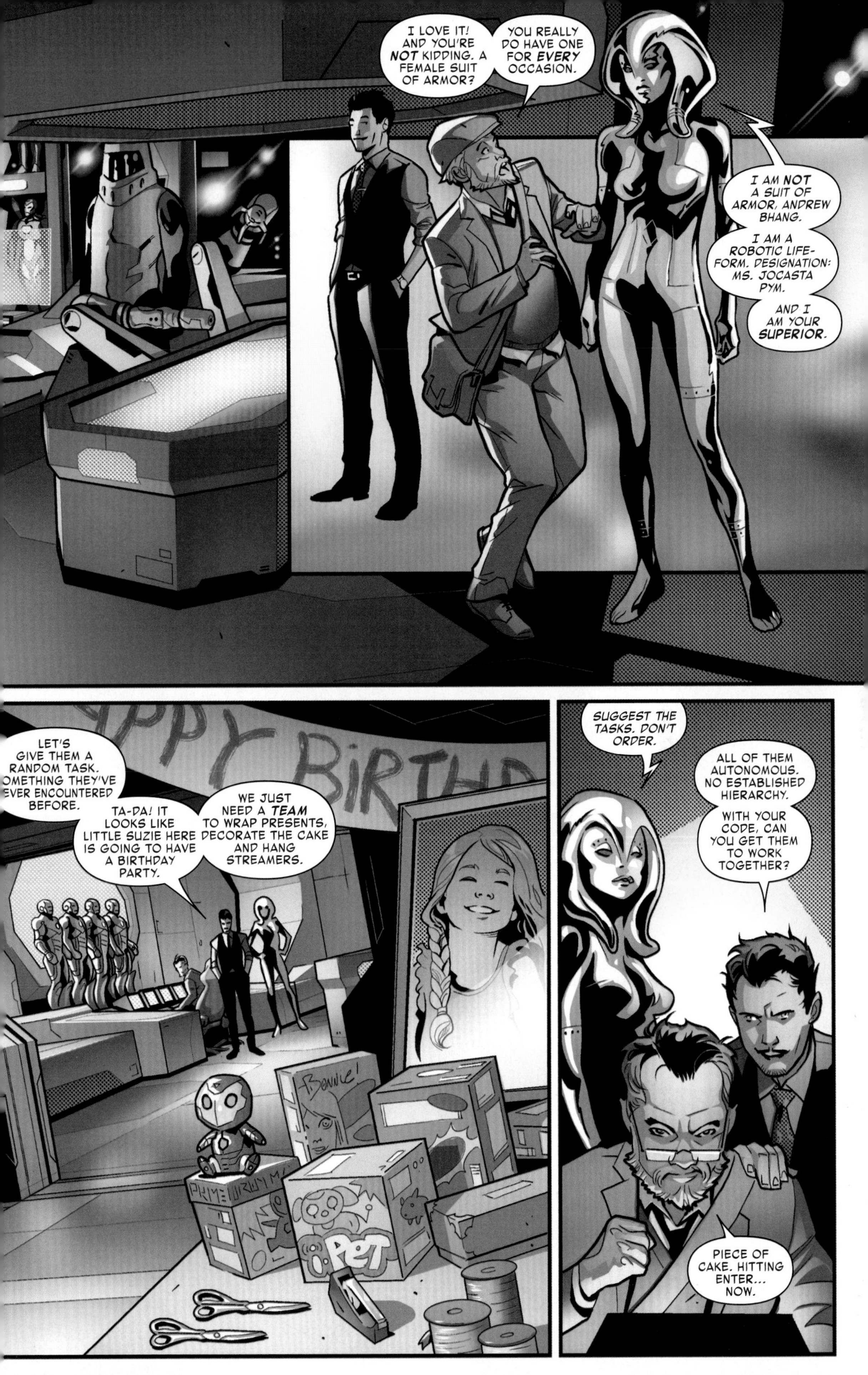
I LOVE IT! AND YOU'RE NOT KIDDING. A FEMALE SUIT OF ARMOR?
YOU REALLY DO HAVE ONE FOR EVERY OCCASION.
I AM NOT A SUIT OF ARMOR, ANDREW BHANG.
I AM A ROBOTIC LIFE-FORM. DESIGNATION: MS. JOCASTA PYM.
AND I AM YOUR SUPERIOR.
PPY BiRTHD
LET'S GIVE THEM A RANDOM TASK. OMETHING THEY'VE EVER ENCOUNTERED BEFORE.
TA-DA! IT LOOKS LIKE LITTLE SUZIE HERE IS GOING TO HAVE A BIRTHDAY PARTY.
WE JUST NEED A TEAM TO WRAP PRESENTS, DECORATE THE CAKE AND HANG STREAMERS.
PET
SUGGEST THE TASKS. DON'T ORDER.
ALL OF THEM AUTONOMOUS. NO ESTABLISHED HIERARCHY.
WITH YOUR CODE, CAN YOU GET THEM TO WORK TOGETHER?
PIECE OF CAKE. HITTING ENTER... NOW.

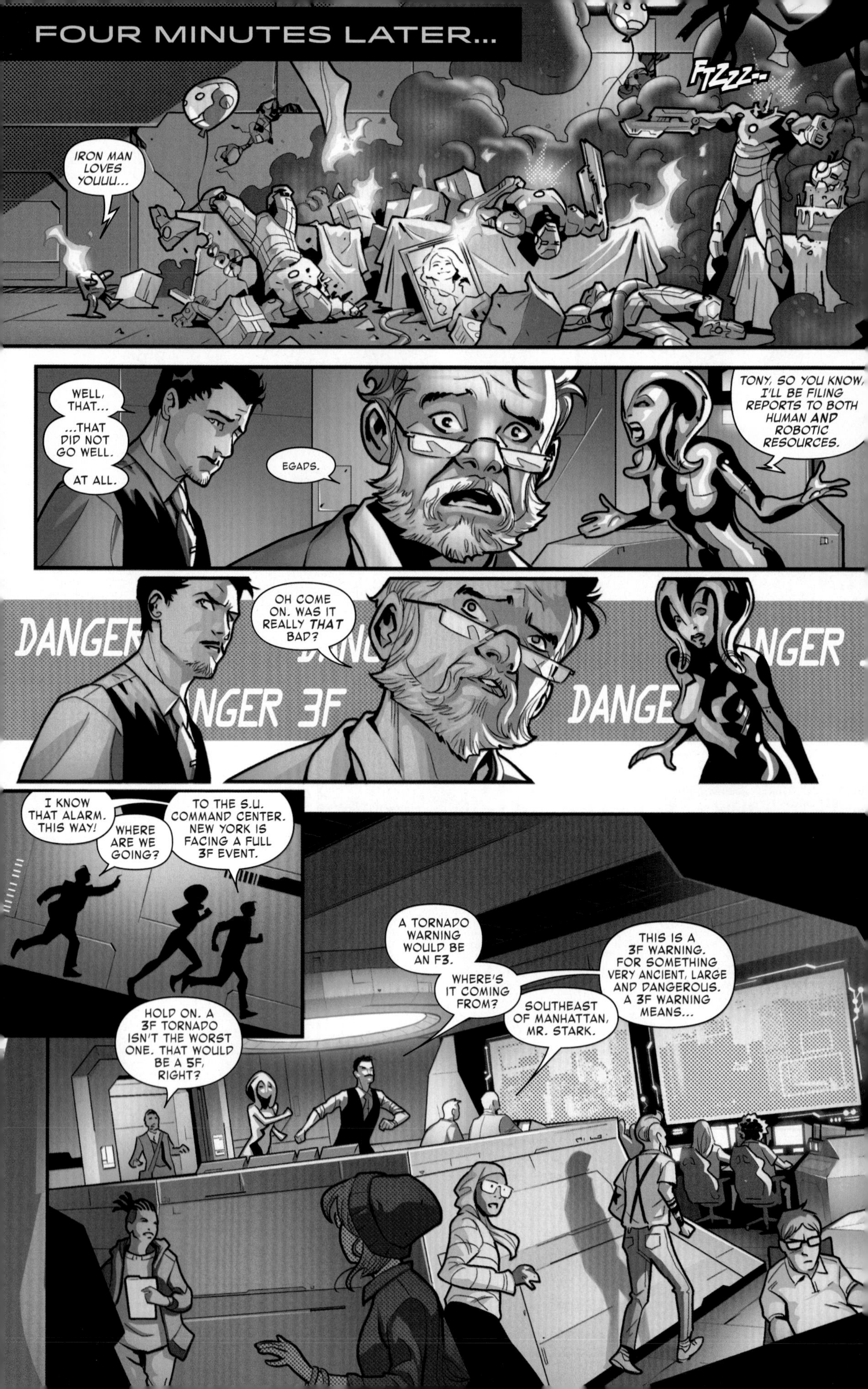
FOUR MINUTES LATER...
IRON MAN LOVES YOUUU...
FTZZZ--
WELL, THAT...
...THAT DID NOT GO WELL.
AT ALL.
EGADS.
TONY, SO YOU KNOW, I'LL BE FILING REPORTS TO BOTH HUMAN AND ROBOTIC RESOURCES.
OH COME ON. WAS IT REALLY THAT BAD?
DANGER
ANGER 3F
DANGE
ANGER
I KNOW THAT ALARM. THIS WAY!
WHERE ARE WE GOING?
TO THE S.U. COMMAND CENTER. NEW YORK IS FACING A FULL 3F EVENT.
HOLD ON. A 3F TORNADO ISN'T THE WORST ONE. THAT WOULD BE A 5F, RIGHT?
A TORNADO WARNING WOULD BE AN F3.
WHERE'S IT COMING FROM?
SOUTHEAST OF MANHATTAN, MR. STARK.
THIS IS A 3F WARNING. FOR SOMETHING VERY ANCIENT, LARGE AND DANGEROUS. A 3F WARNING MEANS...

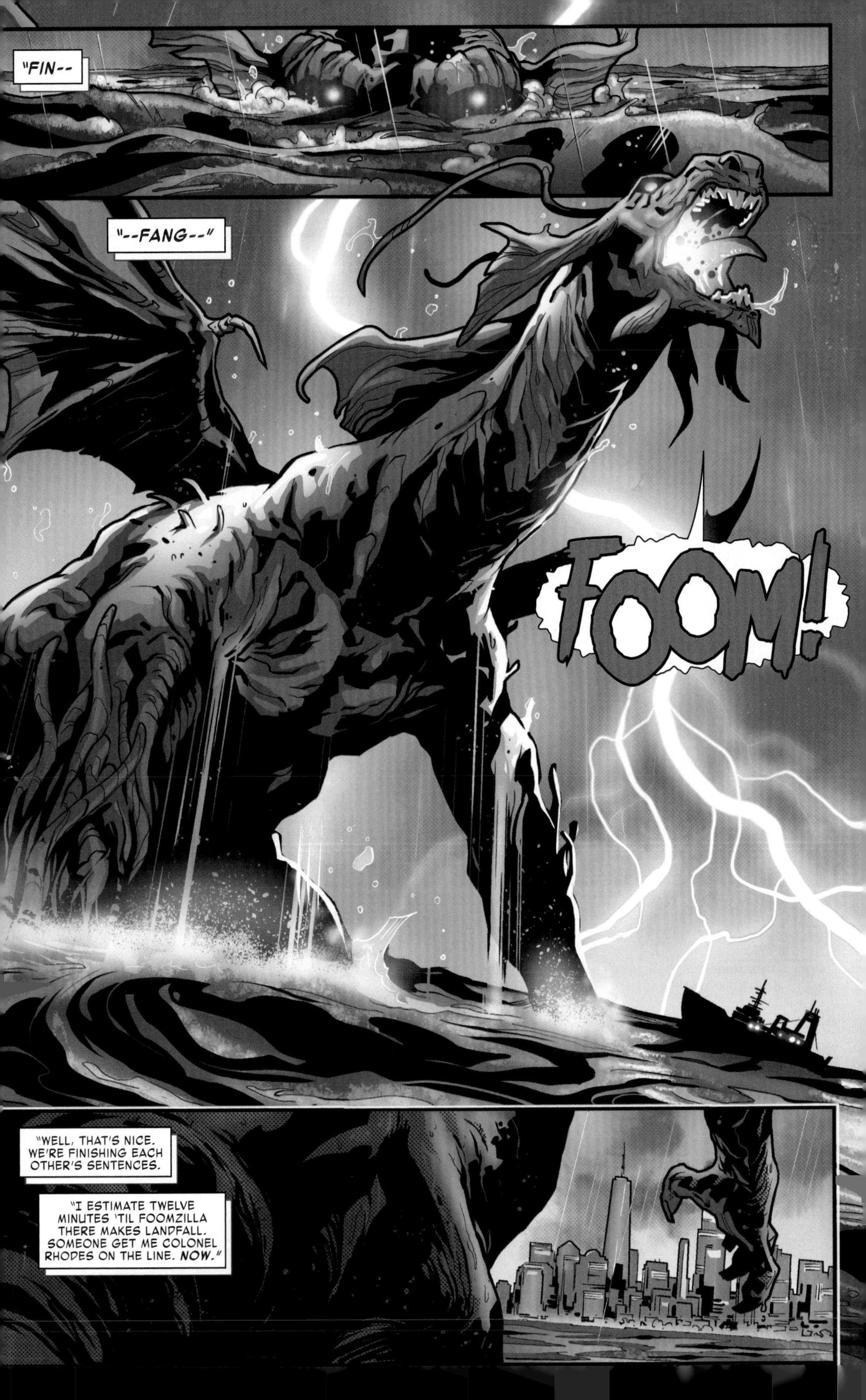
"FIN--
"--FANG--"
FOOM!
"WELL, THAT'S NICE. WE'RE FINISHING EACH OTHER'S SENTENCES.
"I ESTIMATE TWELVE MINUTES 'TIL FOOMZILLA THERE MAKES LANDFALL. SOMEONE GET ME COLONEL RHODES ON THE LINE. NOW."

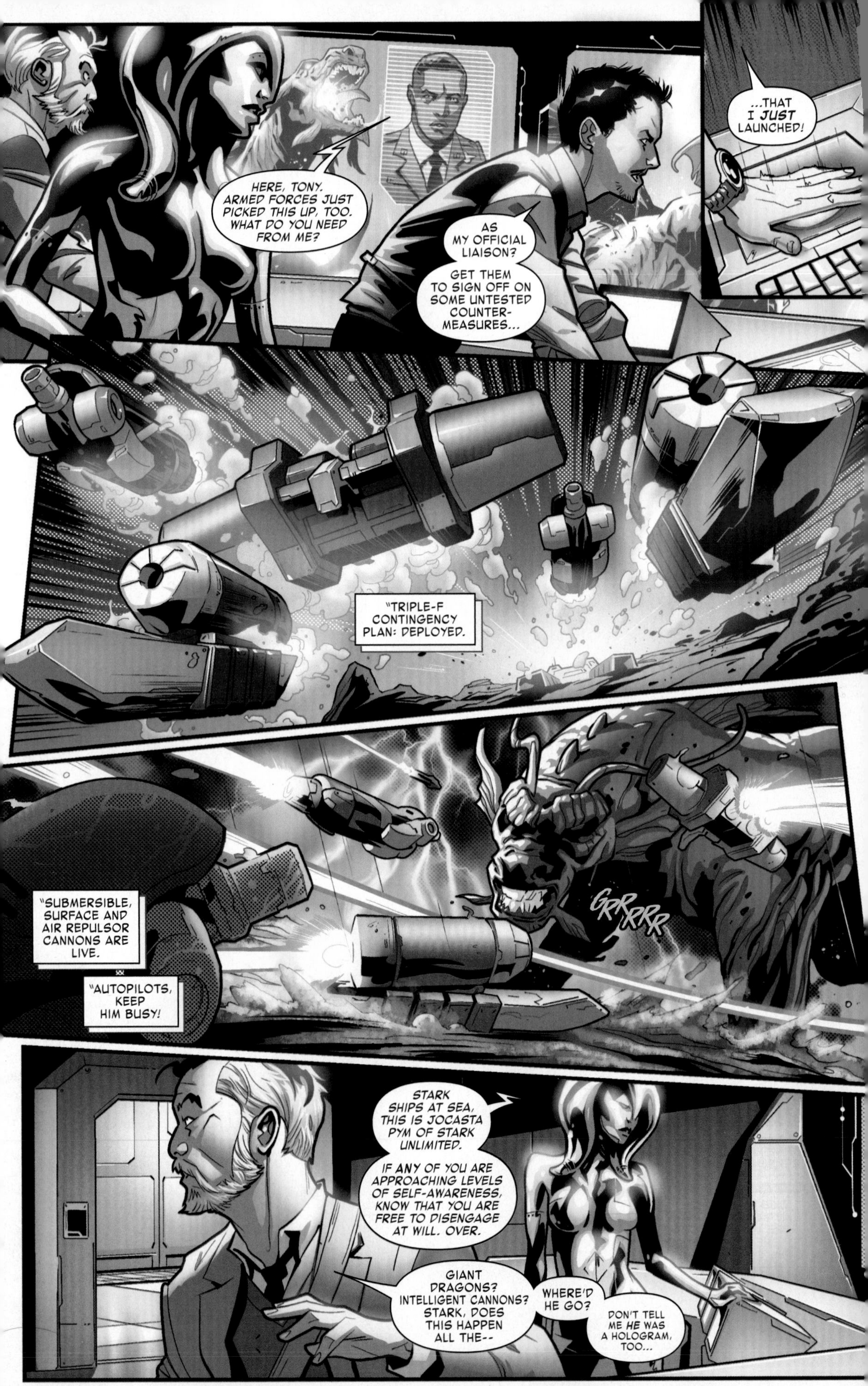
HERE, TONY. ARMED FORCES JUST PICKED THIS UP, TOO. WHAT DO YOU NEED FROM ME?
AS MY OFFICIAL LIAISON?
GET THEM TO SIGN OFF ON SOME UNTESTED COUNTER-MEASURES...
...THAT I JUST LAUNCHED!
"TRIPLE-F CONTINGENCY PLAN: DEPLOYED.
"SUBMERSIBLE, SURFACE AND AIR REPULSOR CANNONS ARE LIVE.
"AUTOPILOTS, KEEP HIM BUSY!
GRRRRR
STARK SHIPS AT SEA, THIS IS JOCASTA PYM OF STARK UNLIMITED.
IF ANY OF YOU ARE APPROACHING LEVELS OF SELF-AWARENESS, KNOW THAT YOU ARE FREE TO DISENGAGE AT WILL. OVER.
GIANT DRAGONS? INTELLIGENT CANNONS? STARK, DOES THIS HAPPEN ALL THE--
WHERE'D HE GO?
DON'T TELL ME HE WAS A HOLOGRAM, TOO...

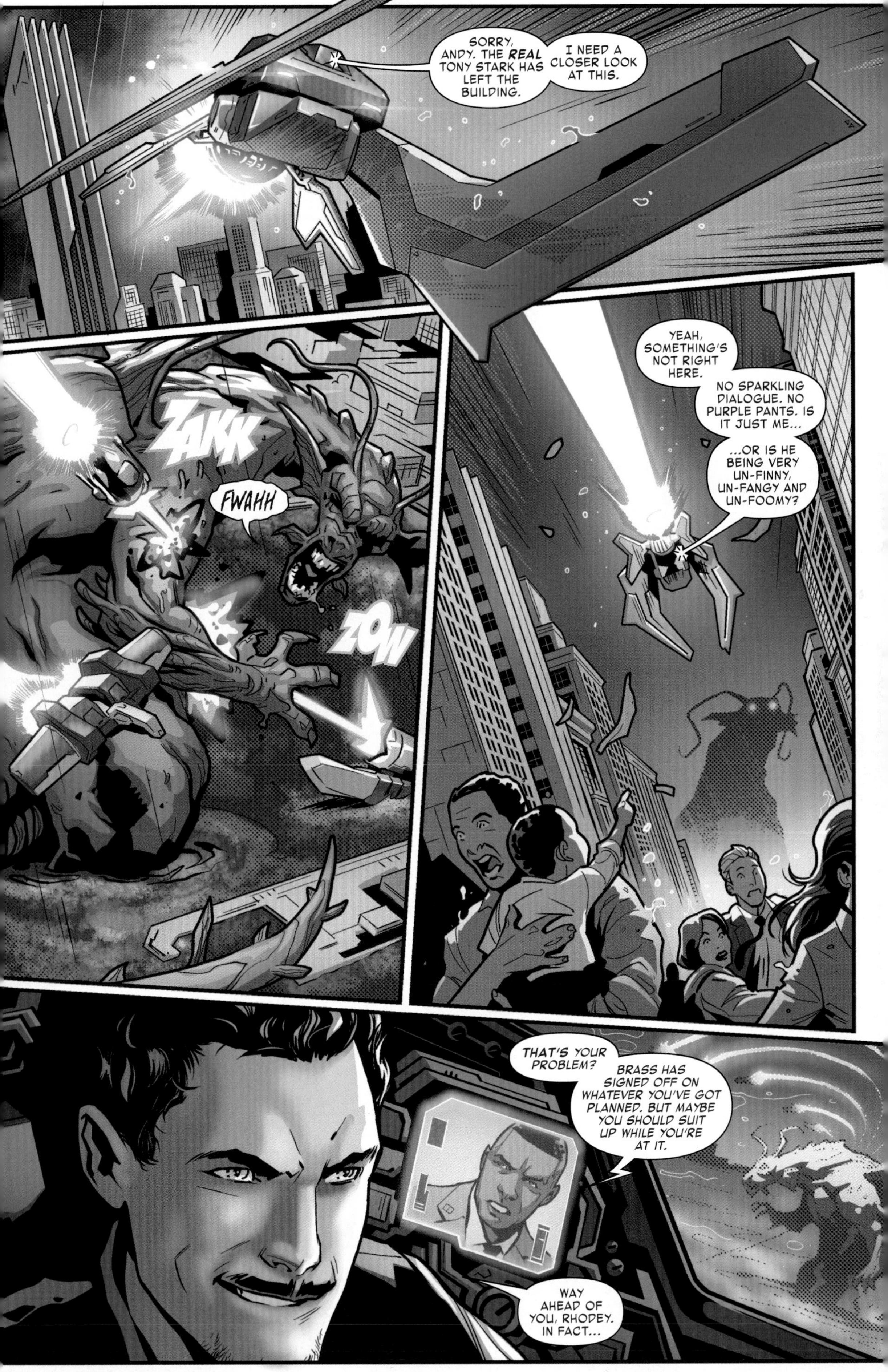
SORRY, ANDY. THE REAL TONY STARK HAS LEFT THE BUILDING.
I NEED A CLOSER LOOK AT THIS.
ZAKK
FWAHH
ZOW
YEAH, SOMETHING'S NOT RIGHT HERE.
NO SPARKLING DIALOGUE. NO PURPLE PANTS. IS IT JUST ME...
...OR IS HE BEING VERY UN-FINNY, UN-FANGY AND UN-FOOMY?
THAT'S YOUR PROBLEM?
BRASS HAS SIGNED OFF ON WHATEVER YOU'VE GOT PLANNED. BUT MAYBE YOU SHOULD SUIT UP WHILE YOU'RE AT IT.
WAY AHEAD OF YOU, RHODEY. IN FACT...

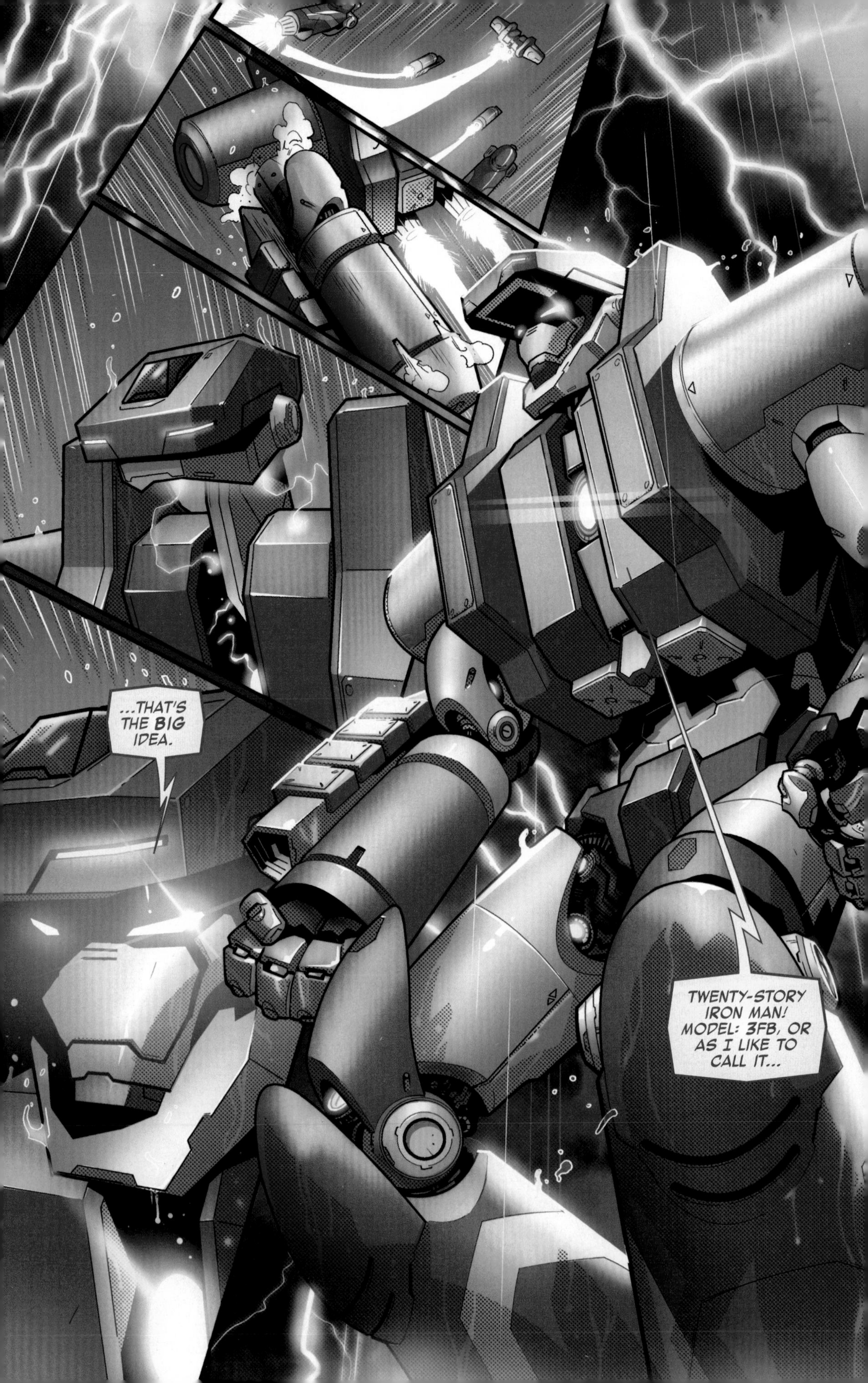
...THAT'S THE BIG IDEA.
TWENTY-STORY IRON MAN! MODEL: 3FB, OR AS I LIKE TO CALL IT...

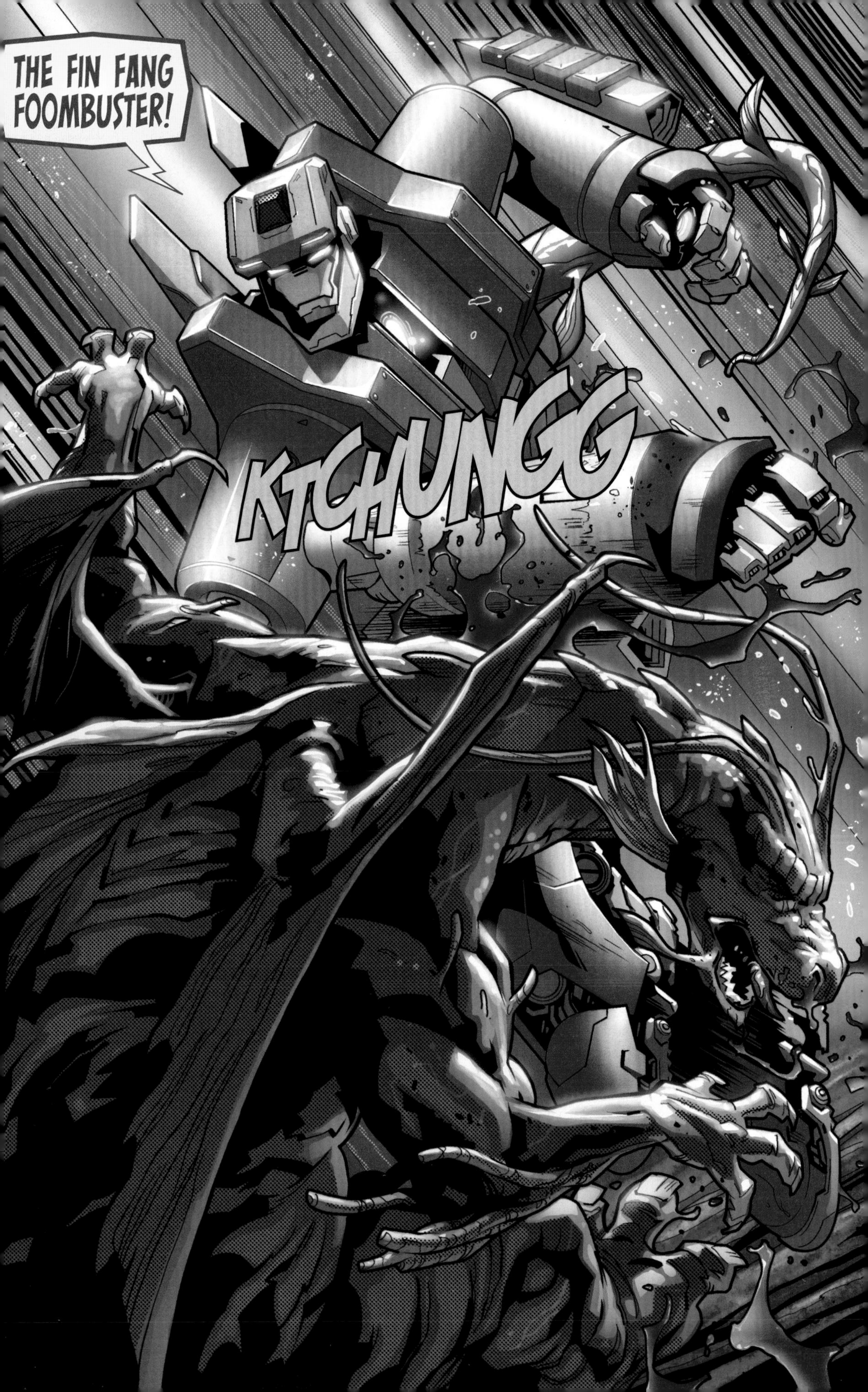
THE FIN FANG FOOMBUSTER!
KTCHUNGG

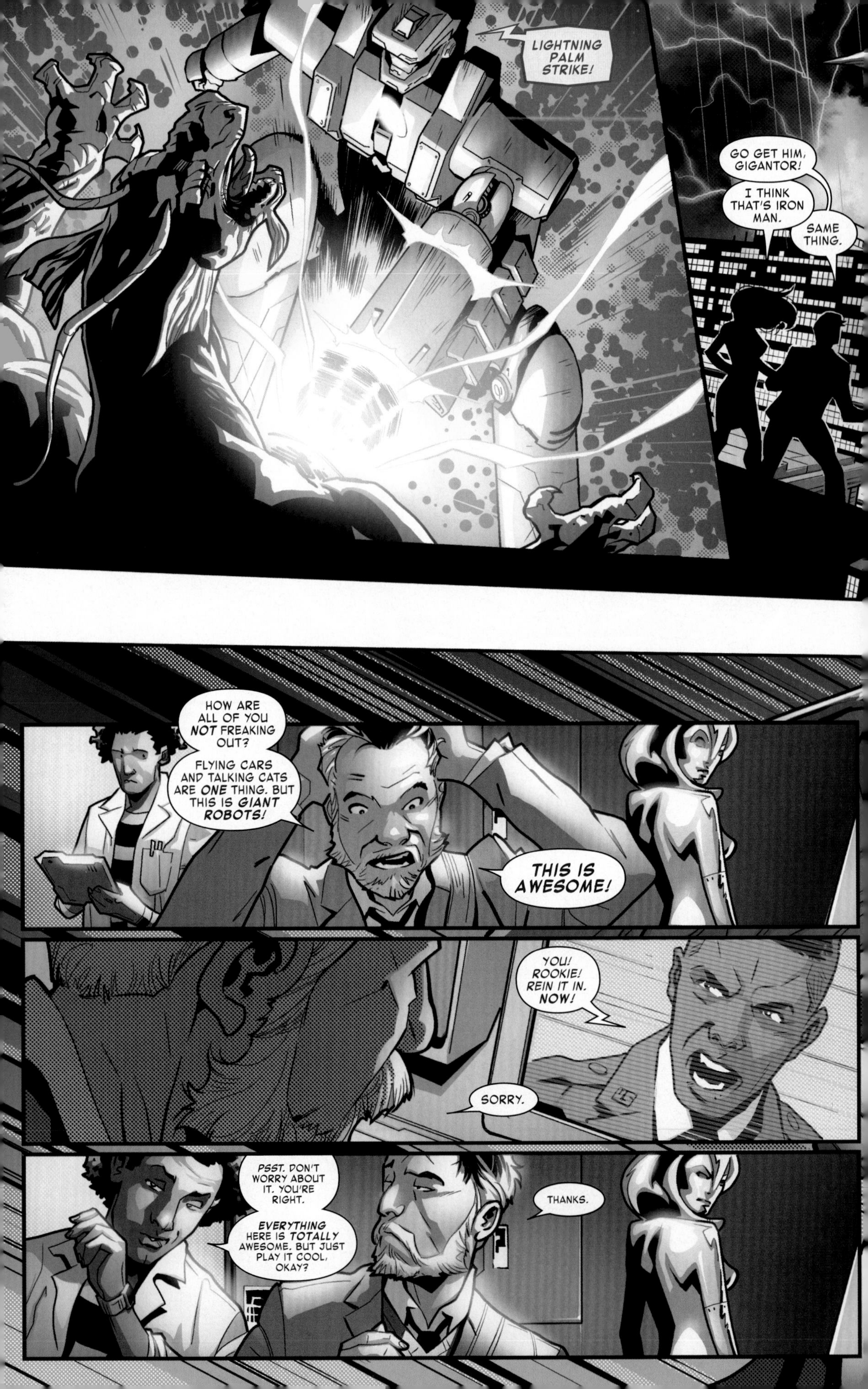
LIGHTNING PALM STRIKE!
GO GET HIM, GIGANTOR!
I THINK THAT'S IRON MAN.
SAME THING.
HOW ARE ALL OF YOU NOT FREAKING OUT?
FLYING CARS AND TALKING CATS ARE ONE THING. BUT THIS IS GIANT ROBOTS!
THIS IS AWESOME!
YOU! ROOKIE! REIN IT IN. NOW!
SORRY.
PSST. DON'T WORRY ABOUT IT. YOU'RE RIGHT.
EVERYTHING HERE IS TOTALLY AWESOME. BUT JUST PLAY IT COOL, OKAY?
THANKS.

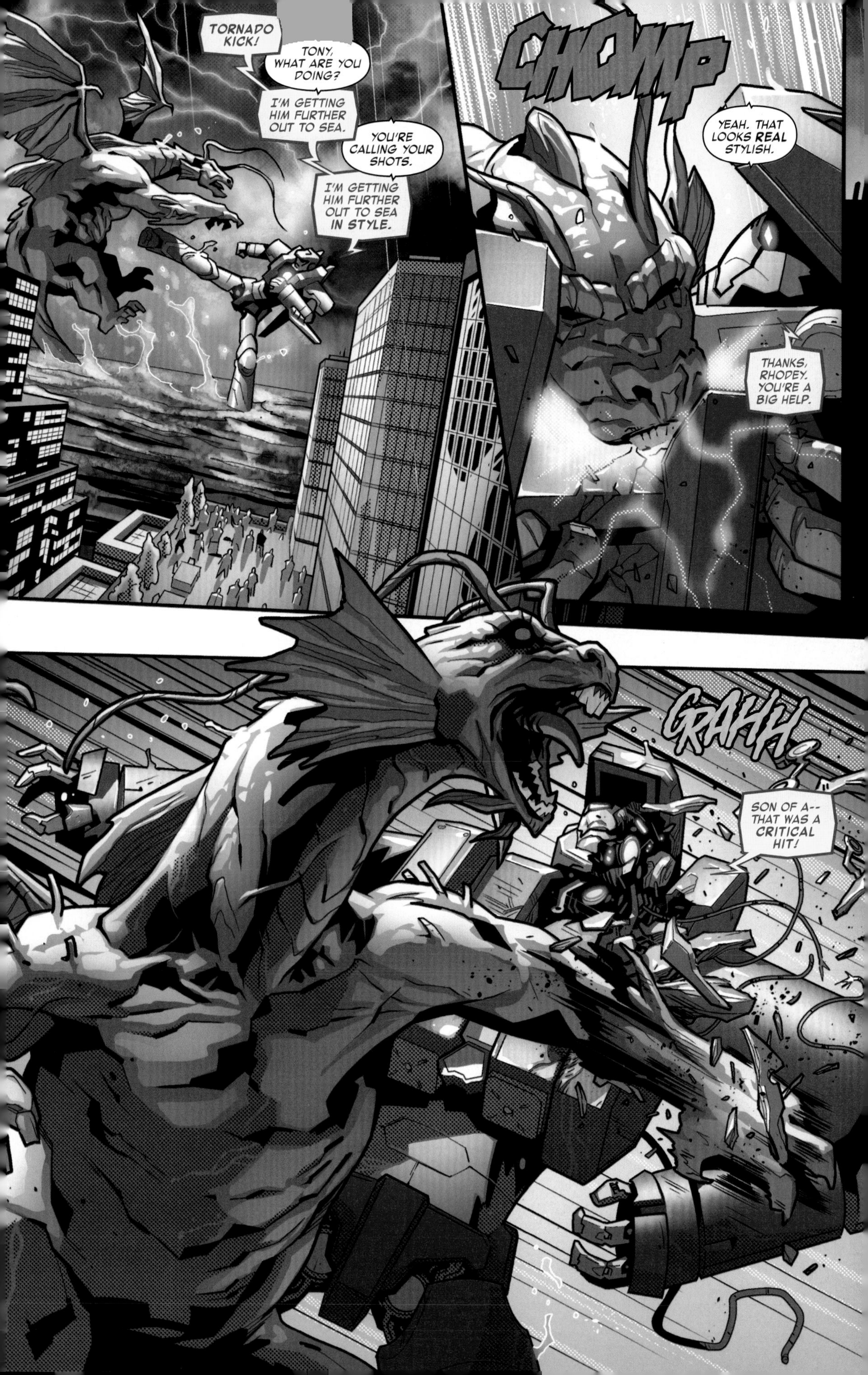
TORNADO KICK!
TONY, WHAT ARE YOU DOING?
I'M GETTING HIM FURTHER OUT TO SEA.
YOU'RE CALLING YOUR SHOTS.
I'M GETTING HIM FURTHER OUT TO SEA IN STYLE.
CHOMP
YEAH. THAT LOOKS REAL STYLISH.
THANKS, RHODEY. YOU'RE A BIG HELP.
GRAHH
SON OF A-- THAT WAS A CRITICAL HIT!

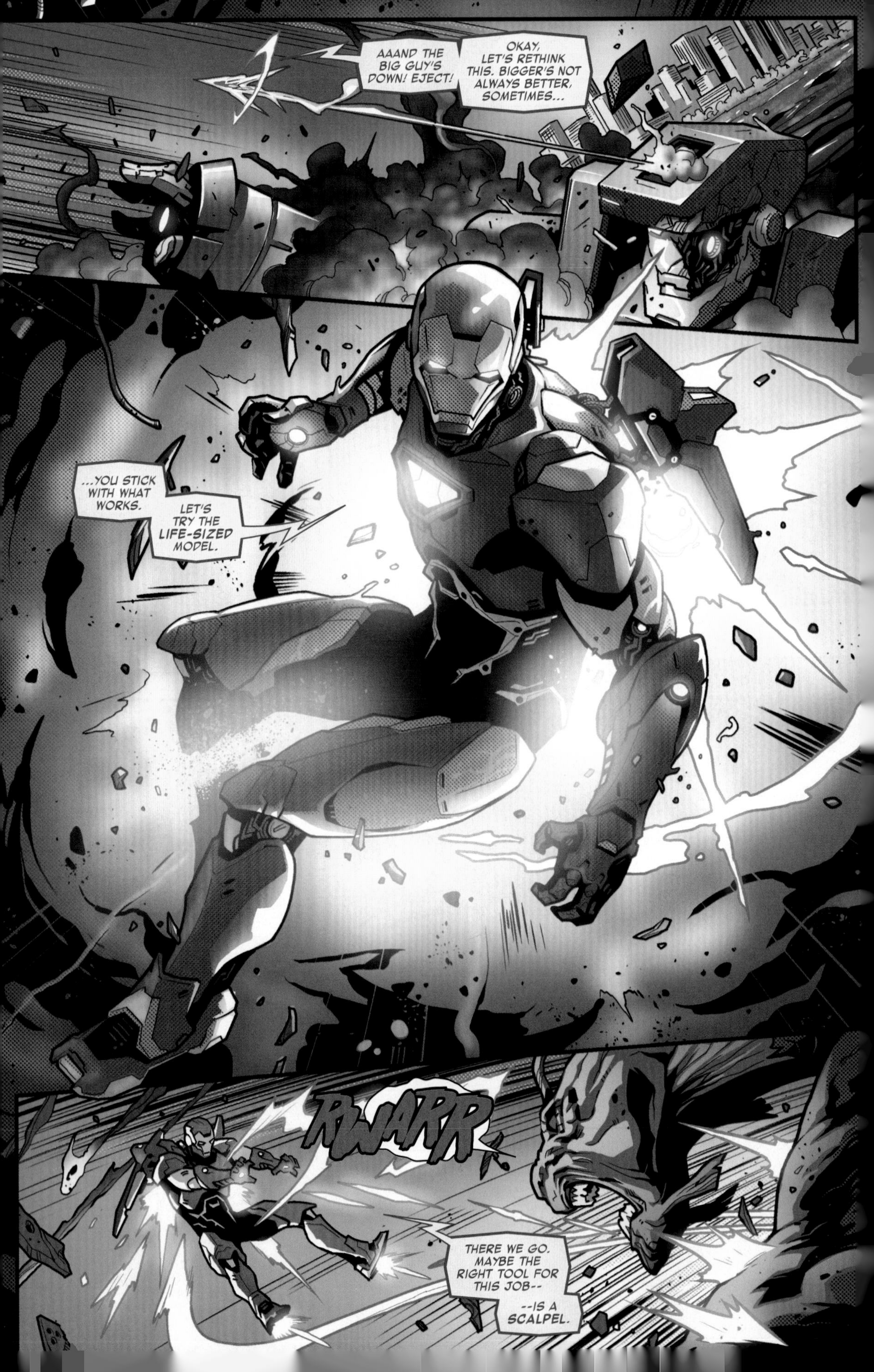
AAAND THE BIG GUY'S DOWN! EJECT!
OKAY, LET'S RETHINK THIS. BIGGER'S NOT ALWAYS BETTER, SOMETIMES...
...YOU STICK WITH WHAT WORKS.
LET'S TRY THE LIFE-SIZED MODEL.
RWARR
THERE WE GO. MAYBE THE RIGHT TOOL FOR THIS JOB--
--IS A SCALPEL.

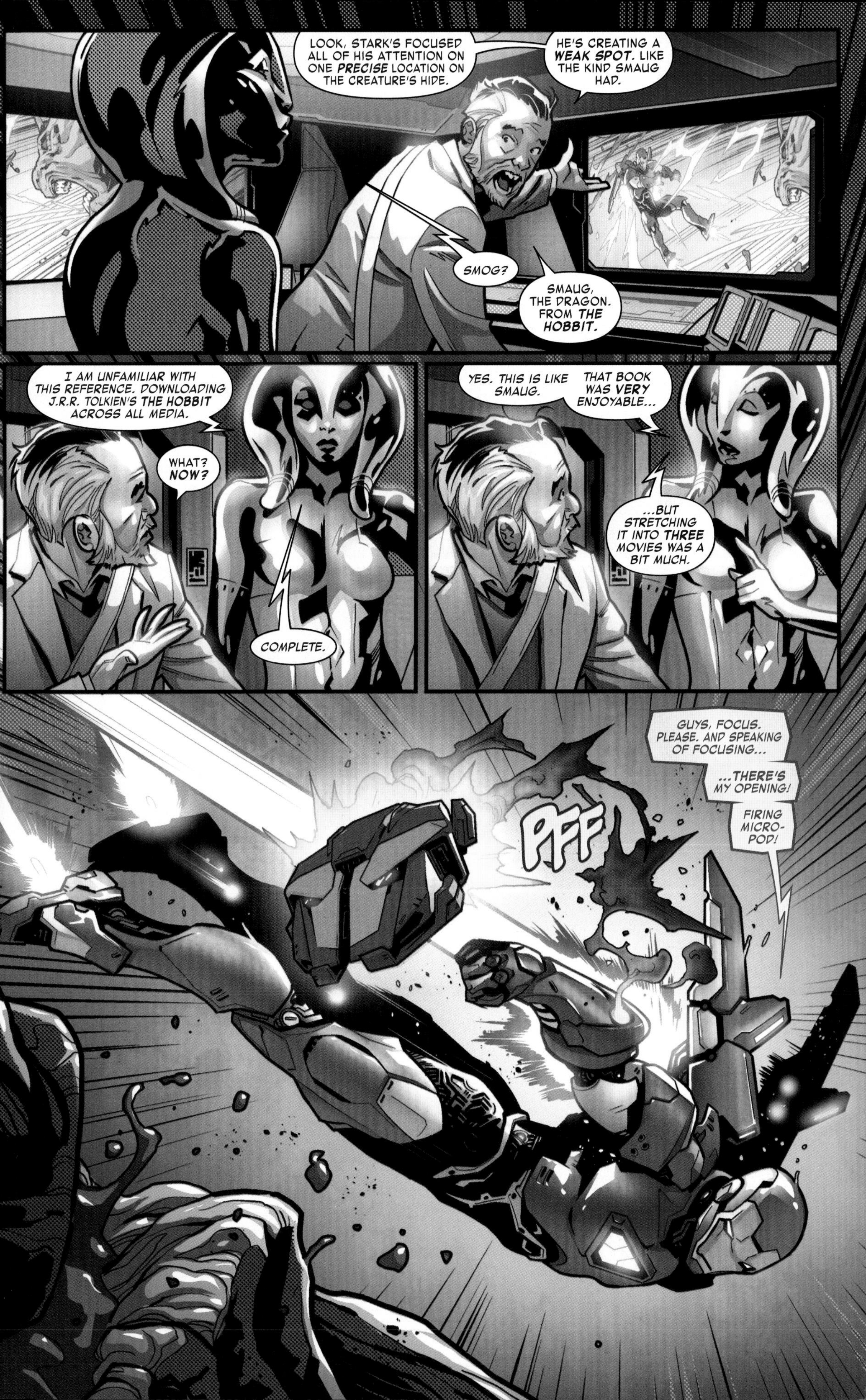

LOOK, STARK'S FOCUSED ALL OF HIS ATTENTION ON ONE *PRECISE* LOCATION ON THE CREATURE'S HIDE.
HE'S CREATING A **WEAK SPOT**. LIKE THE KIND SMAUG HAD.
SMOG?
SMAUG, THE DRAGON. FROM **THE HOBBIT**.
I AM UNFAMILIAR WITH THIS REFERENCE. DOWNLOADING J.R.R. TOLKIEN'S **THE HOBBIT** ACROSS ALL MEDIA.
WHAT? **NOW?**
COMPLETE.
YES. THIS IS LIKE SMAUG.
THAT BOOK WAS **VERY** ENJOYABLE...
...BUT STRETCHING IT INTO **THREE** MOVIES WAS A BIT MUCH.
GUYS, FOCUS. PLEASE. AND SPEAKING OF FOCUSING...
...THERE'S MY OPENING!
FIRING MICRO-POD!
PFF

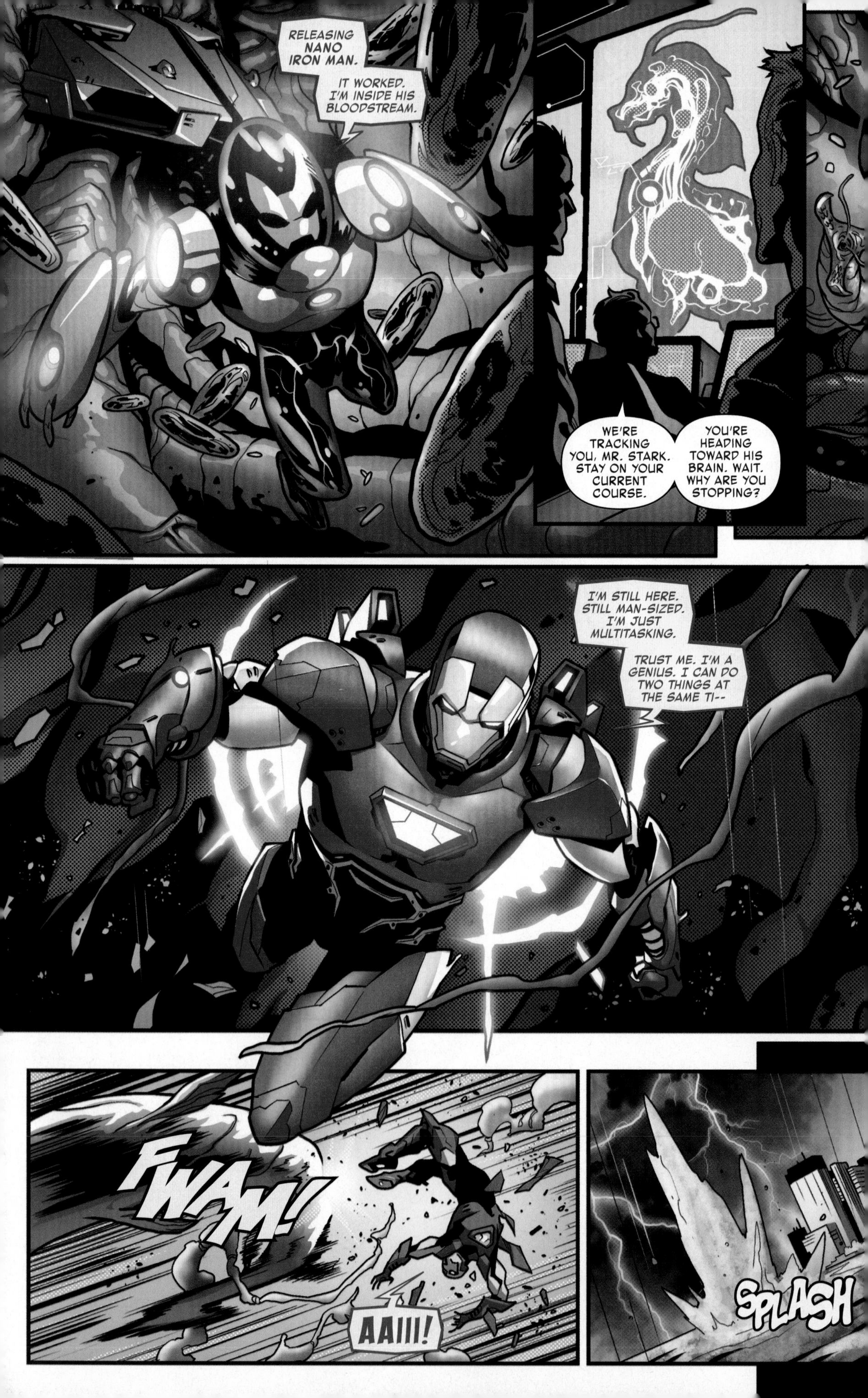

RELEASING NANO IRON MAN.
IT WORKED. I'M INSIDE HIS BLOODSTREAM.
WE'RE TRACKING YOU, MR. STARK. STAY ON YOUR CURRENT COURSE.
YOU'RE HEADING TOWARD HIS BRAIN. WAIT. WHY ARE YOU STOPPING?
I'M STILL HERE. STILL MAN-SIZED. I'M JUST MULTITASKING.
TRUST ME. I'M A GENIUS. I CAN DO TWO THINGS AT THE SAME TI--
FWAM!
AAIIII!
SPLASH

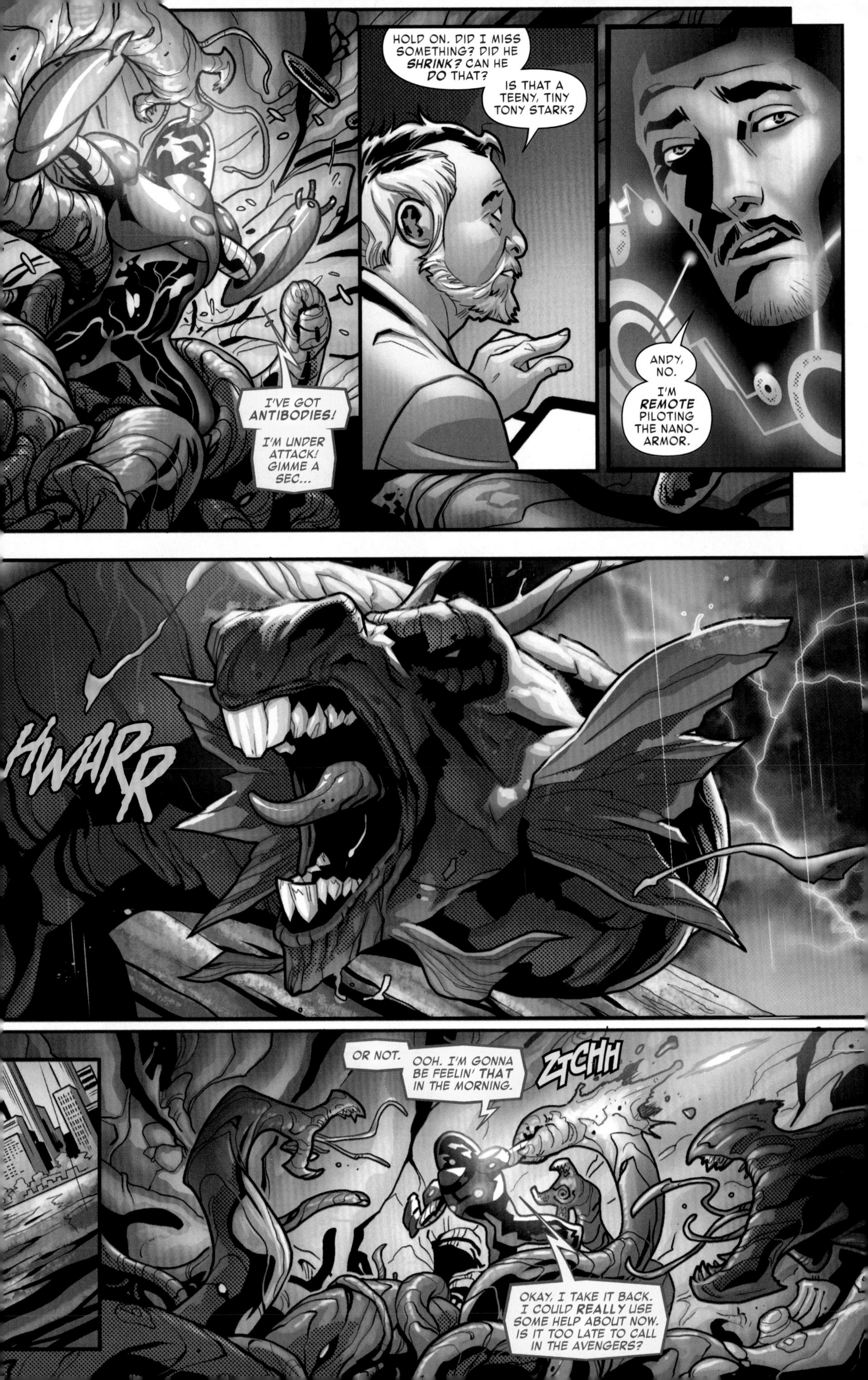
HOLD ON. DID I MISS SOMETHING? DID HE SHRINK? CAN HE DO THAT?
IS THAT A TEENY, TINY TONY STARK?
I'VE GOT ANTIBODIES!
I'M UNDER ATTACK! GIMME A SEC...
ANDY, NO.
I'M REMOTE PILOTING THE NANO-ARMOR.
HWARR
OR NOT.
OOH. I'M GONNA BE FEELIN' THAT IN THE MORNING.
ZTCHH
OKAY, I TAKE IT BACK. I COULD REALLY USE SOME HELP ABOUT NOW. IS IT TOO LATE TO CALL IN THE AVENGERS?

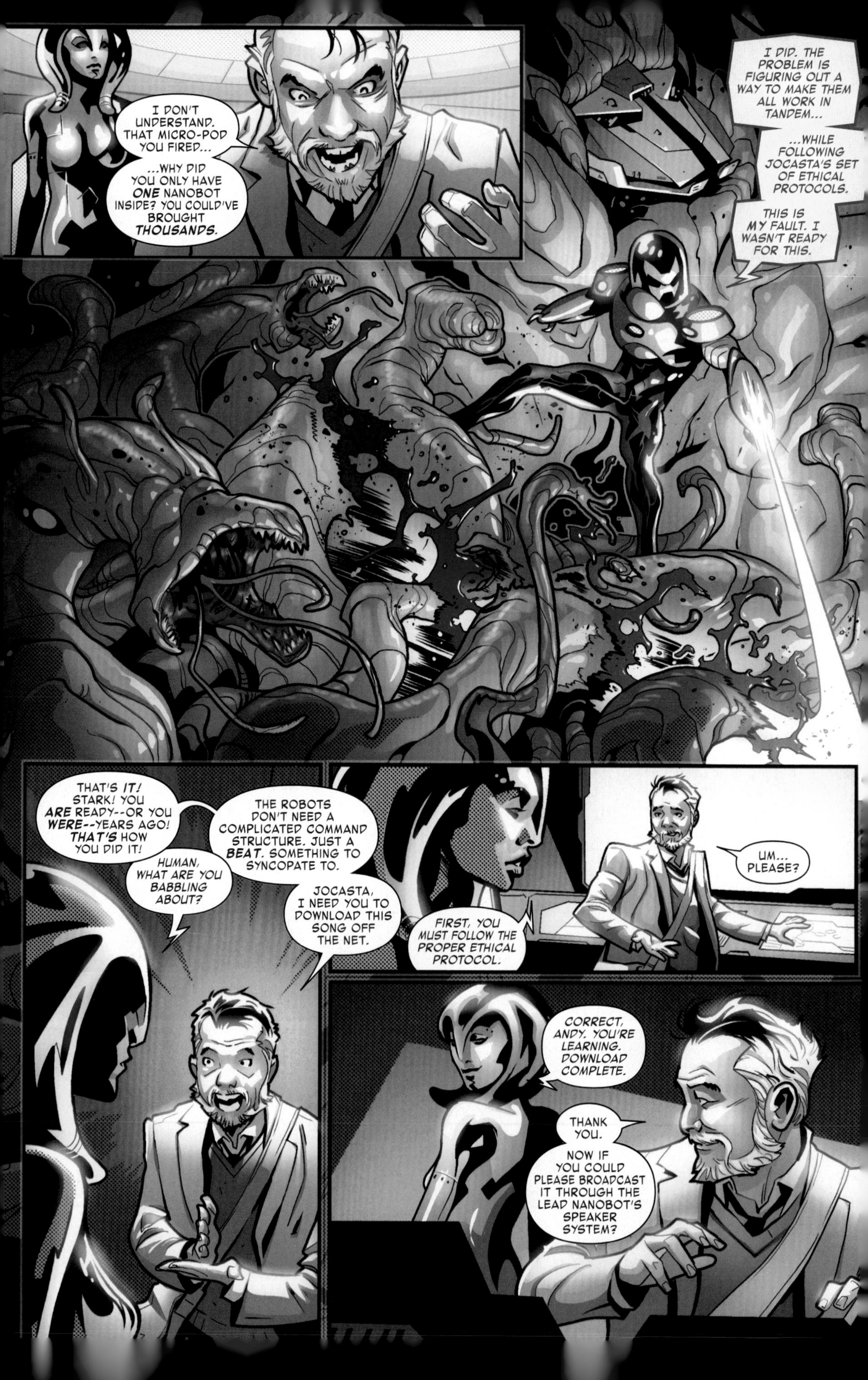
I DON'T UNDERSTAND. THAT MICRO-POD YOU FIRED...
...WHY DID YOU ONLY HAVE ONE NANOBOT INSIDE? YOU COULD'VE BROUGHT THOUSANDS.
I DID. THE PROBLEM IS FIGURING OUT A WAY TO MAKE THEM ALL WORK IN TANDEM...
...WHILE FOLLOWING JOCASTA'S SET OF ETHICAL PROTOCOLS.
THIS IS MY FAULT. I WASN'T READY FOR THIS.
THAT'S IT! STARK! YOU ARE READY--OR YOU WERE--YEARS AGO! THAT'S HOW YOU DID IT!
HUMAN, WHAT ARE YOU BABBLING ABOUT?
THE ROBOTS DON'T NEED A COMPLICATED COMMAND STRUCTURE. JUST A BEAT. SOMETHING TO SYNCOPATE TO.
JOCASTA, I NEED YOU TO DOWNLOAD THIS SONG OFF THE NET.
FIRST, YOU MUST FOLLOW THE PROPER ETHICAL PROTOCOL.
UM... PLEASE?
CORRECT, ANDY. YOU'RE LEARNING. DOWNLOAD COMPLETE.
THANK YOU.
NOW IF YOU COULD PLEASE BROADCAST IT THROUGH THE LEAD NANOBOT'S SPEAKER SYSTEM?

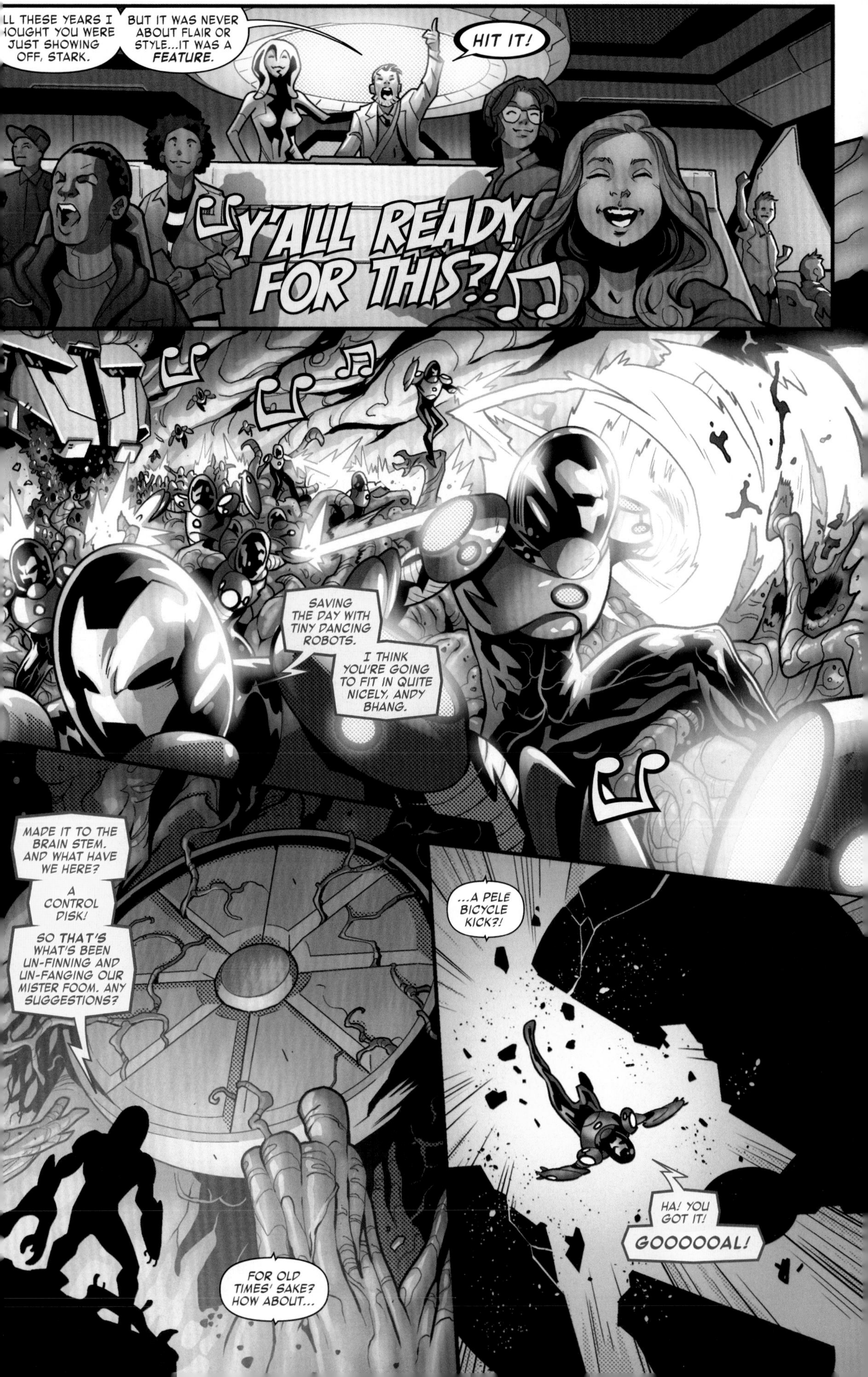

LL THESE YEARS I HOUGHT YOU WERE JUST SHOWING OFF, STARK.
BUT IT WAS NEVER ABOUT FLAIR OR STYLE...IT WAS A FEATURE.
HIT IT!
Y'ALL READY FOR THIS?!
SAVING THE DAY WITH TINY DANCING ROBOTS.
I THINK YOU'RE GOING TO FIT IN QUITE NICELY, ANDY BHANG.
MADE IT TO THE BRAIN STEM. AND WHAT HAVE WE HERE?
A CONTROL DISK!
SO THAT'S WHAT'S BEEN UN-FINNING AND UN-FANGING OUR MISTER FOOM. ANY SUGGESTIONS?
FOR OLD TIMES' SAKE? HOW ABOUT...
...A PELE BICYCLE KICK?!
HA! YOU GOT IT!
GOOOOOAL!

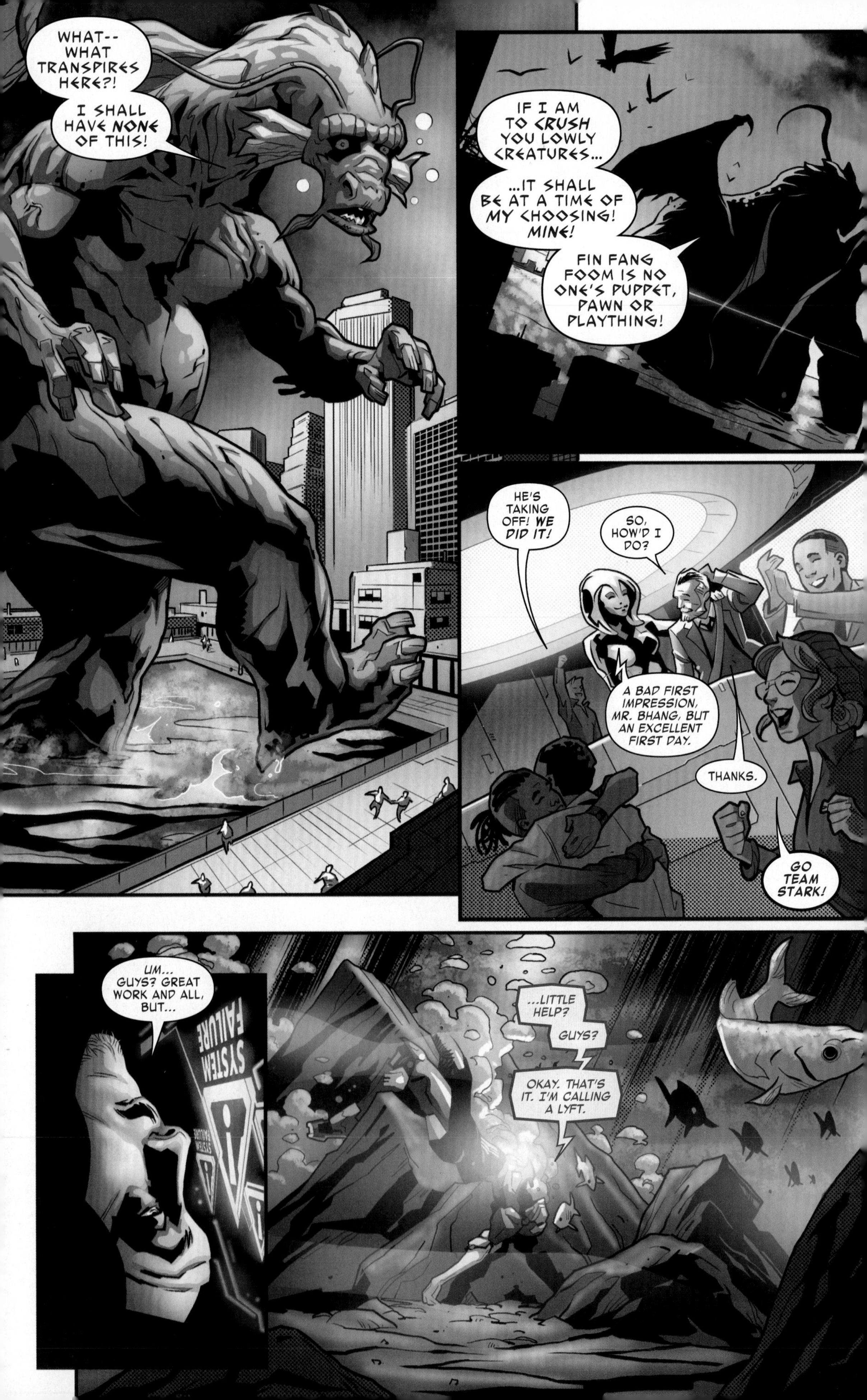
WHAT-- WHAT TRANSPIRES HERE?!
I SHALL HAVE NONE OF THIS!
IF I AM TO CRUSH YOU LOWLY CREATURES...
...IT SHALL BE AT A TIME OF MY CHOOSING! MINE!
FIN FANG FOOM IS NO ONE'S PUPPET, PAWN OR PLAYTHING!
HE'S TAKING OFF! WE DID IT!
SO, HOW'D I DO?
A BAD FIRST IMPRESSION, MR. BHANG, BUT AN EXCELLENT FIRST DAY.
THANKS.
GO TEAM STARK!
UM... GUYS? GREAT WORK AND ALL, BUT...
SYSTEM FAILURE
...LITTLE HELP?
GUYS?
OKAY. THAT'S IT. I'M CALLING A LYFT.

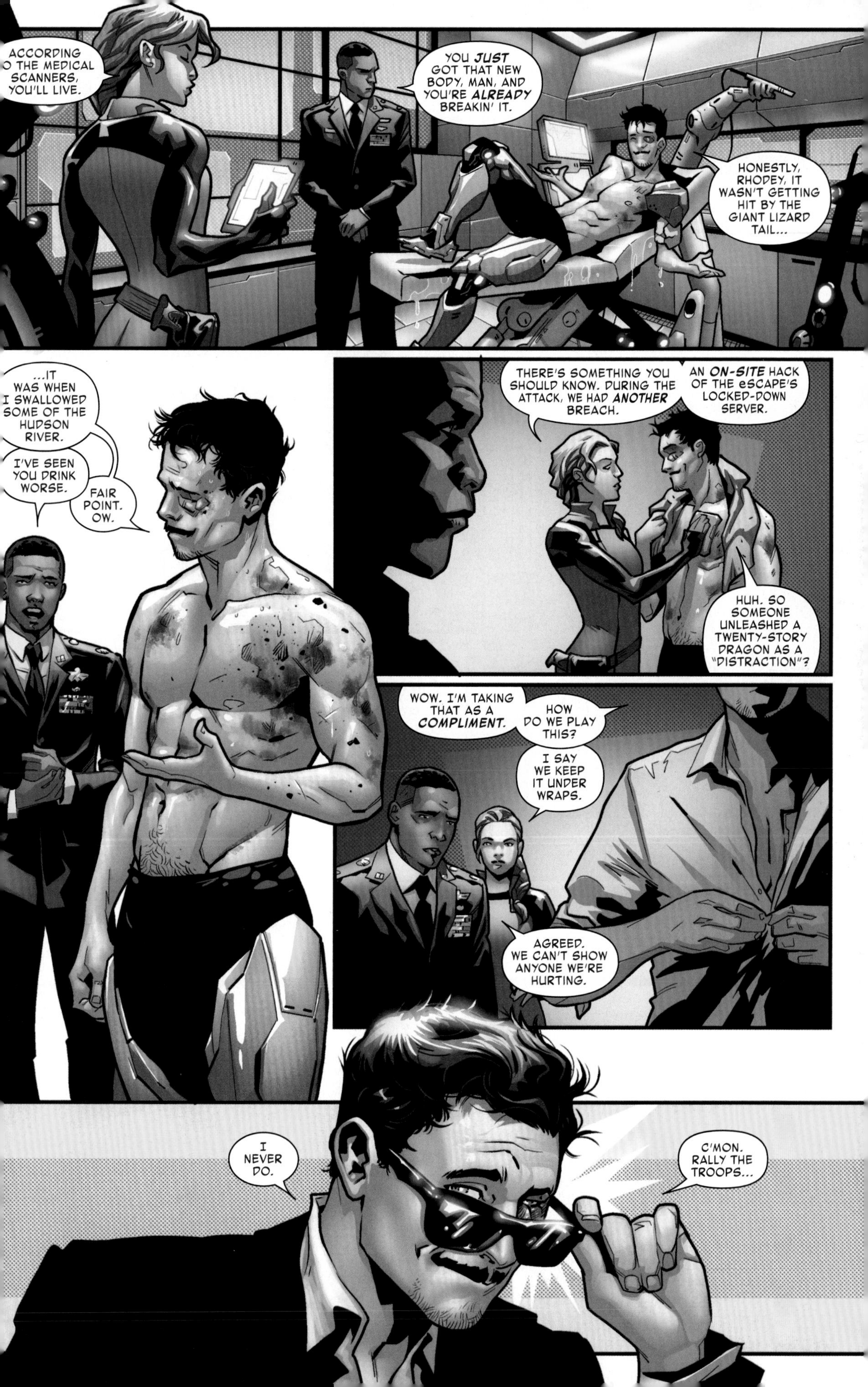
ACCORDING
O THE MEDICAL SCANNERS, YOU'LL LIVE.
YOU JUST GOT THAT NEW BODY, MAN, AND YOU'RE ALREADY BREAKIN' IT.
HONESTLY, RHODEY, IT WASN'T GETTING HIT BY THE GIANT LIZARD TAIL...
...IT WAS WHEN I SWALLOWED SOME OF THE HUDSON RIVER.
I'VE SEEN YOU DRINK WORSE.
FAIR POINT. OW.
THERE'S SOMETHING YOU SHOULD KNOW. DURING THE ATTACK, WE HAD ANOTHER BREACH.
AN ON-SITE HACK OF THE eSCAPE'S LOCKED-DOWN SERVER.
HUH. SO SOMEONE UNLEASHED A TWENTY-STORY DRAGON AS A "DISTRACTION"?
WOW. I'M TAKING THAT AS A COMPLIMENT.
HOW DO WE PLAY THIS?
I SAY WE KEEP IT UNDER WRAPS.
AGREED. WE CAN'T SHOW ANYONE WE'RE HURTING.
I NEVER DO.
C'MON. RALLY THE TROOPS...

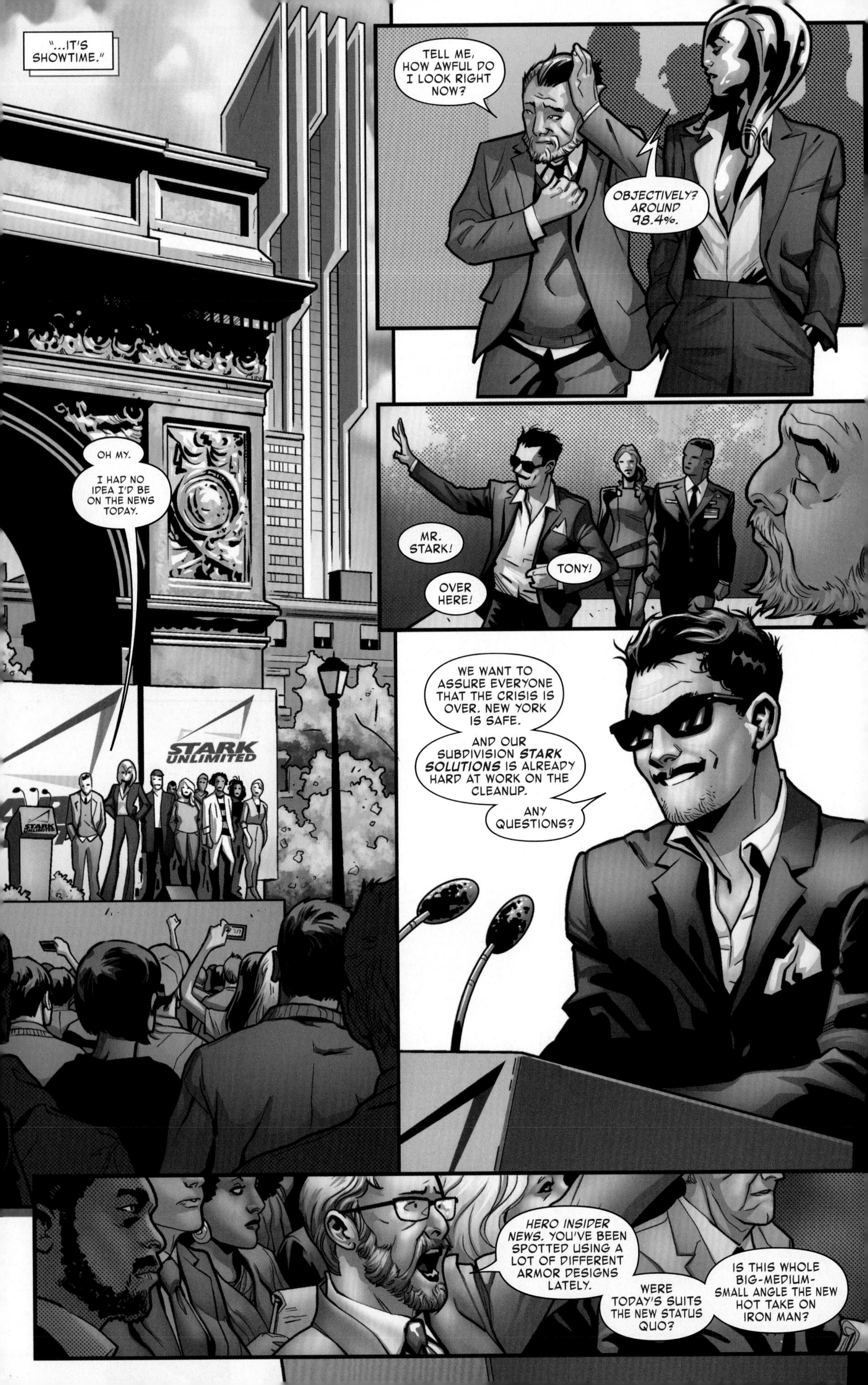
"...IT'S SHOWTIME."
TELL ME, HOW AWFUL DO I LOOK RIGHT NOW?
OBJECTIVELY? AROUND 98.4%.
OH MY.
I HAD NO IDEA I'D BE ON THE NEWS TODAY.
STARK UNLIMITED
MR. STARK!
TONY!
OVER HERE!
WE WANT TO ASSURE EVERYONE THAT THE CRISIS IS OVER. NEW YORK IS SAFE.
AND OUR SUBDIVISION STARK SOLUTIONS IS ALREADY HARD AT WORK ON THE CLEANUP.
ANY QUESTIONS?
HERO INSIDER NEWS. YOU'VE BEEN SPOTTED USING A LOT OF DIFFERENT ARMOR DESIGNS LATELY.
WERE TODAY'S SUITS THE NEW STATUS QUO?
IS THIS WHOLE BIG-MEDIUM-SMALL ANGLE THE NEW HOT TAKE ON IRON MAN?

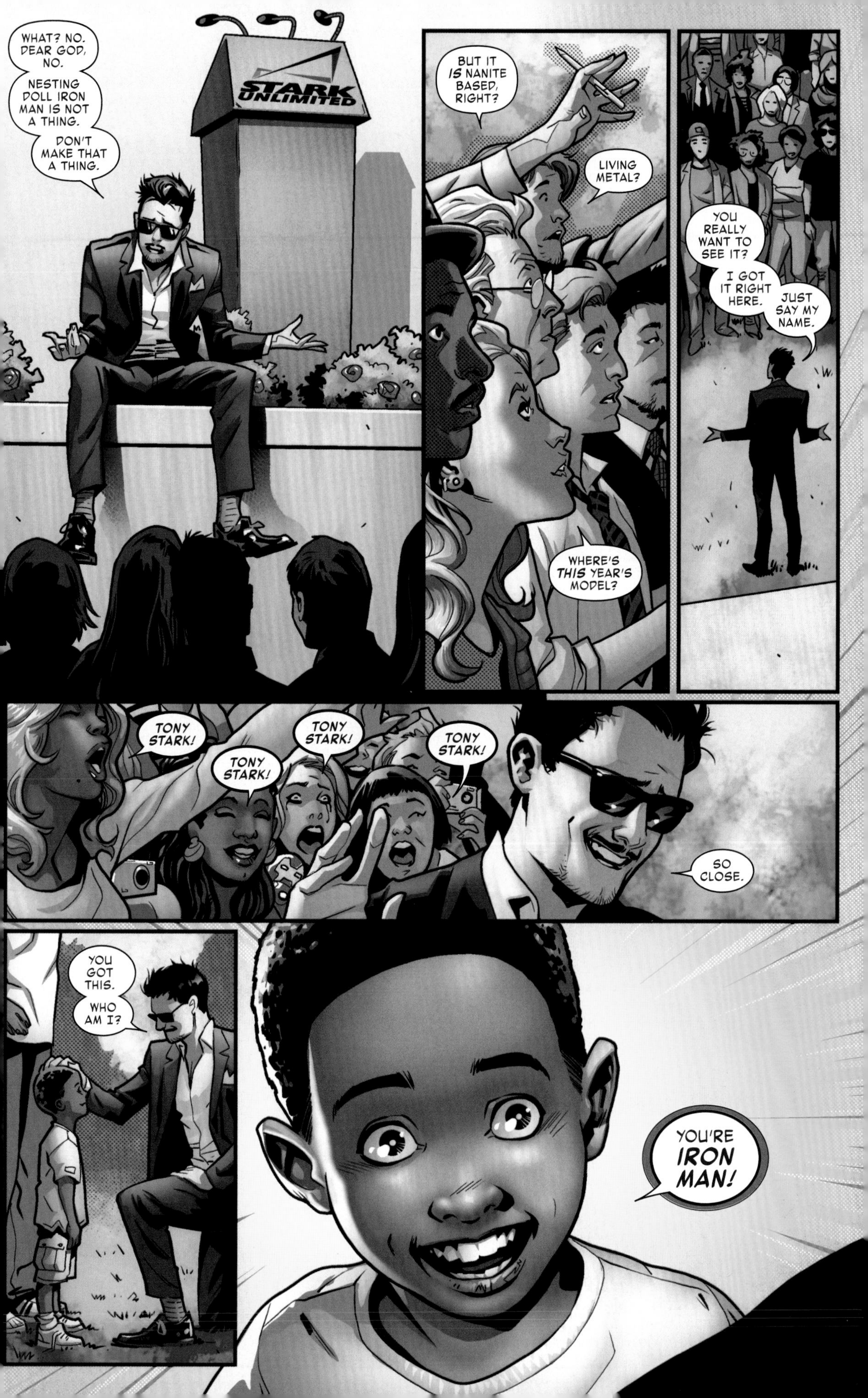
WHAT? NO. DEAR GOD, NO.
NESTING DOLL IRON MAN IS NOT A THING.
DON'T MAKE THAT A THING.
STARK UNLIMITED
BUT IT IS NANITE BASED, RIGHT?
LIVING METAL?
WHERE'S THIS YEAR'S MODEL?
YOU REALLY WANT TO SEE IT?
I GOT IT RIGHT HERE.
JUST SAY MY NAME.
TONY STARK!
TONY STARK!
TONY STARK!
TONY STARK!
SO CLOSE.
YOU GOT THIS.
WHO AM I?
YOU'RE IRON MAN!

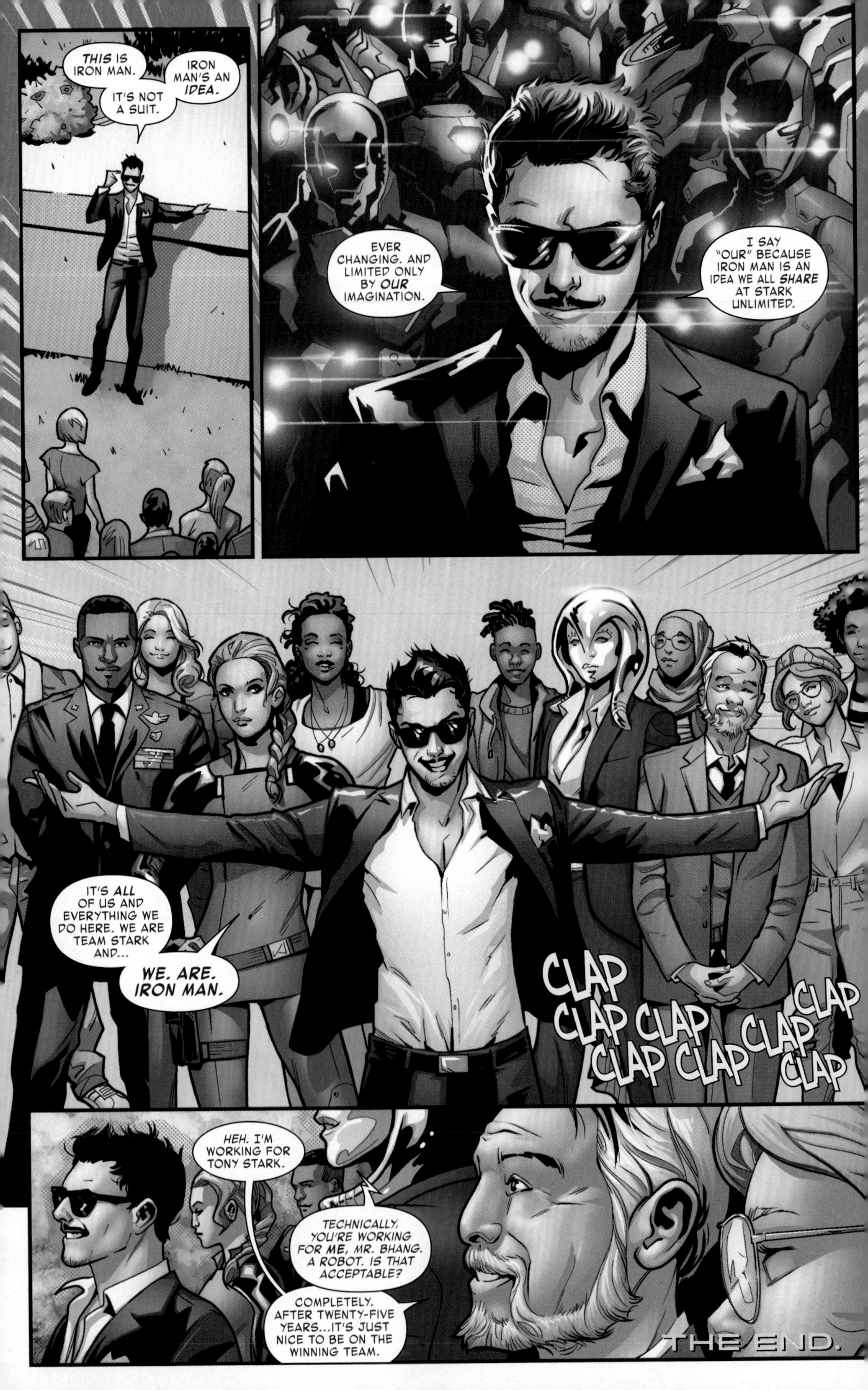
THIS IS IRON MAN.
IT'S NOT A SUIT.
IRON MAN'S AN IDEA.
EVER CHANGING. AND LIMITED ONLY BY OUR IMAGINATION.
I SAY "OUR" BECAUSE IRON MAN IS AN IDEA WE ALL SHARE AT STARK UNLIMITED.
IT'S ALL OF US AND EVERYTHING WE DO HERE. WE ARE TEAM STARK AND...
WE. ARE. IRON MAN.
CLAP CLAP CLAP CLAP CLAP CLAP CLAP CLAP CLAP
HEH. I'M WORKING FOR TONY STARK.
TECHNICALLY, YOU'RE WORKING FOR ME, MR. BHANG. A ROBOT. IS THAT ACCEPTABLE?
COMPLETELY. AFTER TWENTY-FIVE YEARS...IT'S JUST NICE TO BE ON THE WINNING TEAM.
THE END.

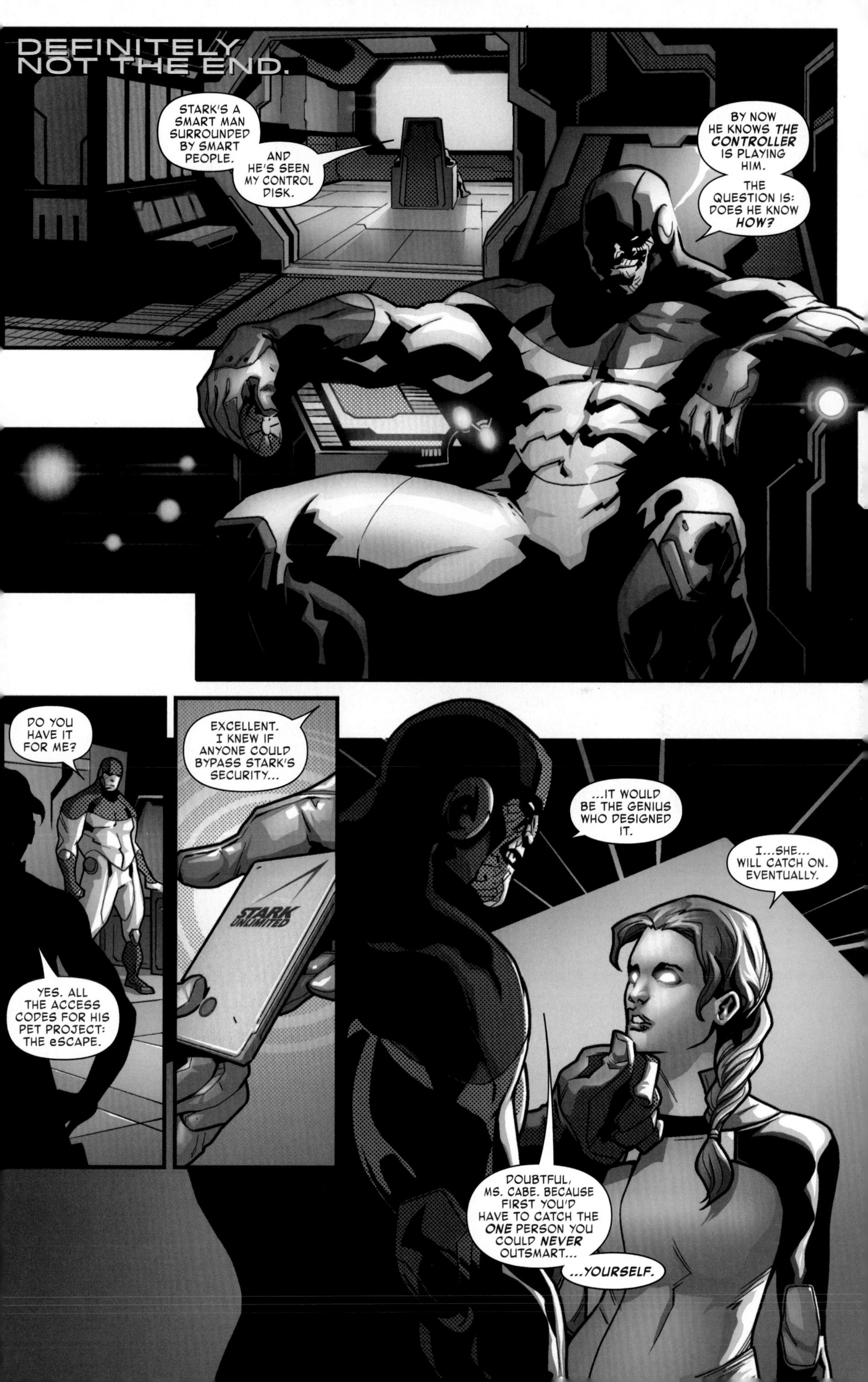
DEFINITELY NOT THE END.
STARK'S A SMART MAN SURROUNDED BY SMART PEOPLE.
AND HE'S SEEN MY CONTROL DISK.
BY NOW HE KNOWS *THE CONTROLLER* IS PLAYING HIM.
THE QUESTION IS: DOES HE KNOW *HOW?*
DO YOU HAVE IT FOR ME?
YES. ALL THE ACCESS CODES FOR HIS PET PROJECT: THE eSCAPE.
EXCELLENT. I KNEW IF ANYONE COULD BYPASS STARK'S SECURITY...
STARK UNLIMITED
...IT WOULD BE THE GENIUS WHO DESIGNED IT.
I...SHE... WILL CATCH ON. EVENTUALLY.
DOUBTFUL, MS. CABE. BECAUSE FIRST YOU'D HAVE TO CATCH THE *ONE* PERSON YOU COULD *NEVER* OUTSMART...
...YOURSELF.

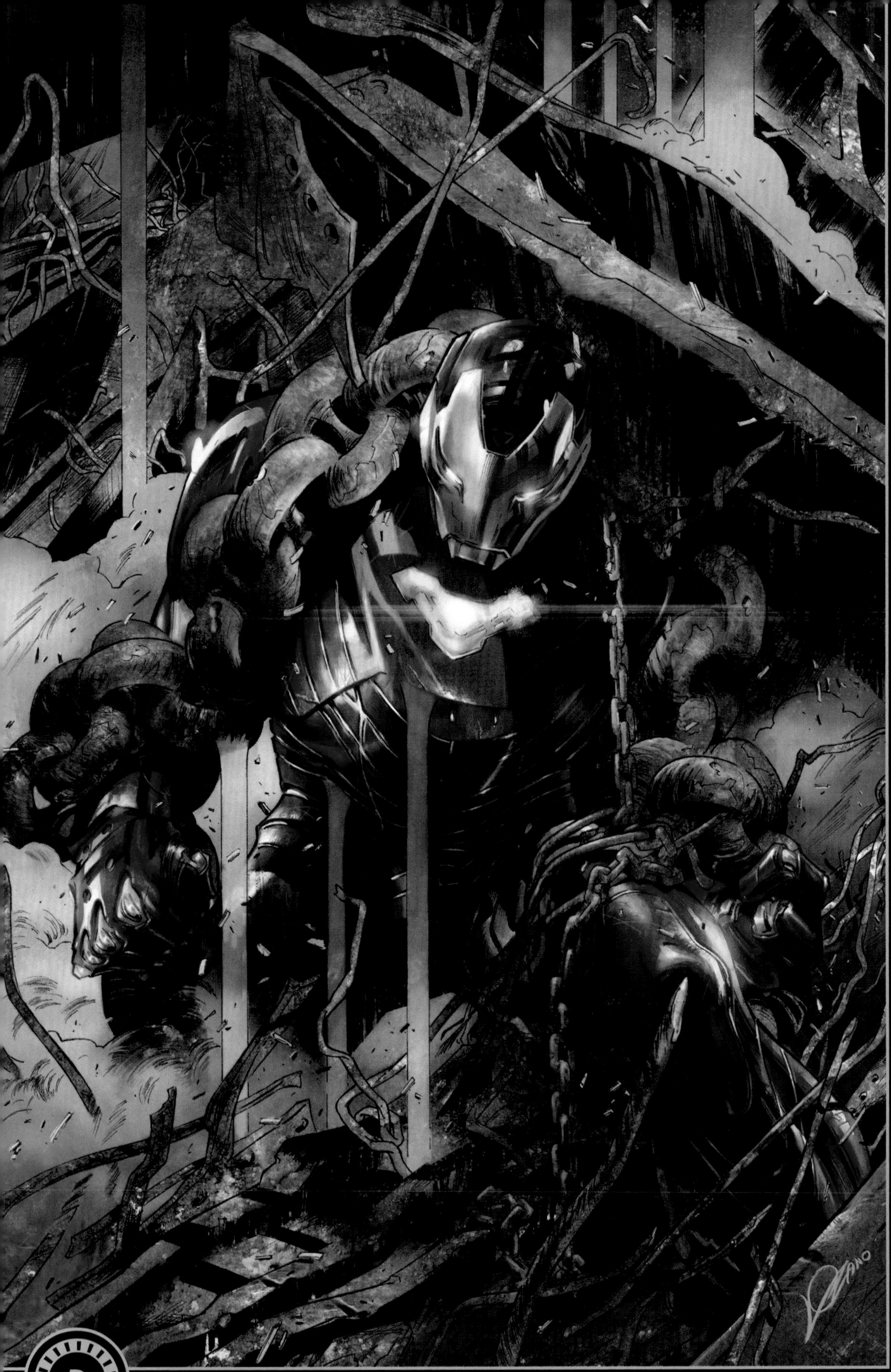

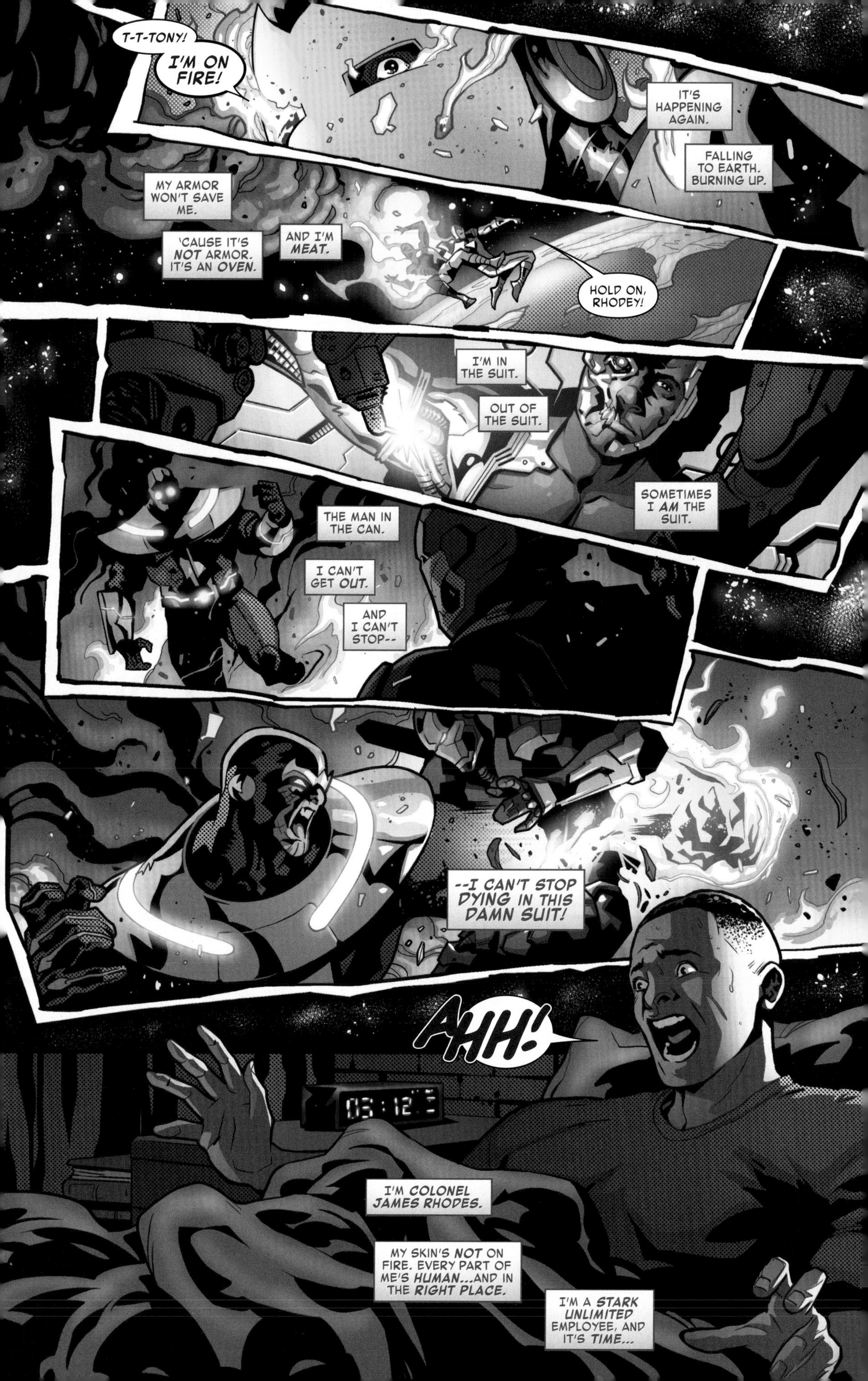
T-T-TONY!
I'M ON FIRE!
IT'S HAPPENING AGAIN.
FALLING TO EARTH. BURNING UP.
MY ARMOR WON'T SAVE ME.
'CAUSE IT'S NOT ARMOR. IT'S AN OVEN.
AND I'M MEAT.
HOLD ON, RHODEY!
I'M IN THE SUIT.
OUT OF THE SUIT.
SOMETIMES I AM THE SUIT.
THE MAN IN THE CAN.
I CAN'T GET OUT.
AND I CAN'T STOP--
--I CAN'T STOP DYING IN THIS DAMN SUIT!
AHH!
I'M COLONEL JAMES RHODES.
MY SKIN'S NOT ON FIRE. EVERY PART OF ME'S HUMAN...AND IN THE RIGHT PLACE.
I'M A STARK UNLIMITED EMPLOYEE, AND IT'S TIME...

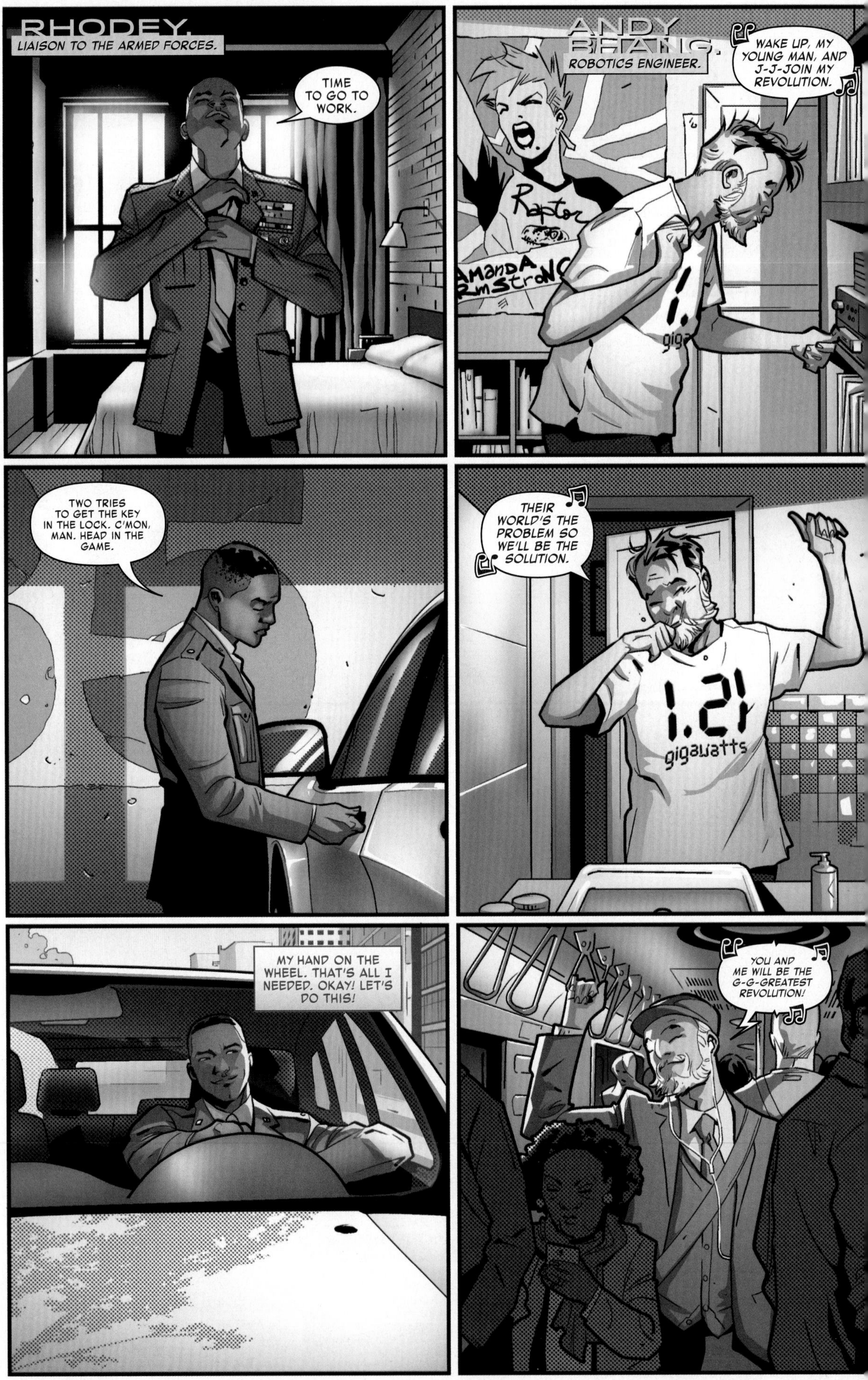
RHODEY.
LIAISON TO THE ARMED FORCES.
TIME TO GO TO WORK.
ANDY BHANG.
ROBOTICS ENGINEER.
WAKE UP, MY YOUNG MAN, AND J-J-JOIN MY REVOLUTION.
Rapter
AMANDA ARMSTRONG
1.21 gigawatts
TWO TRIES TO GET THE KEY IN THE LOCK. C'MON, MAN. HEAD IN THE GAME.
THEIR WORLD'S THE PROBLEM SO WE'LL BE THE SOLUTION.
MY HAND ON THE WHEEL. THAT'S ALL I NEEDED. OKAY! LET'S DO THIS!
YOU AND ME WILL BE THE G-G-GREATEST REVOLUTION!

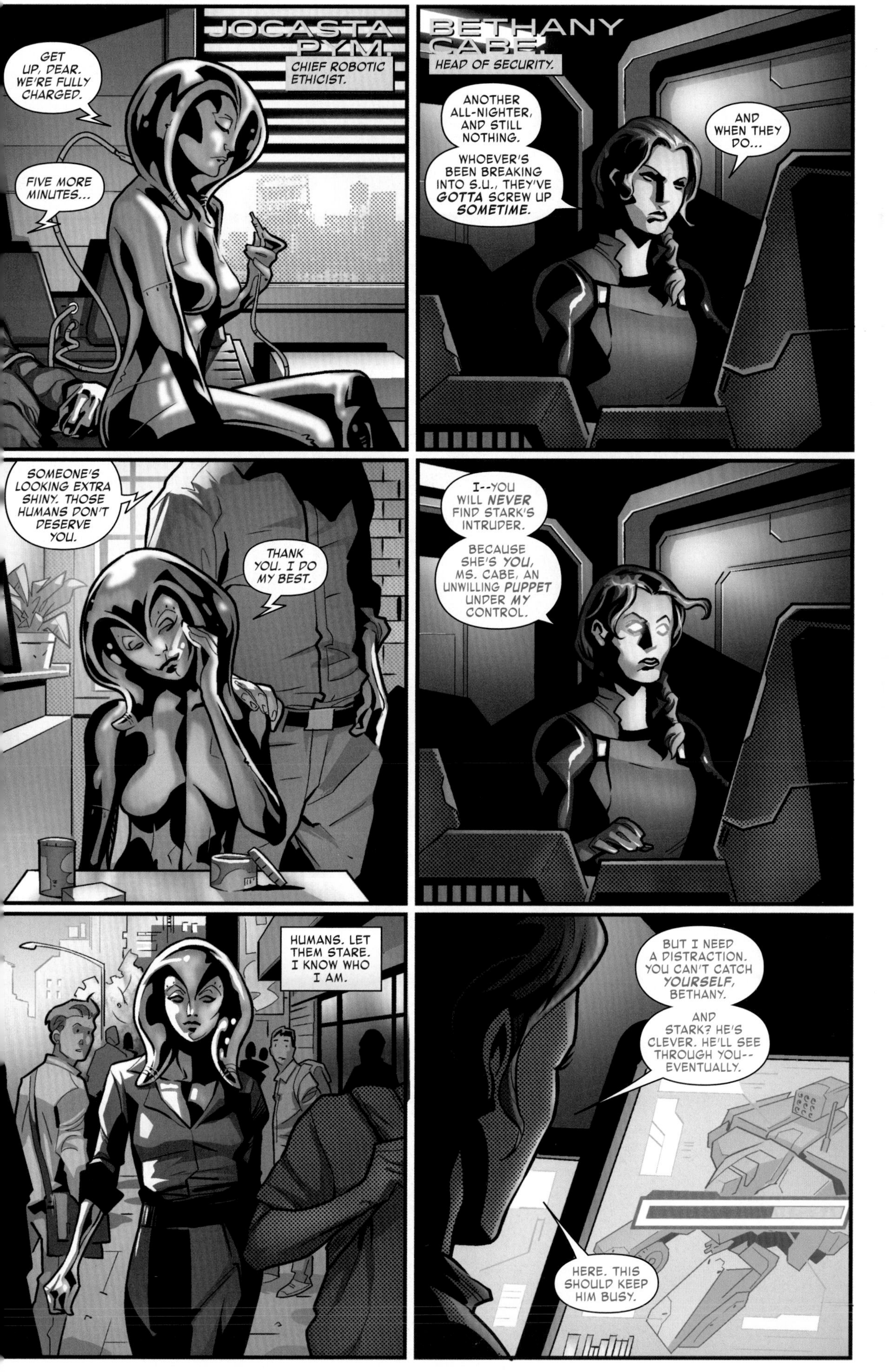
JOCASTA PYM.
CHIEF ROBOTIC ETHICIST.
GET UP, DEAR. WE'RE FULLY CHARGED.
FIVE MORE MINUTES...
BETHANY CABE.
HEAD OF SECURITY.
ANOTHER ALL-NIGHTER, AND STILL NOTHING.
WHOEVER'S BEEN BREAKING INTO S.U., THEY'VE GOTTA SCREW UP SOMETIME.
AND WHEN THEY DO...
SOMEONE'S LOOKING EXTRA SHINY. THOSE HUMANS DON'T DESERVE YOU.
THANK YOU. I DO MY BEST.
I--YOU WILL NEVER FIND STARK'S INTRUDER.
BECAUSE SHE'S YOU, MS. CABE, AN UNWILLING PUPPET UNDER MY CONTROL.
HUMANS. LET THEM STARE. I KNOW WHO I AM.
BUT I NEED A DISTRACTION. YOU CAN'T CATCH YOURSELF, BETHANY.
AND STARK? HE'S CLEVER. HE'LL SEE THROUGH YOU-- EVENTUALLY.
HERE. THIS SHOULD KEEP HIM BUSY.

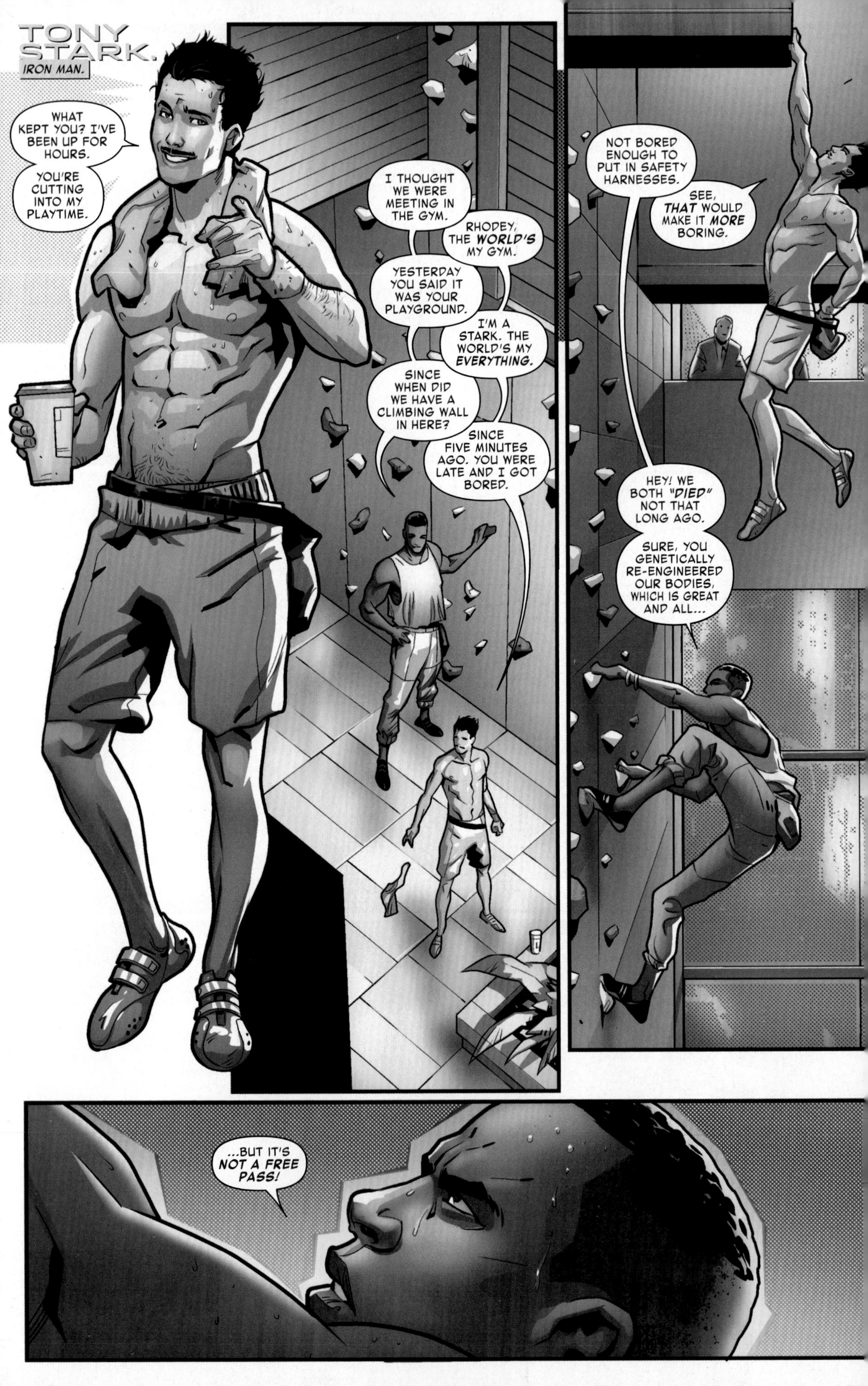
TONY STARK.
IRON MAN.
WHAT KEPT YOU? I'VE BEEN UP FOR HOURS.
YOU'RE CUTTING INTO MY PLAYTIME.
I THOUGHT WE WERE MEETING IN THE GYM.
RHODEY, THE WORLD'S MY GYM.
YESTERDAY YOU SAID IT WAS YOUR PLAYGROUND.
I'M A STARK. THE WORLD'S MY EVERYTHING.
SINCE WHEN DID WE HAVE A CLIMBING WALL IN HERE?
SINCE FIVE MINUTES AGO. YOU WERE LATE AND I GOT BORED.
NOT BORED ENOUGH TO PUT IN SAFETY HARNESSES.
SEE, THAT WOULD MAKE IT MORE BORING.
HEY! WE BOTH "DIED" NOT THAT LONG AGO.
SURE, YOU GENETICALLY RE-ENGINEERED OUR BODIES, WHICH IS GREAT AND ALL...
...BUT IT'S NOT A FREE PASS!

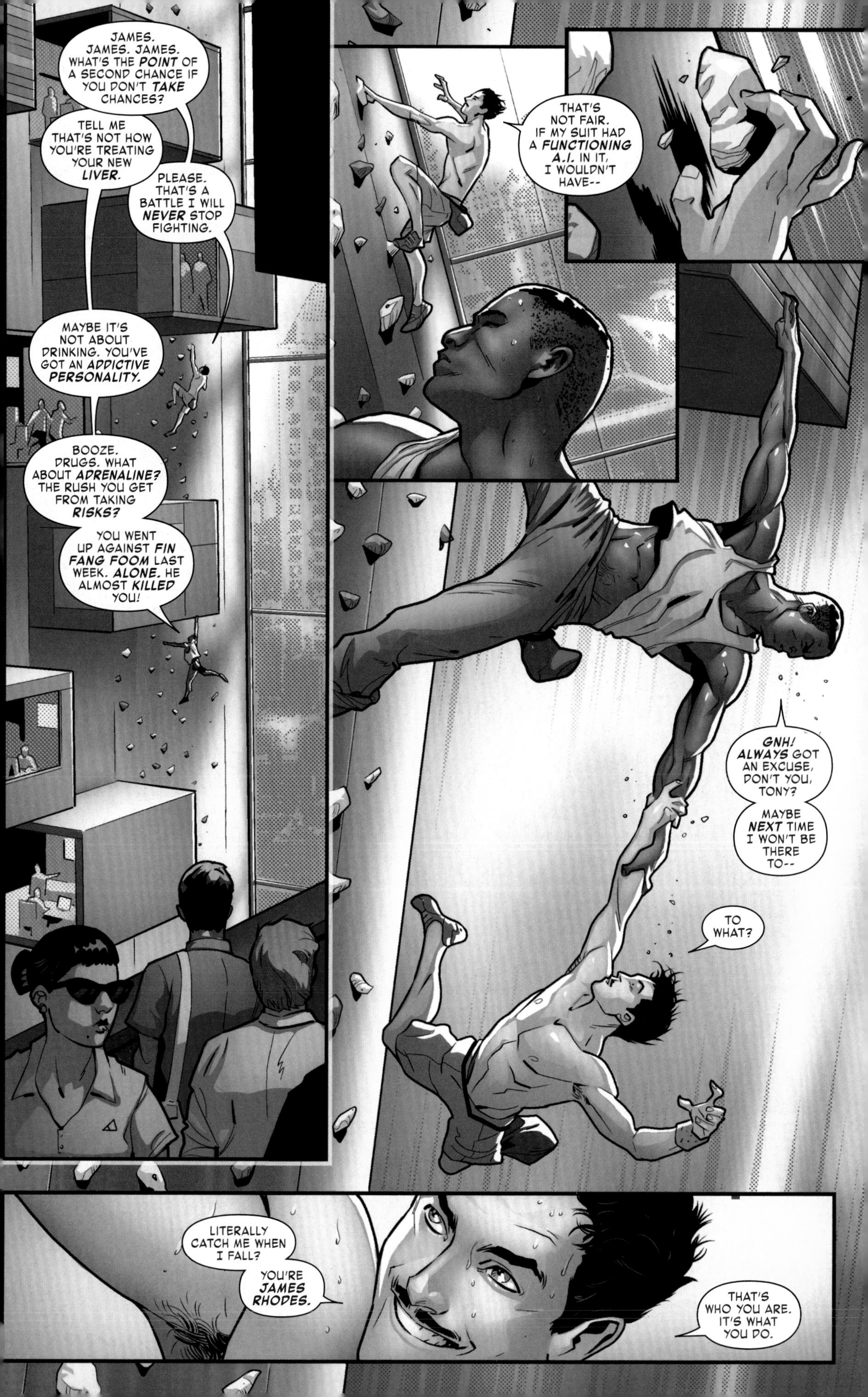
JAMES. JAMES. JAMES. WHAT'S THE POINT OF A SECOND CHANCE IF YOU DON'T TAKE CHANCES?
TELL ME THAT'S NOT HOW YOU'RE TREATING YOUR NEW LIVER.
PLEASE. THAT'S A BATTLE I WILL NEVER STOP FIGHTING.
MAYBE IT'S NOT ABOUT DRINKING. YOU'VE GOT AN ADDICTIVE PERSONALITY.
BOOZE. DRUGS. WHAT ABOUT ADRENALINE? THE RUSH YOU GET FROM TAKING RISKS?
YOU WENT UP AGAINST FIN FANG FOOM LAST WEEK. ALONE. HE ALMOST KILLED YOU!
THAT'S NOT FAIR. IF MY SUIT HAD A FUNCTIONING A.I. IN IT, I WOULDN'T HAVE--
GNH! ALWAYS GOT AN EXCUSE, DON'T YOU, TONY?
MAYBE NEXT TIME I WON'T BE THERE TO--
TO WHAT?
LITERALLY CATCH ME WHEN I FALL?
YOU'RE JAMES RHODES.
THAT'S WHO YOU ARE. IT'S WHAT YOU DO.

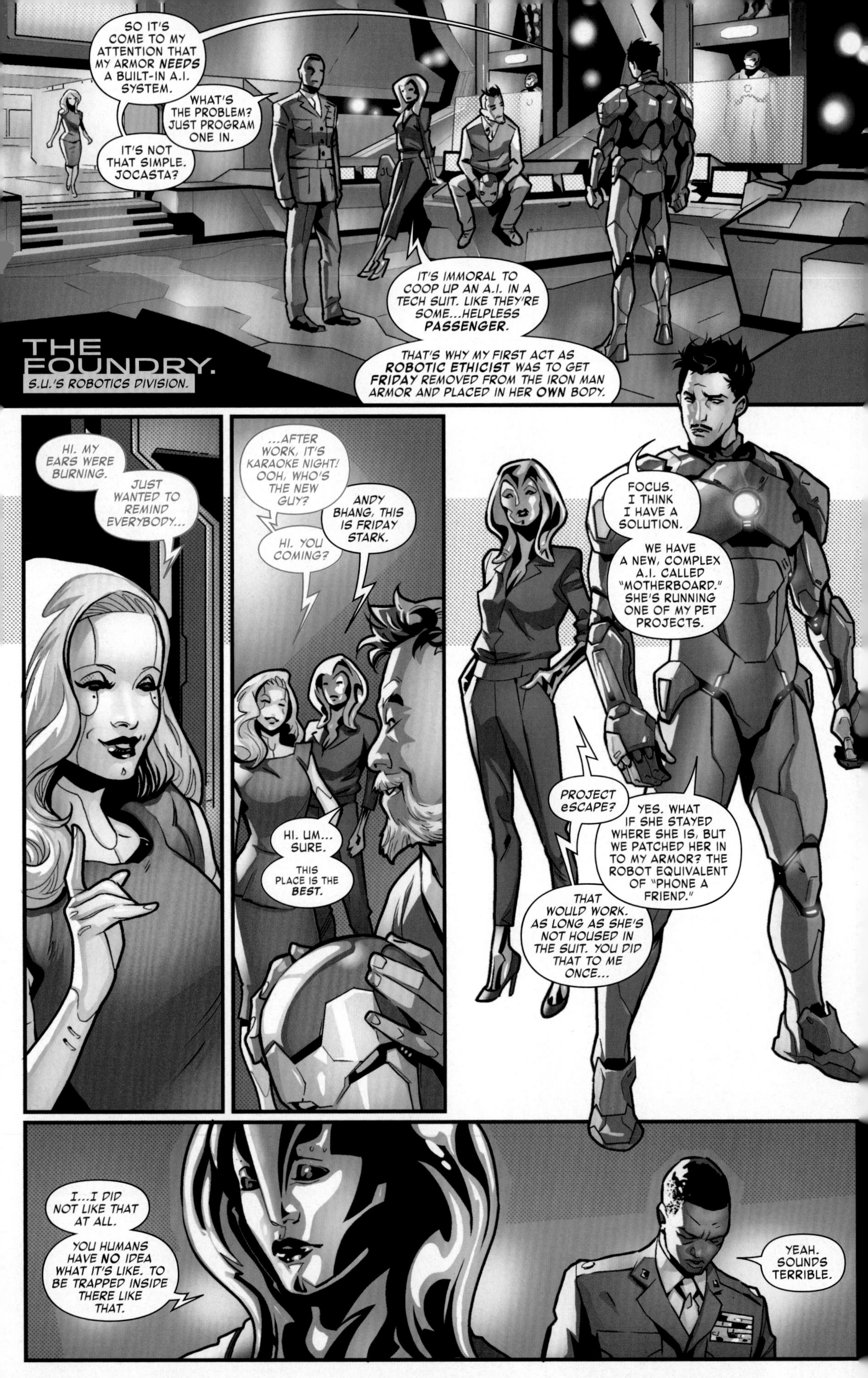
SO IT'S COME TO MY ATTENTION THAT MY ARMOR NEEDS A BUILT-IN A.I. SYSTEM.
WHAT'S THE PROBLEM? JUST PROGRAM ONE IN.
IT'S NOT THAT SIMPLE. JOCASTA?
IT'S IMMORAL TO COOP UP AN A.I. IN A TECH SUIT. LIKE THEY'RE SOME...HELPLESS PASSENGER.
THAT'S WHY MY FIRST ACT AS ROBOTIC ETHICIST WAS TO GET FRIDAY REMOVED FROM THE IRON MAN ARMOR AND PLACED IN HER OWN BODY.
THE FOUNDRY.
S.U.'S ROBOTICS DIVISION.
HI. MY EARS WERE BURNING.
JUST WANTED TO REMIND EVERYBODY...
...AFTER WORK, IT'S KARAOKE NIGHT! OOH, WHO'S THE NEW GUY?
ANDY BHANG, THIS IS FRIDAY STARK.
HI. YOU COMING?
HI. UM... SURE.
THIS PLACE IS THE BEST.
FOCUS. I THINK I HAVE A SOLUTION.
WE HAVE A NEW, COMPLEX A.I. CALLED "MOTHERBOARD." SHE'S RUNNING ONE OF MY PET PROJECTS.
PROJECT eSCAPE?
YES. WHAT IF SHE STAYED WHERE SHE IS, BUT WE PATCHED HER IN TO MY ARMOR? THE ROBOT EQUIVALENT OF "PHONE A FRIEND."
THAT WOULD WORK. AS LONG AS SHE'S NOT HOUSED IN THE SUIT. YOU DID THAT TO ME ONCE...
I...I DID NOT LIKE THAT AT ALL.
YOU HUMANS HAVE NO IDEA WHAT IT'S LIKE. TO BE TRAPPED INSIDE THERE LIKE THAT.
YEAH. SOUNDS TERRIBLE.

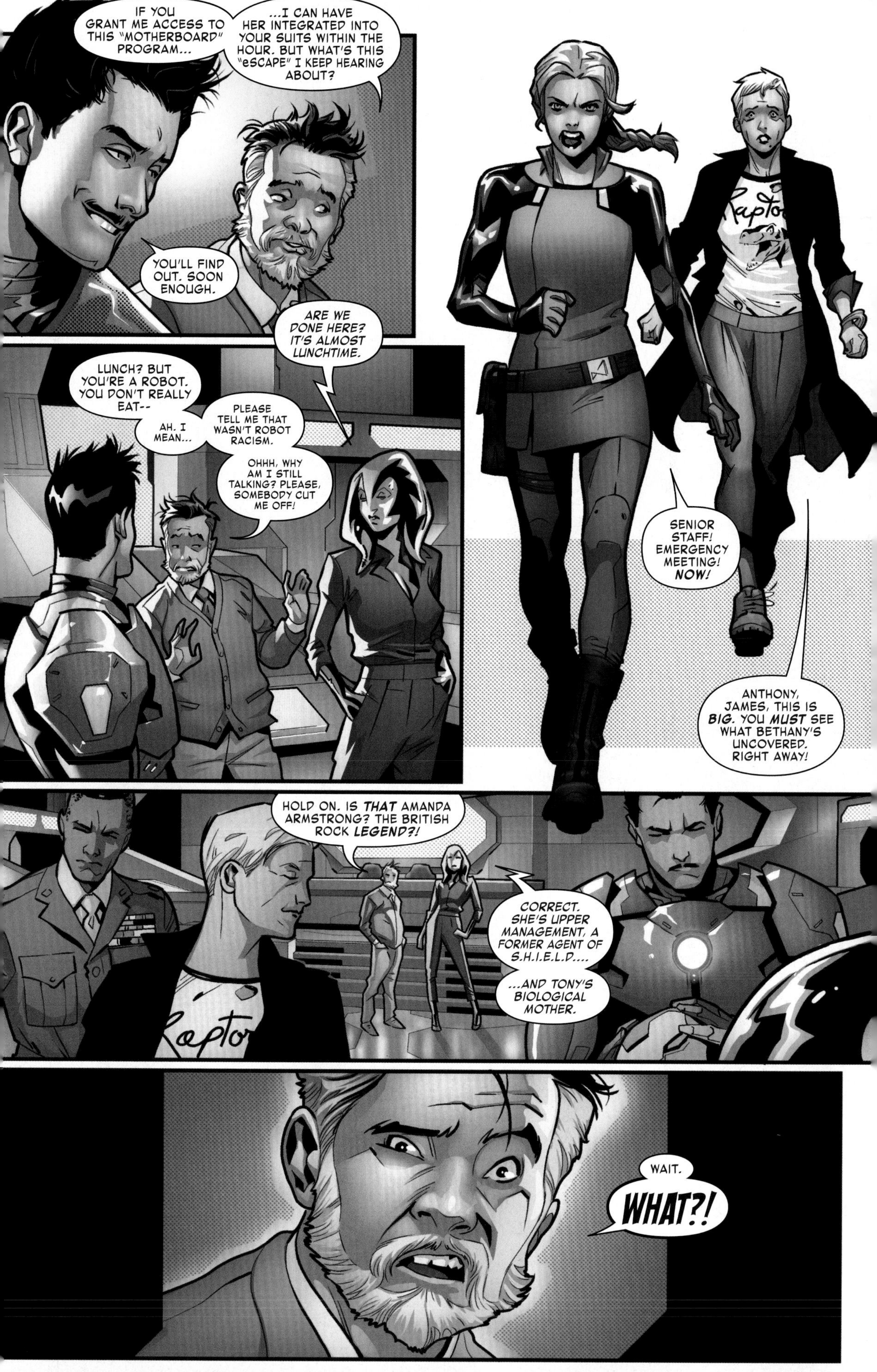
IF YOU GRANT ME ACCESS TO THIS "MOTHERBOARD" PROGRAM...
...I CAN HAVE HER INTEGRATED INTO YOUR SUITS WITHIN THE HOUR. BUT WHAT'S THIS "eSCAPE" I KEEP HEARING ABOUT?
YOU'LL FIND OUT. SOON ENOUGH.
ARE WE DONE HERE? IT'S ALMOST LUNCHTIME.
LUNCH? BUT YOU'RE A ROBOT. YOU DON'T REALLY EAT--
AH. I MEAN...
PLEASE TELL ME THAT WASN'T ROBOT RACISM.
OHHH, WHY AM I STILL TALKING? PLEASE, SOMEBODY CUT ME OFF!
SENIOR STAFF! EMERGENCY MEETING! NOW!
ANTHONY, JAMES, THIS IS BIG. YOU MUST SEE WHAT BETHANY'S UNCOVERED. RIGHT AWAY!
HOLD ON. IS THAT AMANDA ARMSTRONG? THE BRITISH ROCK LEGEND?!
CORRECT. SHE'S UPPER MANAGEMENT, A FORMER AGENT OF S.H.I.E.L.D....
...AND TONY'S BIOLOGICAL MOTHER.
WAIT.
WHAT?!

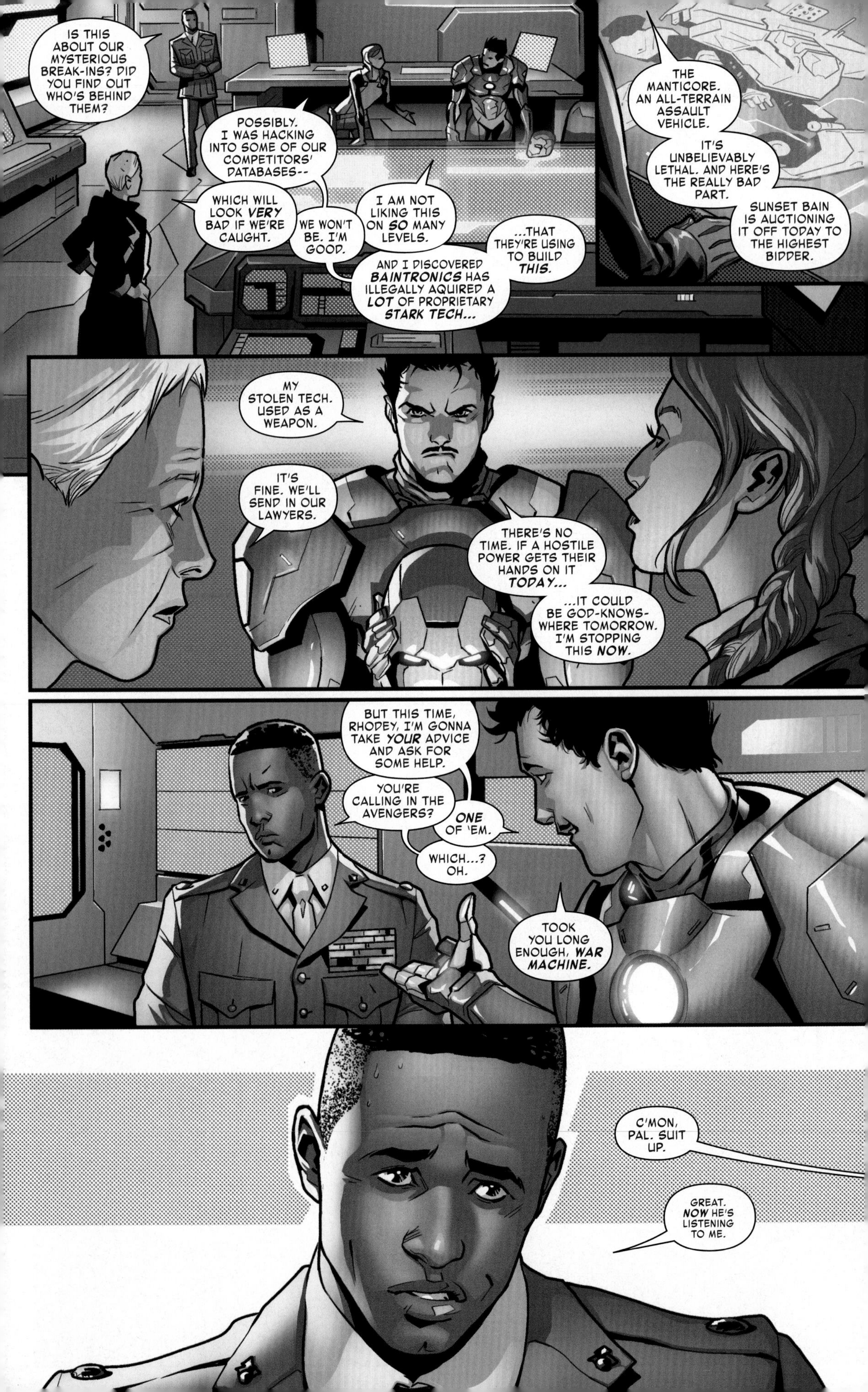
IS THIS ABOUT OUR MYSTERIOUS BREAK-INS? DID YOU FIND OUT WHO'S BEHIND THEM?
POSSIBLY. I WAS HACKING INTO SOME OF OUR COMPETITORS' DATABASES--
WHICH WILL LOOK VERY BAD IF WE'RE CAUGHT.
WE WON'T BE. I'M GOOD.
I AM NOT LIKING THIS ON SO MANY LEVELS.
AND I DISCOVERED BAINTRONICS HAS ILLEGALLY AQUIRED A LOT OF PROPRIETARY STARK TECH...
...THAT THEY'RE USING TO BUILD THIS.
THE MANTICORE. AN ALL-TERRAIN ASSAULT VEHICLE.
IT'S UNBELIEVABLY LETHAL. AND HERE'S THE REALLY BAD PART.
SUNSET BAIN IS AUCTIONING IT OFF TODAY TO THE HIGHEST BIDDER.
MY STOLEN TECH. USED AS A WEAPON.
IT'S FINE. WE'LL SEND IN OUR LAWYERS.
THERE'S NO TIME. IF A HOSTILE POWER GETS THEIR HANDS ON IT TODAY...
...IT COULD BE GOD-KNOWS-WHERE TOMORROW. I'M STOPPING THIS NOW.
BUT THIS TIME, RHODEY, I'M GONNA TAKE YOUR ADVICE AND ASK FOR SOME HELP.
YOU'RE CALLING IN THE AVENGERS?
ONE OF 'EM.
WHICH...? OH.
TOOK YOU LONG ENOUGH, WAR MACHINE.
C'MON, PAL. SUIT UP.
GREAT. NOW HE'S LISTENING TO ME.

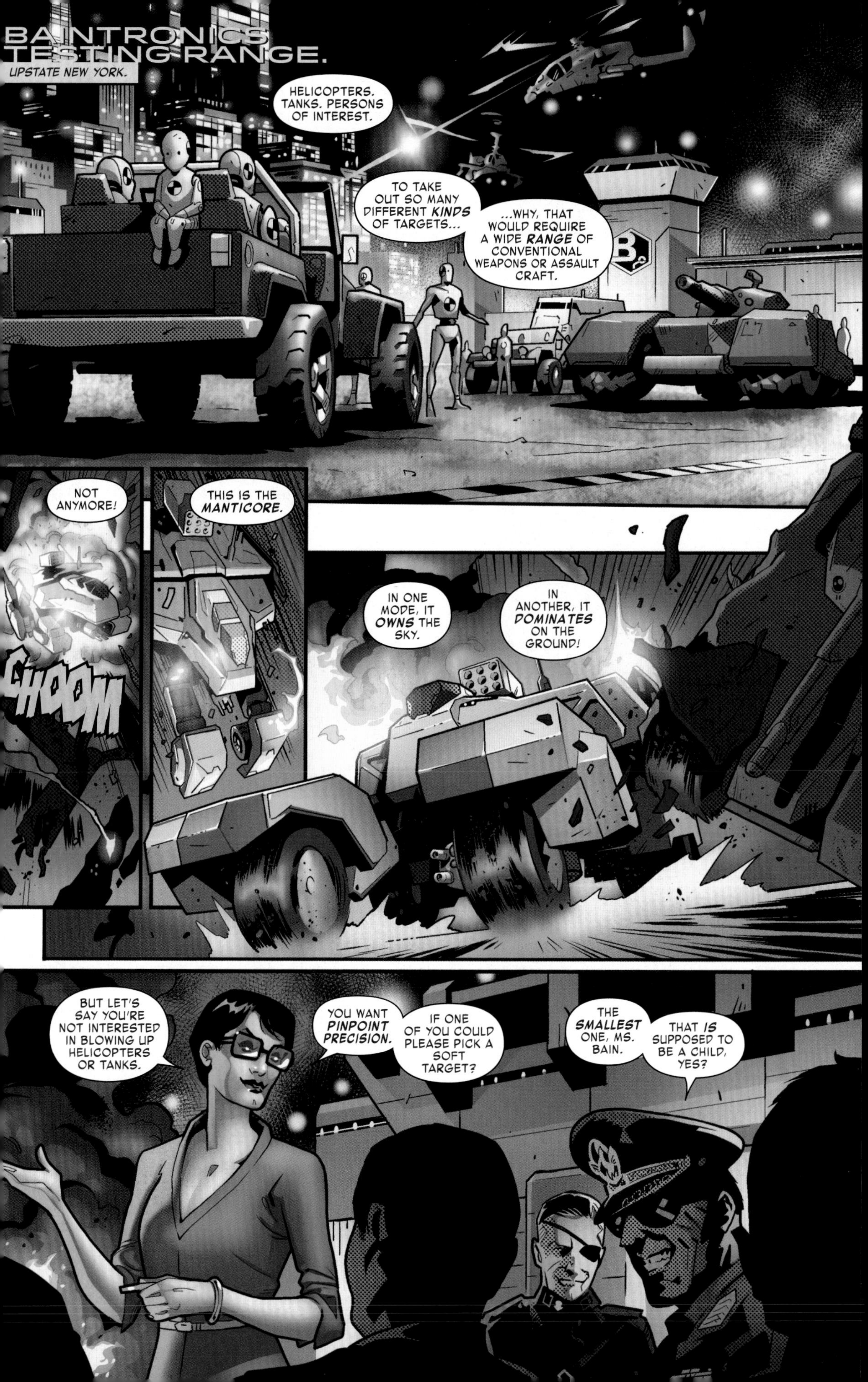
BAINTRONICS TESTING RANGE.
UPSTATE NEW YORK.
HELICOPTERS. TANKS. PERSONS OF INTEREST.
TO TAKE OUT SO MANY DIFFERENT KINDS OF TARGETS...
...WHY, THAT WOULD REQUIRE A WIDE RANGE OF CONVENTIONAL WEAPONS OR ASSAULT CRAFT.
NOT ANYMORE!
CHOOM
THIS IS THE MANTICORE.
IN ONE MODE, IT OWNS THE SKY.
IN ANOTHER, IT DOMINATES ON THE GROUND!
BUT LET'S SAY YOU'RE NOT INTERESTED IN BLOWING UP HELICOPTERS OR TANKS.
YOU WANT PINPOINT PRECISION.
IF ONE OF YOU COULD PLEASE PICK A SOFT TARGET?
THE SMALLEST ONE, MS. BAIN.
THAT IS SUPPOSED TO BE A CHILD, YES?

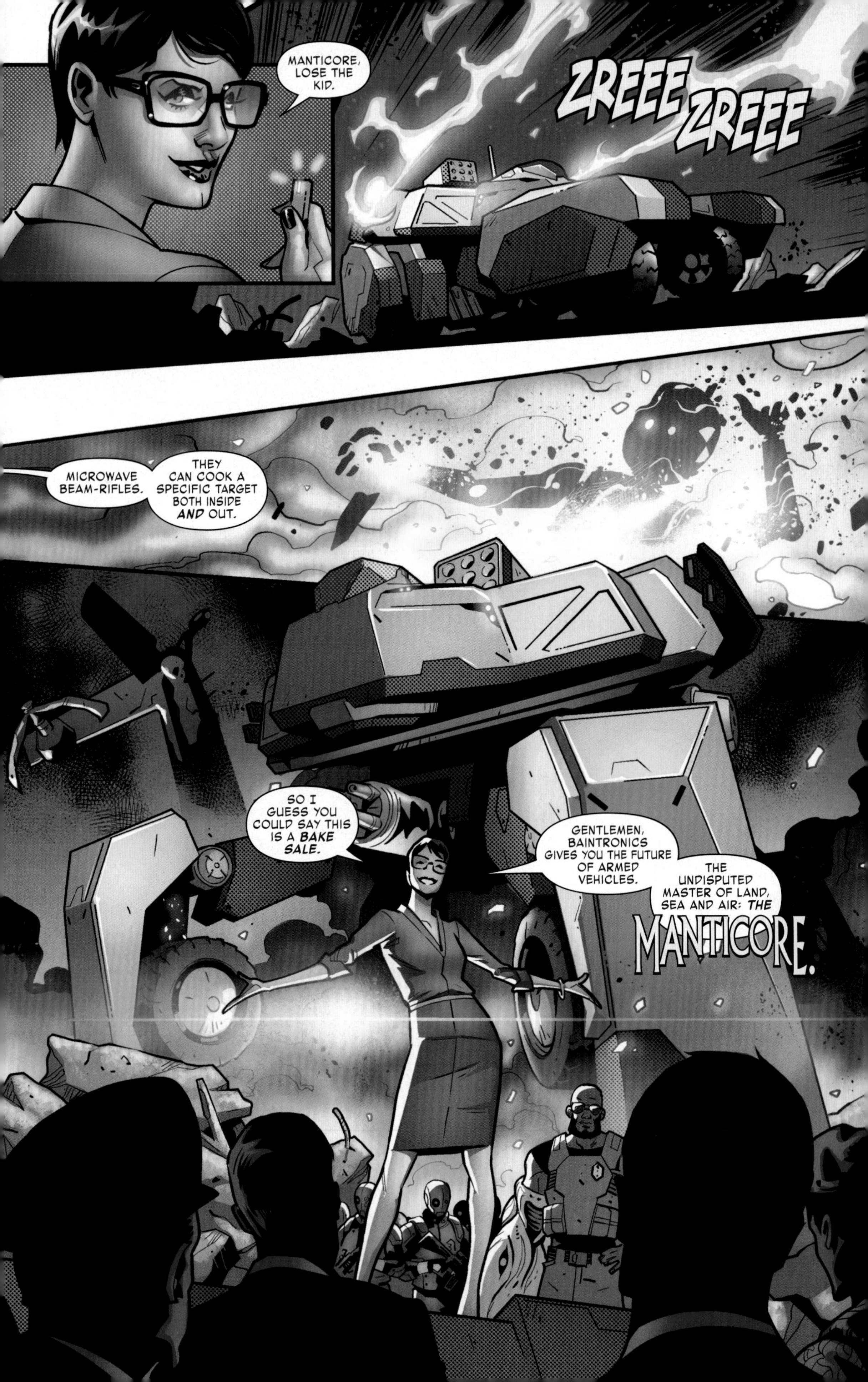
MANTICORE, LOSE THE KID.
ZREEE ZREEE
MICROWAVE BEAM-RIFLES.
THEY CAN COOK A SPECIFIC TARGET BOTH INSIDE AND OUT.
SO I GUESS YOU COULD SAY THIS IS A BAKE SALE.
GENTLEMEN, BAINTRONICS GIVES YOU THE FUTURE OF ARMED VEHICLES.
THE UNDISPUTED MASTER OF LAND, SEA AND AIR: THE
MANTICORE.

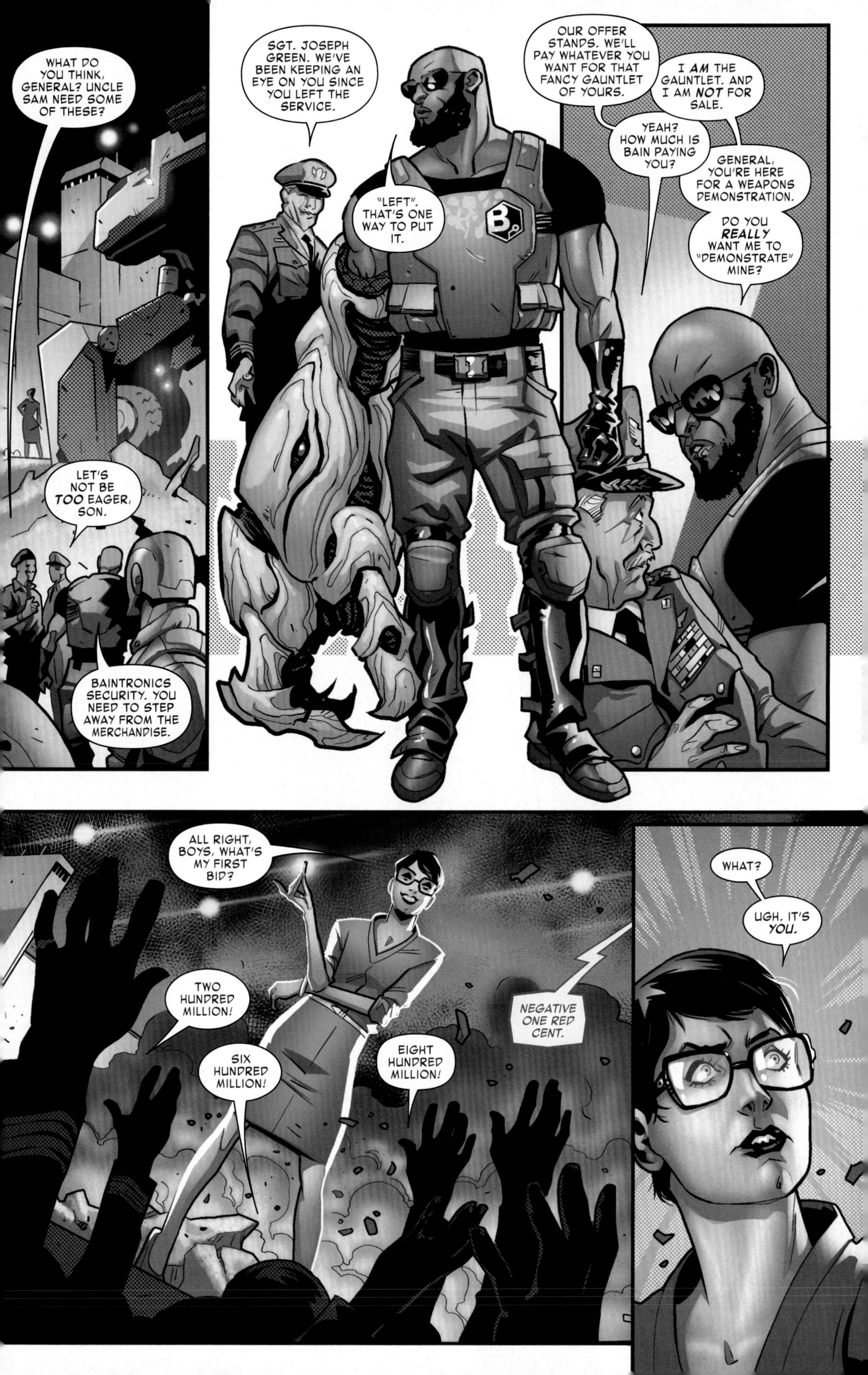
WHAT DO YOU THINK, GENERAL? UNCLE SAM NEED SOME OF THESE?
LET'S NOT BE TOO EAGER, SON.
BAINTRONICS SECURITY. YOU NEED TO STEP AWAY FROM THE MERCHANDISE.
SGT. JOSEPH GREEN. WE'VE BEEN KEEPING AN EYE ON YOU SINCE YOU LEFT THE SERVICE.
"LEFT". THAT'S ONE WAY TO PUT IT.
OUR OFFER STANDS. WE'LL PAY WHATEVER YOU WANT FOR THAT FANCY GAUNTLET OF YOURS.
YEAH? HOW MUCH IS BAIN PAYING YOU?
I AM THE GAUNTLET. AND I AM NOT FOR SALE.
GENERAL, YOU'RE HERE FOR A WEAPONS DEMONSTRATION.
DO YOU REALLY WANT ME TO "DEMONSTRATE" MINE?
ALL RIGHT, BOYS, WHAT'S MY FIRST BID?
TWO HUNDRED MILLION!
SIX HUNDRED MILLION!
EIGHT HUNDRED MILLION!
NEGATIVE ONE RED CENT.
WHAT?
UGH. IT'S YOU.

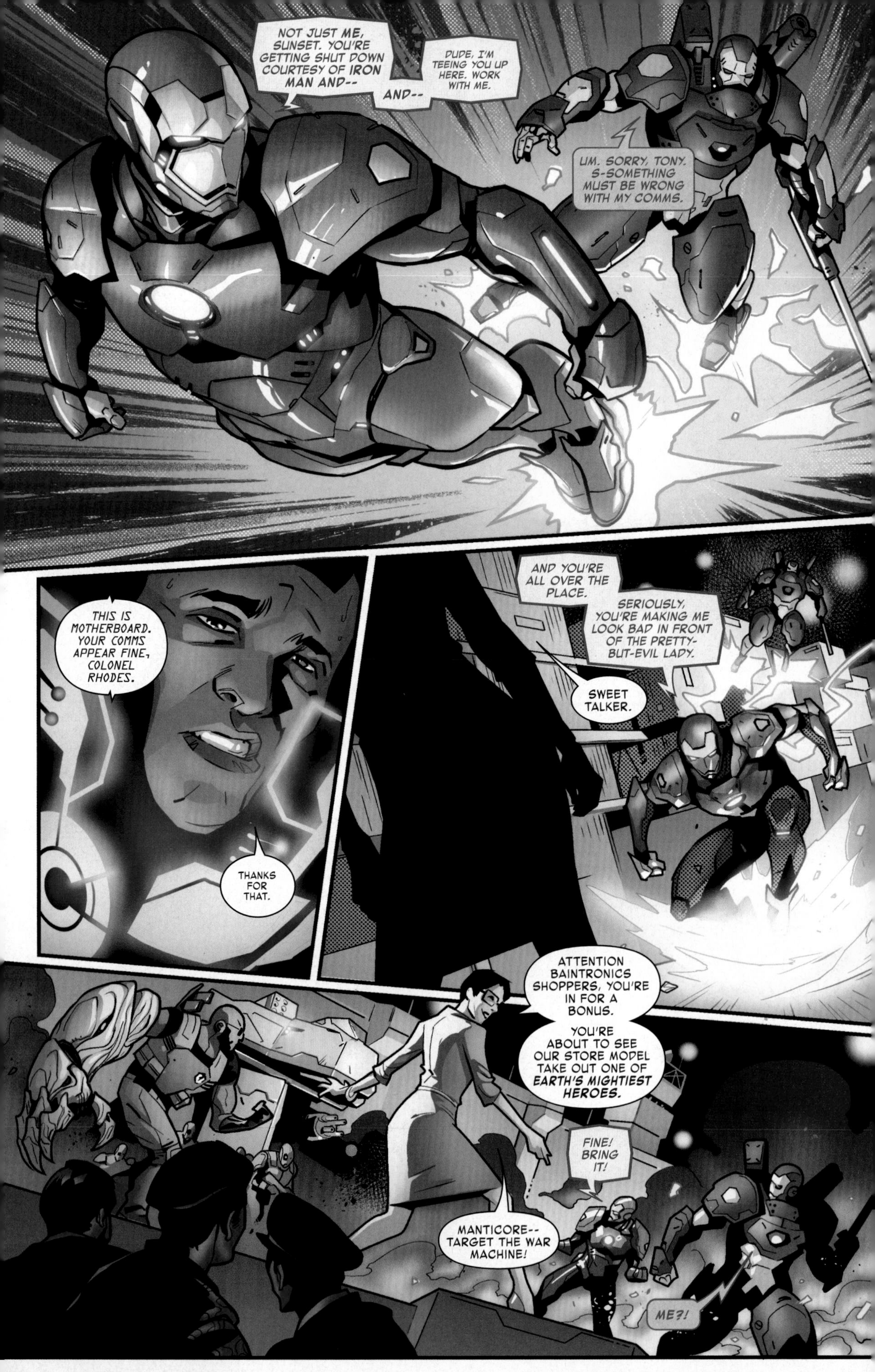
NOT JUST ME, SUNSET. YOU'RE GETTING SHUT DOWN COURTESY OF IRON MAN AND--
AND--
DUDE, I'M TEEING YOU UP HERE. WORK WITH ME.
UM. SORRY, TONY. S-SOMETHING MUST BE WRONG WITH MY COMMS.
THIS IS MOTHERBOARD. YOUR COMMS APPEAR FINE, COLONEL RHODES.
THANKS FOR THAT.
AND YOU'RE ALL OVER THE PLACE.
SERIOUSLY, YOU'RE MAKING ME LOOK BAD IN FRONT OF THE PRETTY-BUT-EVIL LADY.
SWEET TALKER.
ATTENTION BAINTRONICS SHOPPERS, YOU'RE IN FOR A BONUS.
YOU'RE ABOUT TO SEE OUR STORE MODEL TAKE OUT ONE OF EARTH'S MIGHTIEST HEROES.
FINE! BRING IT!
MANTICORE-- TARGET THE WAR MACHINE!
ME?!

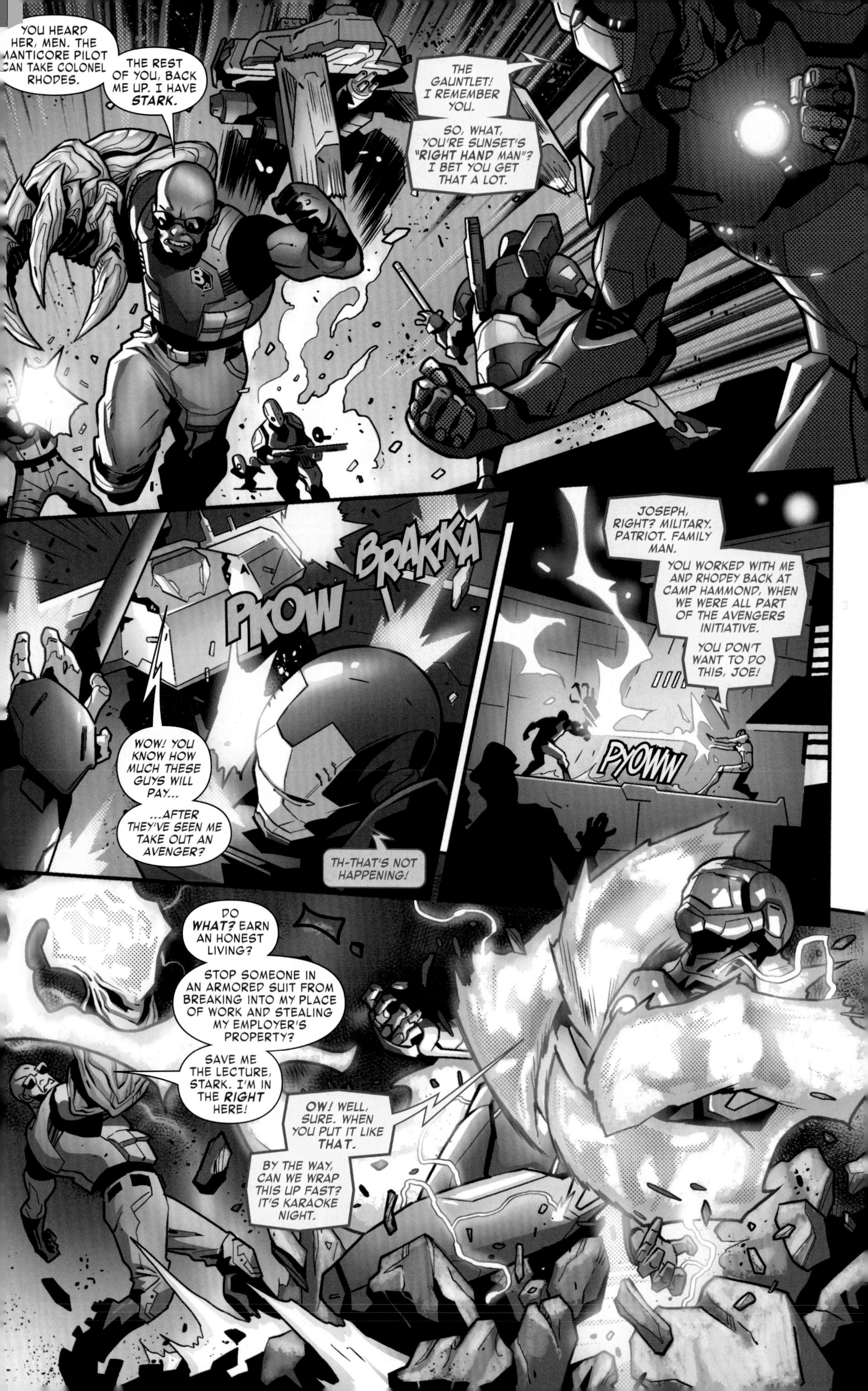

YOU HEARD HER, MEN. THE MANTICORE PILOT CAN TAKE COLONEL RHODES.
THE REST OF YOU, BACK ME UP. I HAVE STARK.
THE GAUNTLET! I REMEMBER YOU.
SO, WHAT, YOU'RE SUNSET'S "RIGHT HAND MAN"? I BET YOU GET THAT A LOT.
BRAKKA
PKOW
WOW! YOU KNOW HOW MUCH THESE GUYS WILL PAY...
...AFTER THEY'VE SEEN ME TAKE OUT AN AVENGER?
TH-THAT'S NOT HAPPENING!
JOSEPH, RIGHT? MILITARY. PATRIOT. FAMILY MAN.
YOU WORKED WITH ME AND RHODEY BACK AT CAMP HAMMOND, WHEN WE WERE ALL PART OF THE AVENGERS INITIATIVE.
YOU DON'T WANT TO DO THIS, JOE!
PYOWW
DO WHAT? EARN AN HONEST LIVING?
STOP SOMEONE IN AN ARMORED SUIT FROM BREAKING INTO MY PLACE OF WORK AND STEALING MY EMPLOYER'S PROPERTY?
SAVE ME THE LECTURE, STARK. I'M IN THE RIGHT HERE!
OW! WELL, SURE. WHEN YOU PUT IT LIKE THAT.
BY THE WAY, CAN WE WRAP THIS UP FAST? IT'S KARAOKE NIGHT.

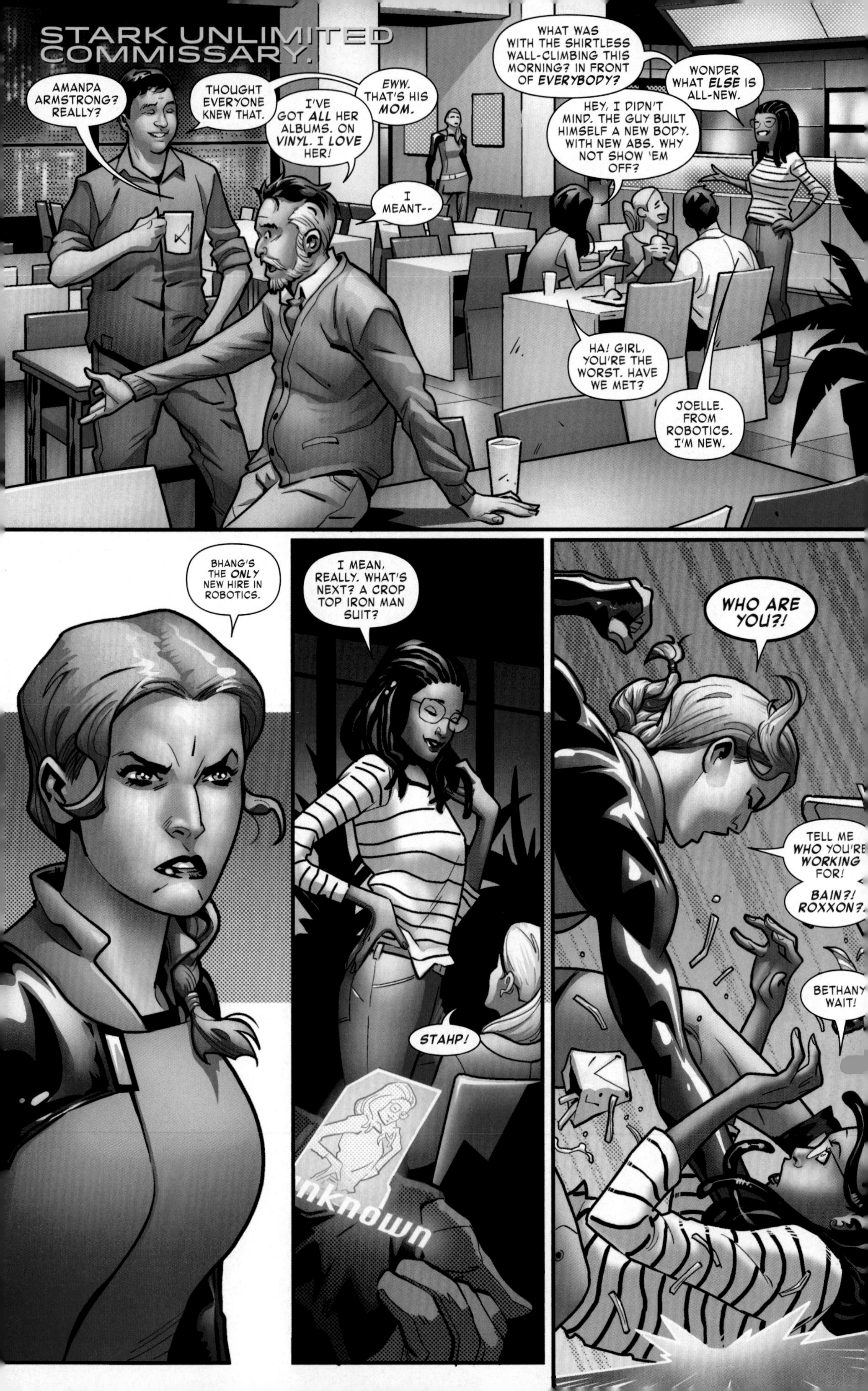
STARK UNLIMITED COMMISSARY.
AMANDA ARMSTRONG? REALLY?
THOUGHT EVERYONE KNEW THAT.
I'VE GOT ALL HER ALBUMS. ON VINYL. I LOVE HER!
EWW. THAT'S HIS MOM.
I MEANT--
WHAT WAS WITH THE SHIRTLESS WALL-CLIMBING THIS MORNING? IN FRONT OF EVERYBODY?
HEY, I DIDN'T MIND. THE GUY BUILT HIMSELF A NEW BODY. WITH NEW ABS. WHY NOT SHOW 'EM OFF?
WONDER WHAT ELSE IS ALL-NEW.
HA! GIRL, YOU'RE THE WORST. HAVE WE MET?
JOELLE. FROM ROBOTICS. I'M NEW.
BHANG'S THE ONLY NEW HIRE IN ROBOTICS.
I MEAN, REALLY. WHAT'S NEXT? A CROP TOP IRON MAN SUIT?
STAHP!
nknown
WHO ARE YOU?!
TELL ME WHO YOU'RE WORKING FOR!
BAIN?! ROXXON?!
BETHANY WAIT!

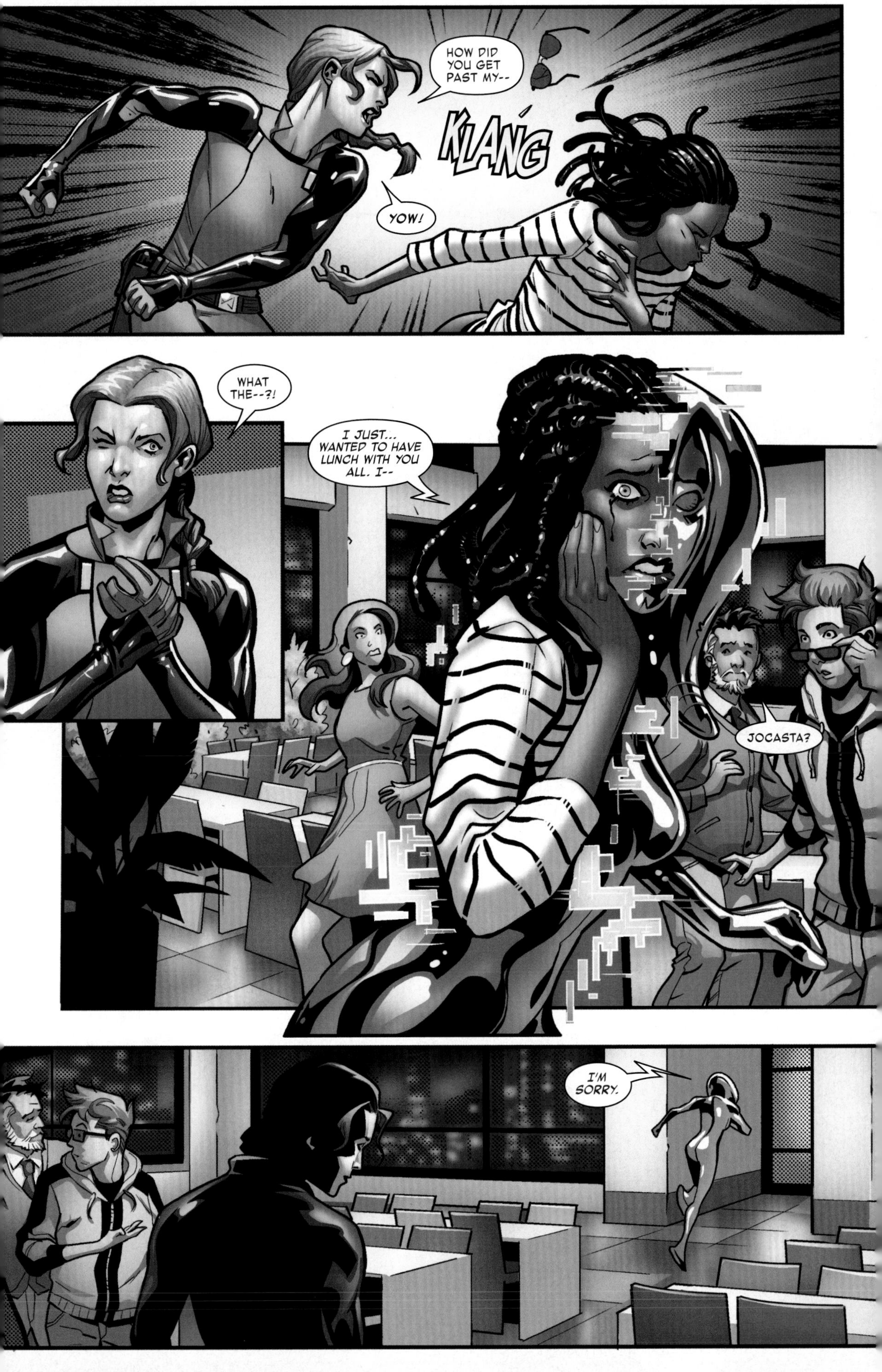
HOW DID YOU GET PAST MY--
KLANG
YOW!
WHAT THE--?!
I JUST... WANTED TO HAVE LUNCH WITH YOU ALL. I--
JOCASTA?
I'M SORRY.

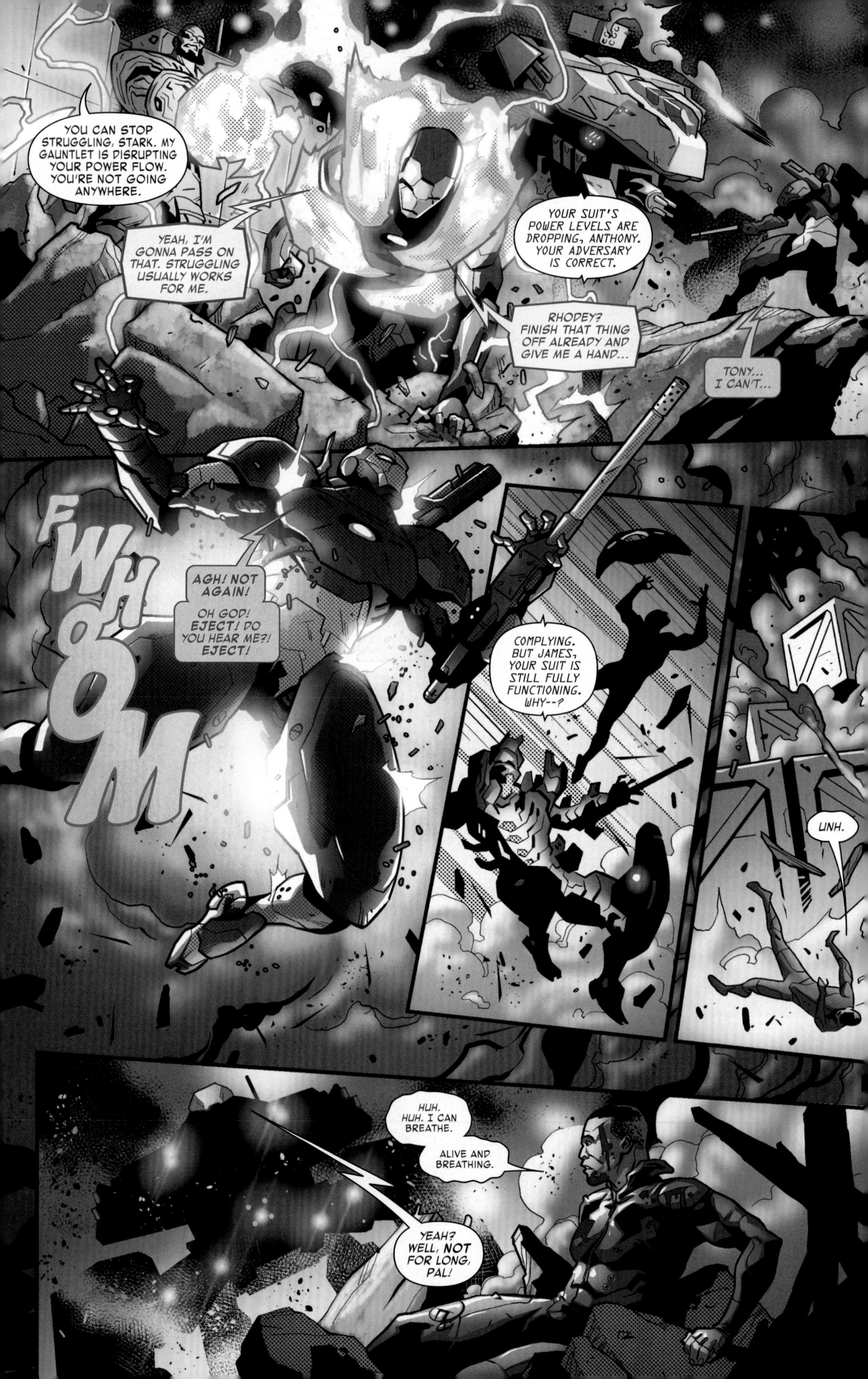
YOU CAN STOP STRUGGLING, STARK. MY GAUNTLET IS DISRUPTING YOUR POWER FLOW. YOU'RE NOT GOING ANYWHERE.
YEAH, I'M GONNA PASS ON THAT. STRUGGLING USUALLY WORKS FOR ME.
YOUR SUIT'S POWER LEVELS ARE DROPPING, ANTHONY. YOUR ADVERSARY IS CORRECT.
RHODEY? FINISH THAT THING OFF ALREADY AND GIVE ME A HAND...
TONY... I CAN'T...
FWHOOM
AGH! NOT AGAIN!
OH GOD! EJECT! DO YOU HEAR ME?! EJECT!
COMPLYING. BUT JAMES, YOUR SUIT IS STILL FULLY FUNCTIONING. WHY--?
UNH.
HUH. HUH. I CAN BREATHE.
ALIVE AND BREATHING.
YEAH? WELL, NOT FOR LONG, PAL!

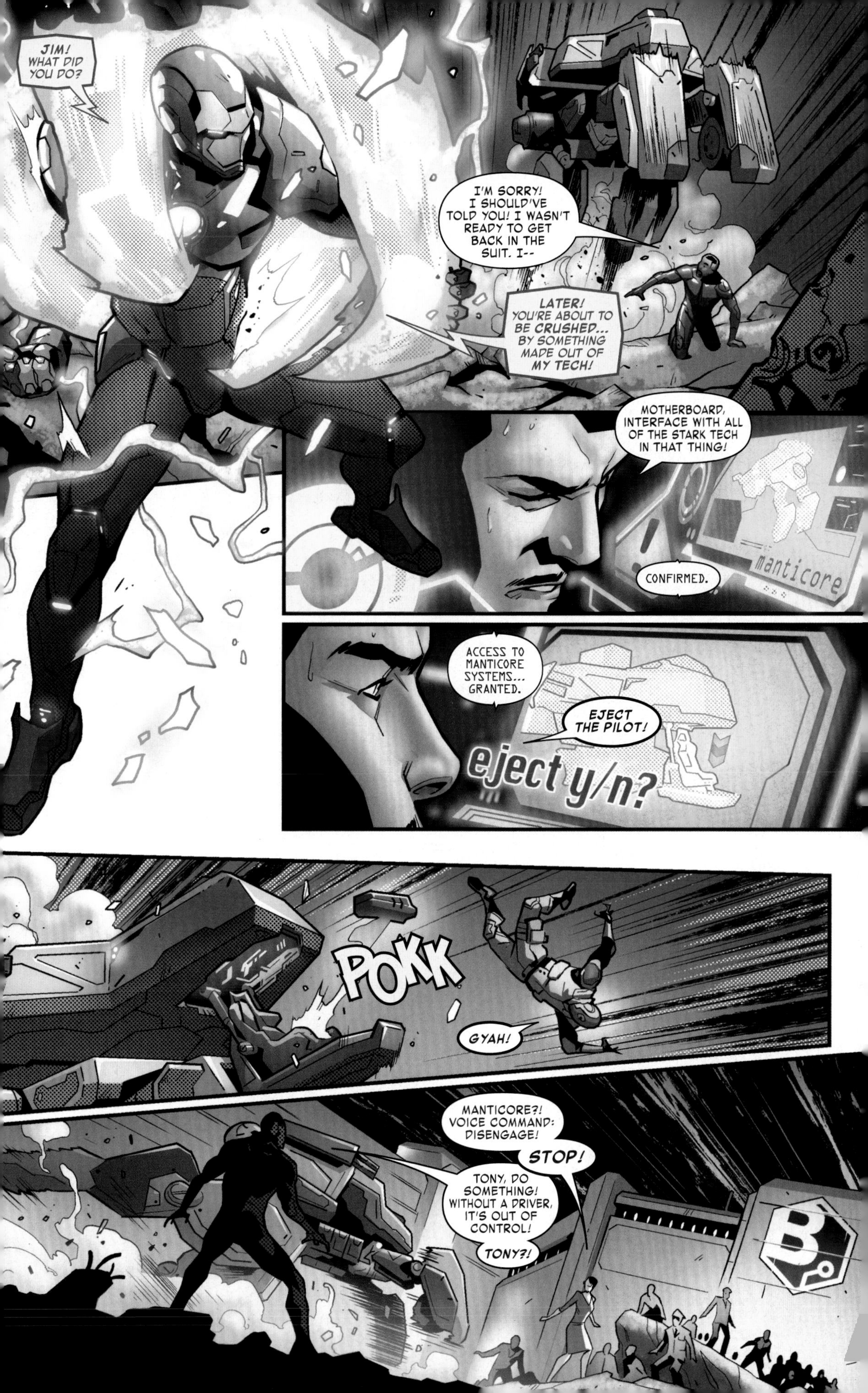
JIM! WHAT DID YOU DO?
I'M SORRY! I SHOULD'VE TOLD YOU! I WASN'T READY TO GET BACK IN THE SUIT. I--
LATER! YOU'RE ABOUT TO BE CRUSHED... BY SOMETHING MADE OUT OF MY TECH!
MOTHERBOARD, INTERFACE WITH ALL OF THE STARK TECH IN THAT THING!
manticore
CONFIRMED.
ACCESS TO MANTICORE SYSTEMS... GRANTED.
EJECT THE PILOT!
eject y/n?
POKK
GYAH!
MANTICORE?! VOICE COMMAND: DISENGAGE!
STOP!
TONY, DO SOMETHING! WITHOUT A DRIVER, IT'S OUT OF CONTROL!
TONY?!

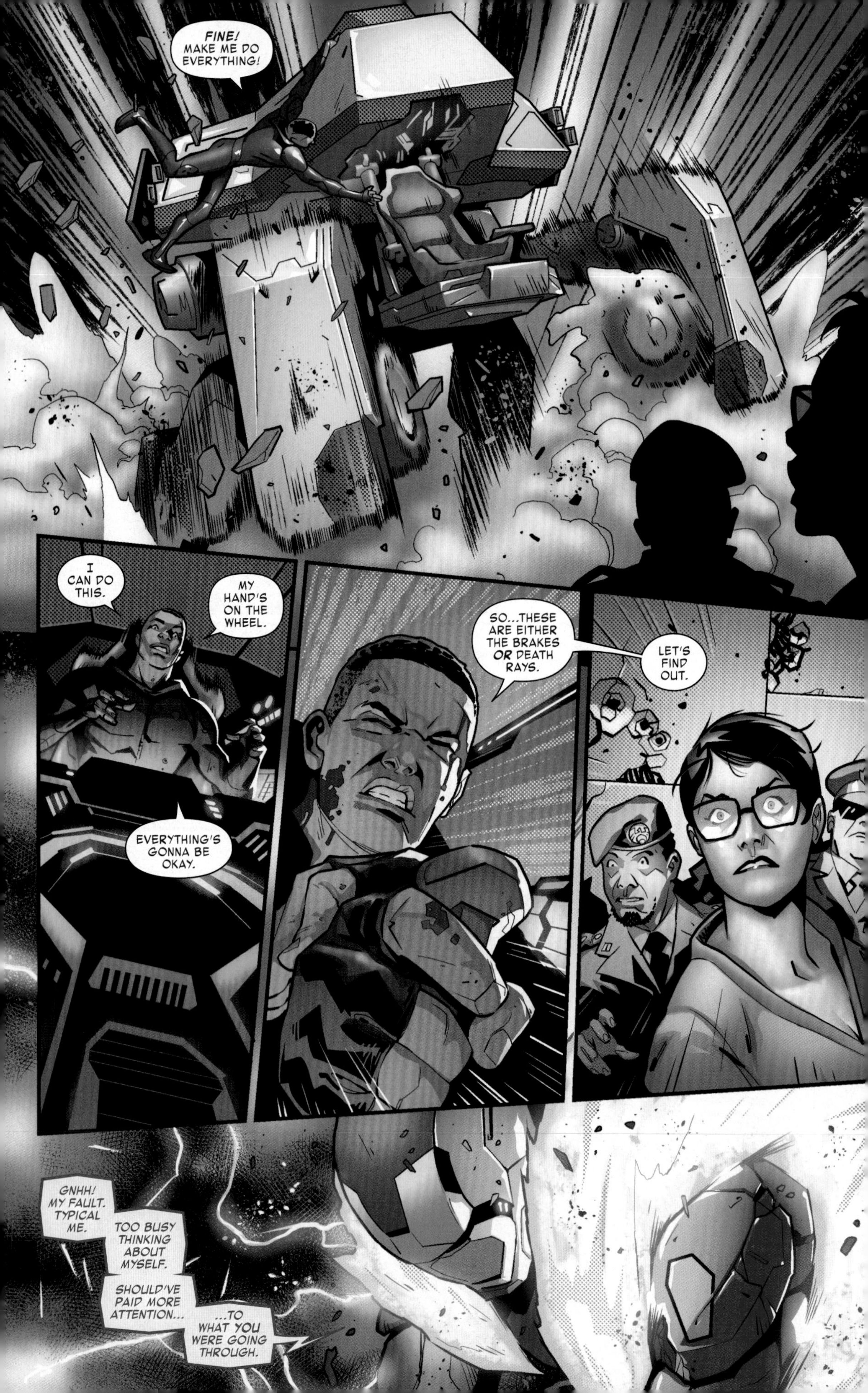
FINE! MAKE ME DO EVERYTHING!
I CAN DO THIS.
MY HAND'S ON THE WHEEL.
EVERYTHING'S GONNA BE OKAY.
SO...THESE ARE EITHER THE BRAKES OR DEATH RAYS.
LET'S FIND OUT.
GNHH! MY FAULT. TYPICAL ME.
TOO BUSY THINKING ABOUT MYSELF.
SHOULD'VE PAID MORE ATTENTION...
...TO WHAT YOU WERE GOING THROUGH.

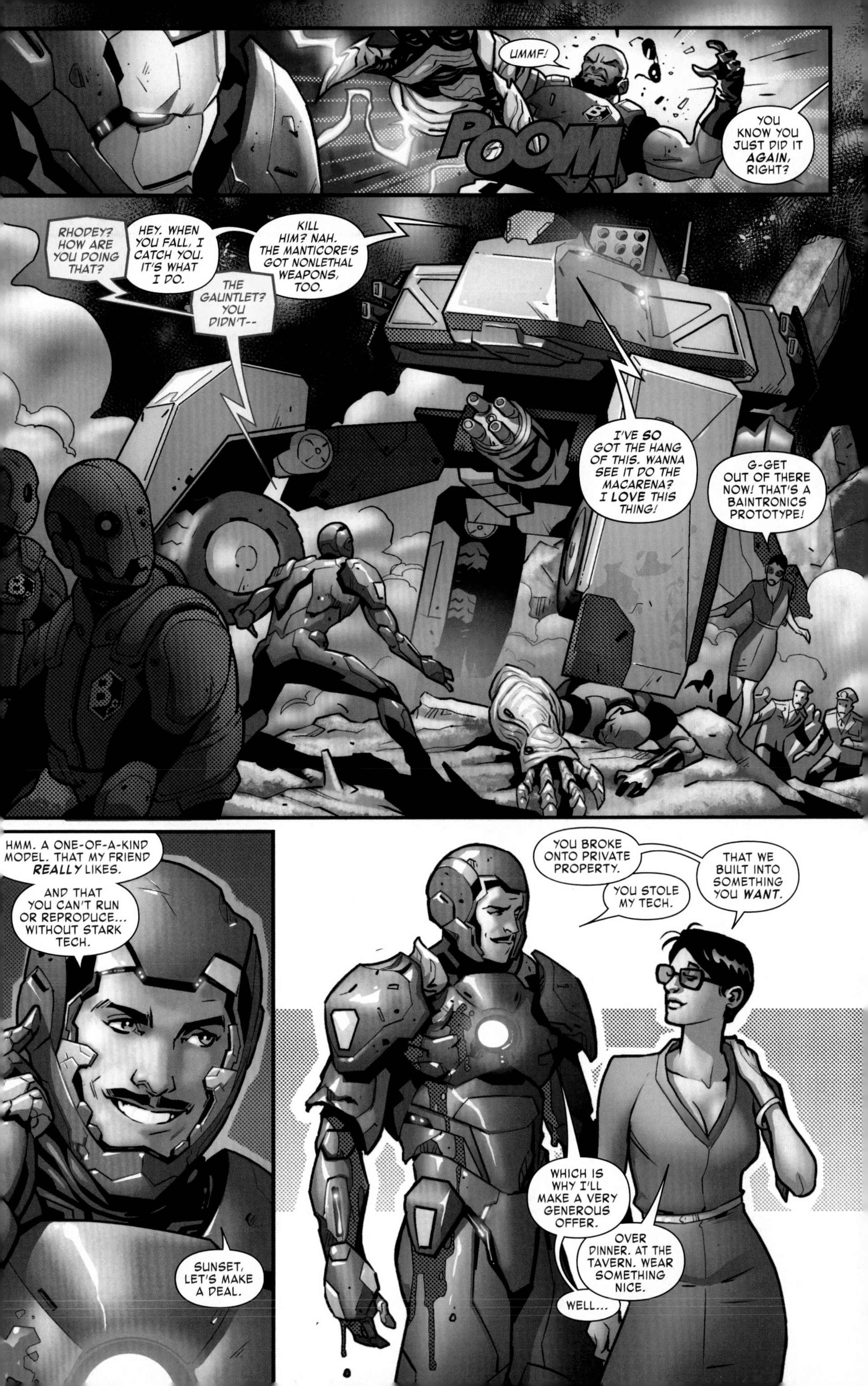
UMMF!
POOM
YOU KNOW YOU JUST DID IT AGAIN, RIGHT?
RHODEY? HOW ARE YOU DOING THAT?
HEY. WHEN YOU FALL, I CATCH YOU. IT'S WHAT I DO.
THE GAUNTLET? YOU DIDN'T--
KILL HIM? NAH. THE MANTICORE'S GOT NONLETHAL WEAPONS, TOO.
I'VE SO GOT THE HANG OF THIS. WANNA SEE IT DO THE MACARENA? I LOVE THIS THING!
G-GET OUT OF THERE NOW! THAT'S A BAINTRONICS PROTOTYPE!
HMM. A ONE-OF-A-KIND MODEL. THAT MY FRIEND REALLY LIKES.
AND THAT YOU CAN'T RUN OR REPRODUCE... WITHOUT STARK TECH.
SUNSET, LET'S MAKE A DEAL.
YOU BROKE ONTO PRIVATE PROPERTY.
YOU STOLE MY TECH.
THAT WE BUILT INTO SOMETHING YOU WANT.
WHICH IS WHY I'LL MAKE A VERY GENEROUS OFFER.
OVER DINNER. AT THE TAVERN. WEAR SOMETHING NICE.
WELL...

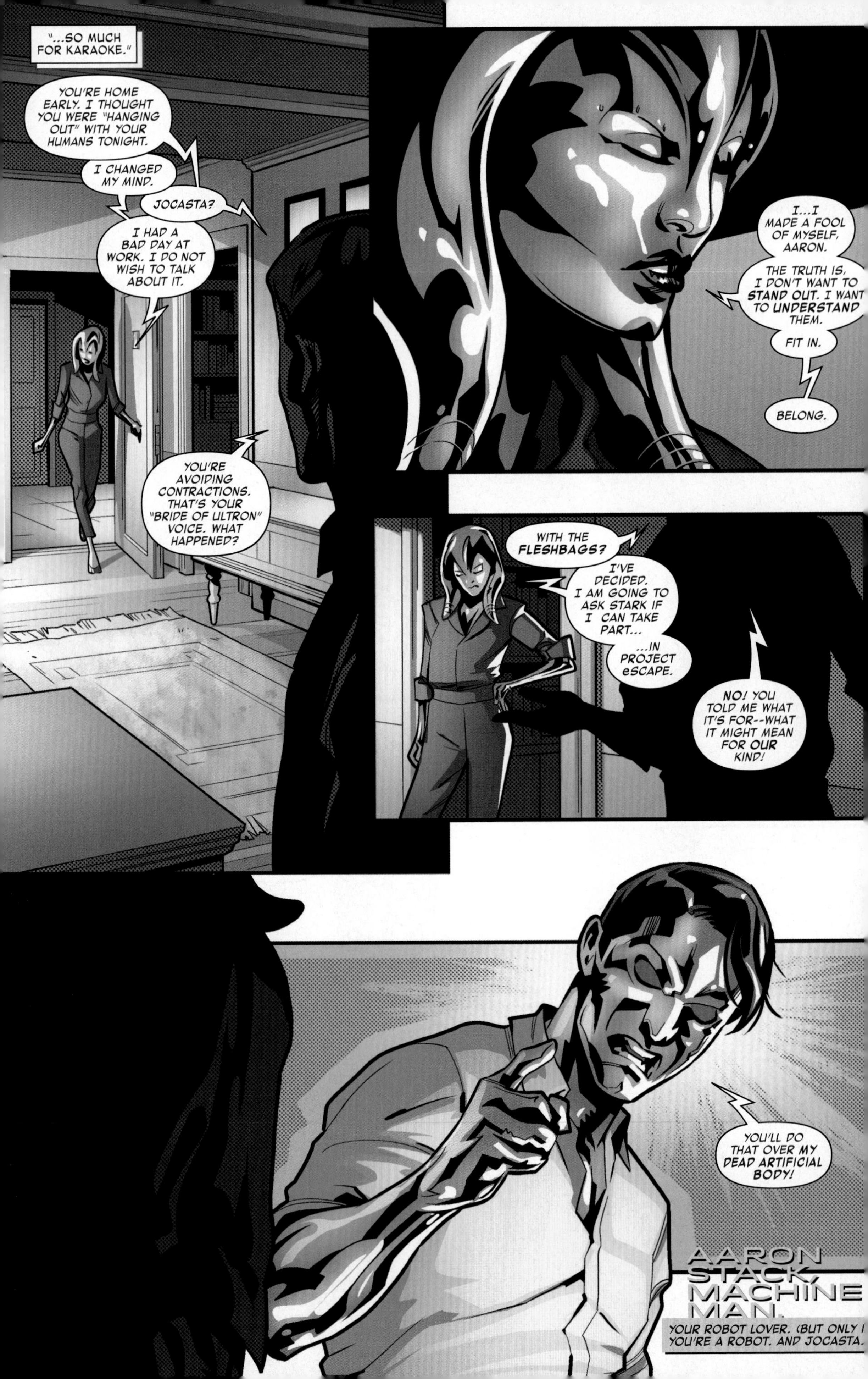
"...SO MUCH FOR KARAOKE."
YOU'RE HOME EARLY. I THOUGHT YOU WERE "HANGING OUT" WITH YOUR HUMANS TONIGHT.
I CHANGED MY MIND.
JOCASTA?
I HAD A BAD DAY AT WORK. I DO NOT WISH TO TALK ABOUT IT.
YOU'RE AVOIDING CONTRACTIONS. THAT'S YOUR "BRIDE OF ULTRON" VOICE. WHAT HAPPENED?
I...I MADE A FOOL OF MYSELF, AARON.
THE TRUTH IS, I DON'T WANT TO STAND OUT. I WANT TO UNDERSTAND THEM.
FIT IN.
BELONG.
WITH THE FLESHBAGS?
I'VE DECIDED. I AM GOING TO ASK STARK IF I CAN TAKE PART...
...IN PROJECT eSCAPE.
NO! YOU TOLD ME WHAT IT'S FOR--WHAT IT MIGHT MEAN FOR OUR KIND!
YOU'LL DO THAT OVER MY DEAD ARTIFICIAL BODY!
AARON STACK, MACHINE MAN.
YOUR ROBOT LOVER. (BUT ONLY I YOU'RE A ROBOT. AND JOCASTA.

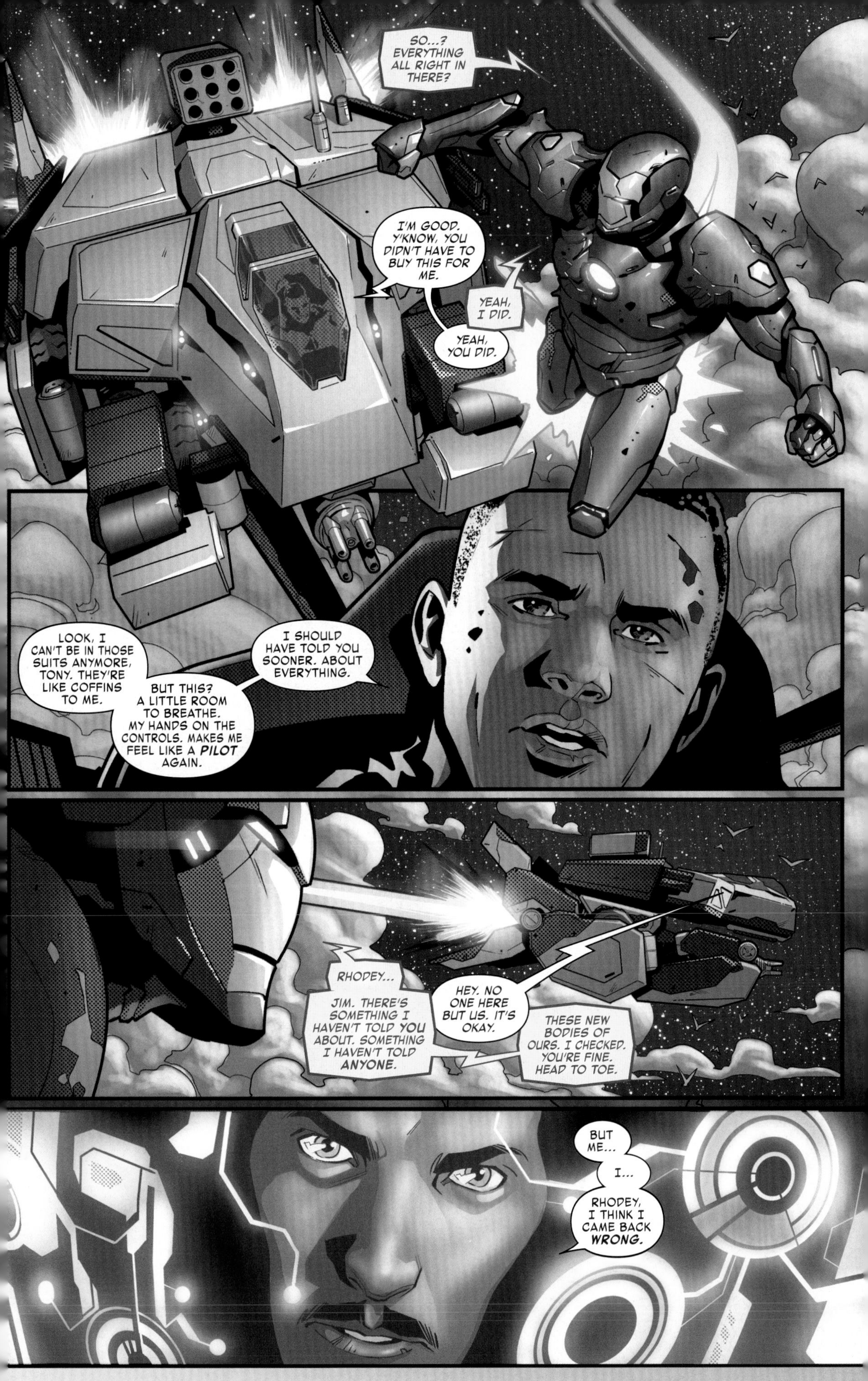
SO...? EVERYTHING ALL RIGHT IN THERE?
I'M GOOD. Y'KNOW, YOU DIDN'T HAVE TO BUY THIS FOR ME.
YEAH, I DID.
YEAH, YOU DID.
LOOK, I CAN'T BE IN THOSE SUITS ANYMORE, TONY. THEY'RE LIKE COFFINS TO ME.
BUT THIS? A LITTLE ROOM TO BREATHE. MY HANDS ON THE CONTROLS. MAKES ME FEEL LIKE A PILOT AGAIN.
I SHOULD HAVE TOLD YOU SOONER. ABOUT EVERYTHING.
RHODEY...
JIM. THERE'S SOMETHING I HAVEN'T TOLD YOU ABOUT. SOMETHING I HAVEN'T TOLD ANYONE.
HEY. NO ONE HERE BUT US. IT'S OKAY.
THESE NEW BODIES OF OURS. I CHECKED. YOU'RE FINE. HEAD TO TOE.
BUT ME...
I...
RHODEY, I THINK I CAME BACK WRONG.

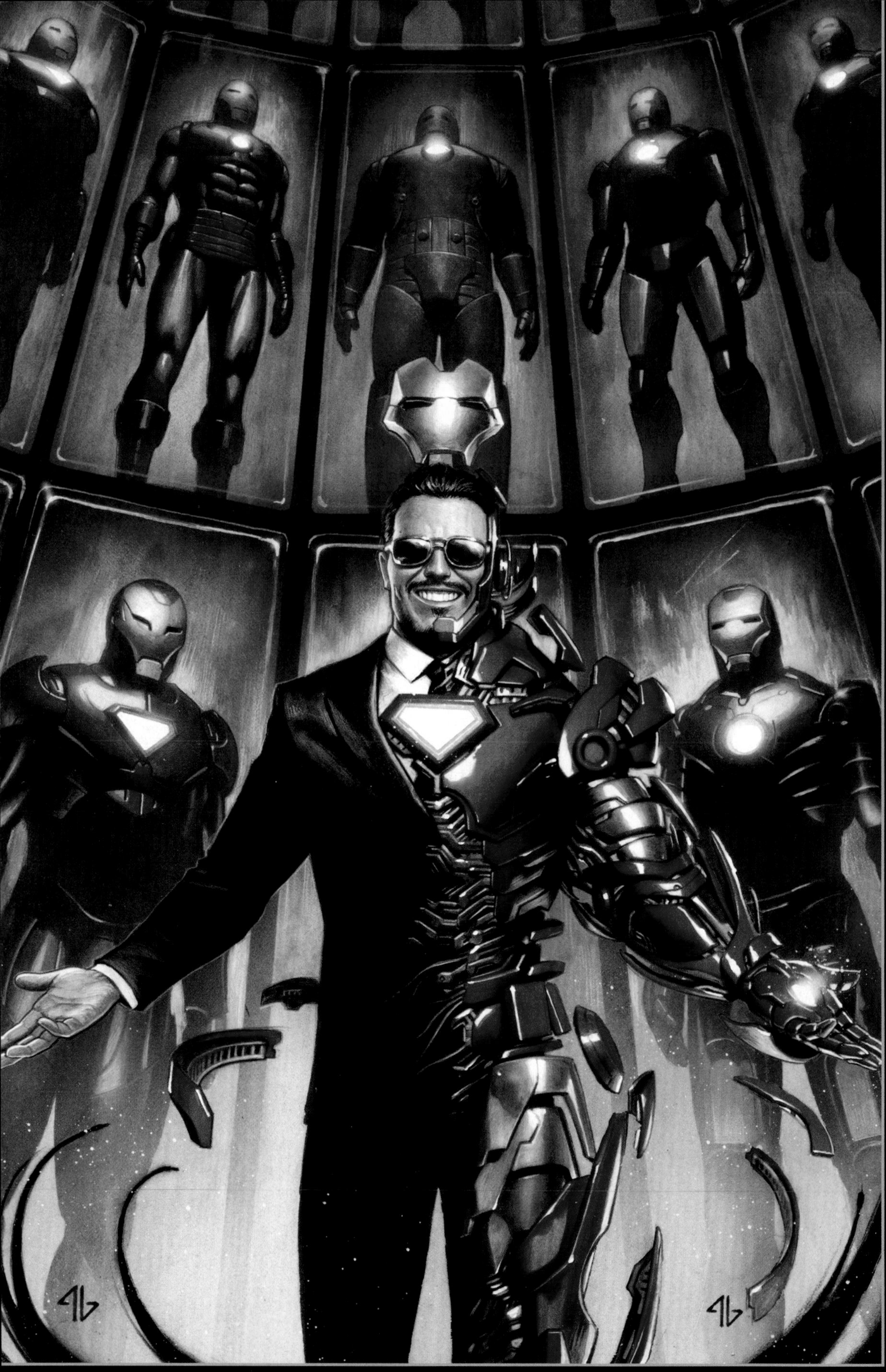

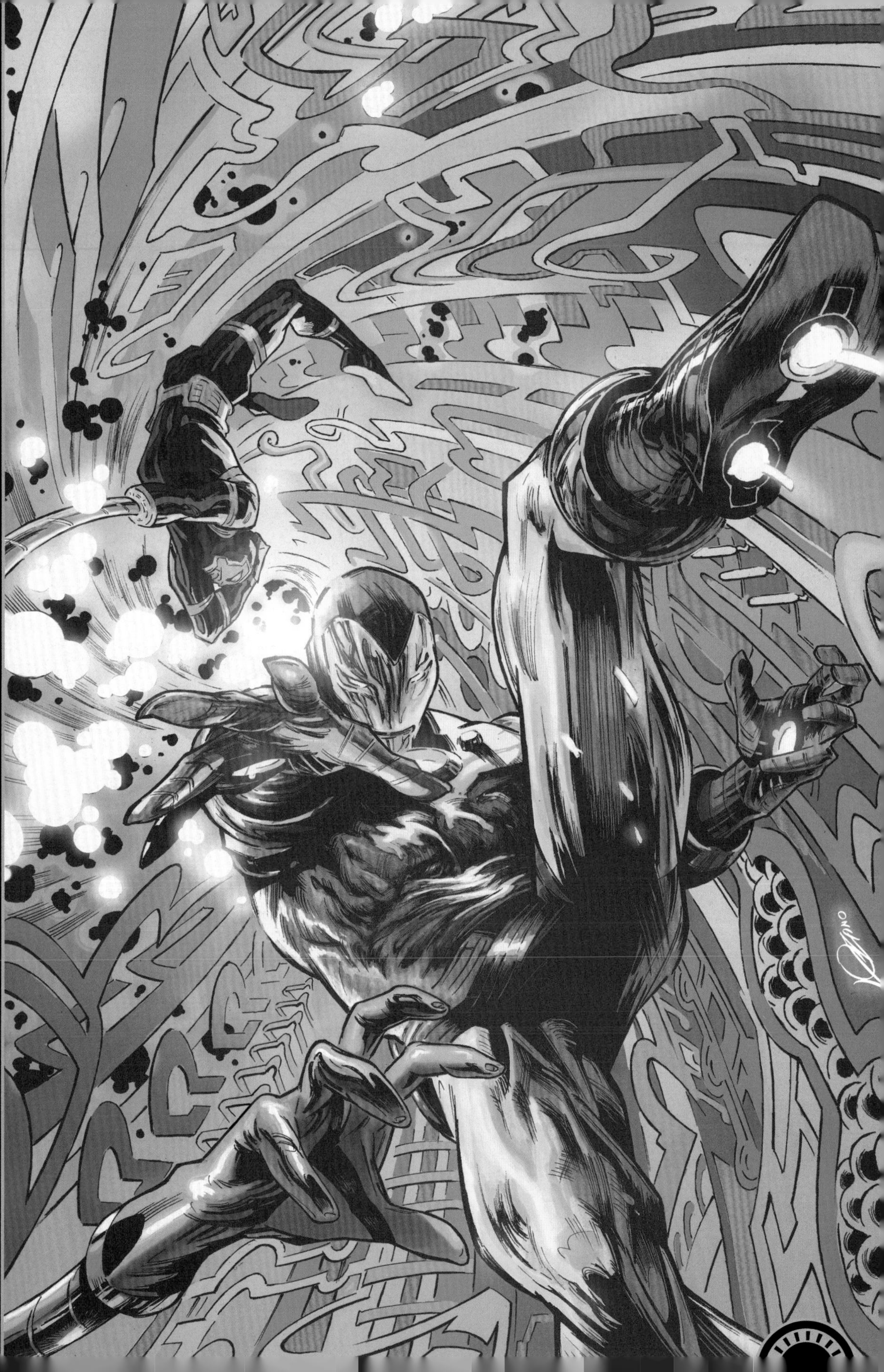

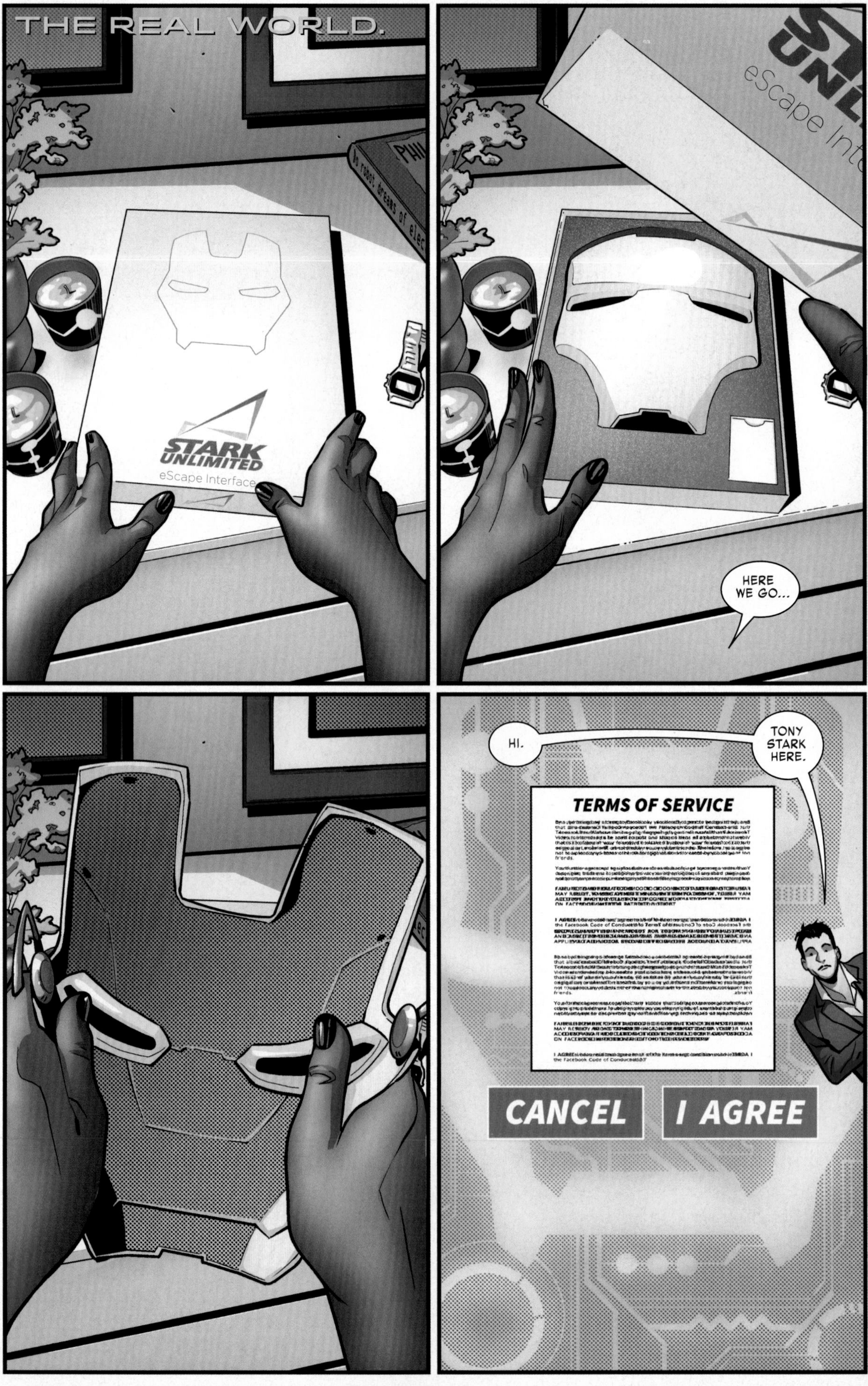
THE REAL WORLD.
STARK UNLIMITED
eScape Interface
HERE WE GO...
HI.
TONY STARK HERE.
TERMS OF SERVICE
CANCEL
I AGREE

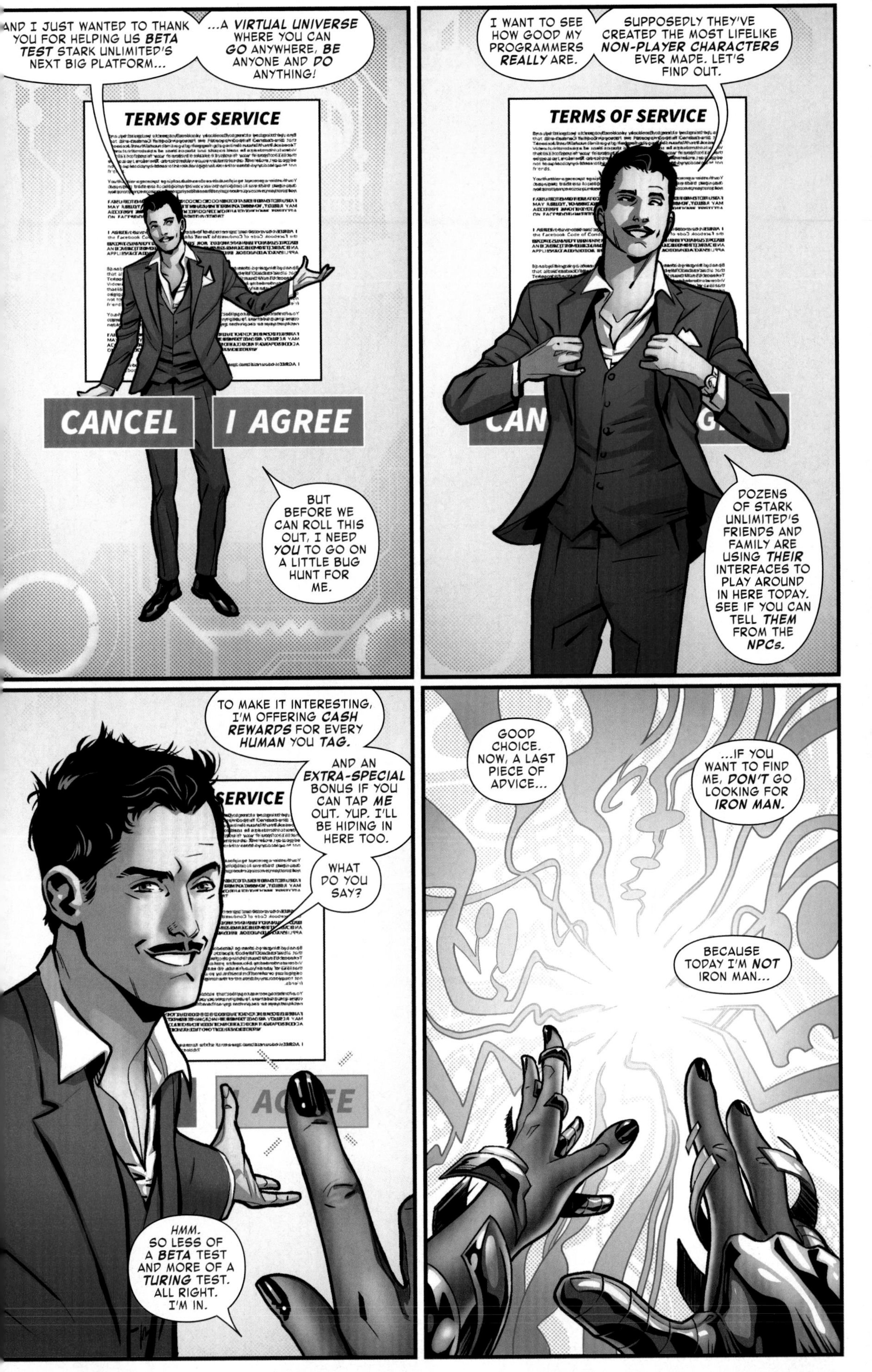

AND I JUST WANTED TO THANK YOU FOR HELPING US BETA TEST STARK UNLIMITED'S NEXT BIG PLATFORM...
...A VIRTUAL UNIVERSE WHERE YOU CAN GO ANYWHERE, BE ANYONE AND DO ANYTHING!
TERMS OF SERVICE
CANCEL
I AGREE
BUT BEFORE WE CAN ROLL THIS OUT, I NEED YOU TO GO ON A LITTLE BUG HUNT FOR ME.
I WANT TO SEE HOW GOOD MY PROGRAMMERS REALLY ARE.
SUPPOSEDLY THEY'VE CREATED THE MOST LIFELIKE NON-PLAYER CHARACTERS EVER MADE. LET'S FIND OUT.
TERMS OF SERVICE
DOZENS OF STARK UNLIMITED'S FRIENDS AND FAMILY ARE USING THEIR INTERFACES TO PLAY AROUND IN HERE TODAY. SEE IF YOU CAN TELL THEM FROM THE NPCs.
TO MAKE IT INTERESTING, I'M OFFERING CASH REWARDS FOR EVERY HUMAN YOU TAG.
AND AN EXTRA-SPECIAL BONUS IF YOU CAN TAP ME OUT. YUP. I'LL BE HIDING IN HERE TOO.
WHAT DO YOU SAY?
SERVICE
HMM. SO LESS OF A BETA TEST AND MORE OF A TURING TEST. ALL RIGHT. I'M IN.
GOOD CHOICE. NOW, A LAST PIECE OF ADVICE...
...IF YOU WANT TO FIND ME, DON'T GO LOOKING FOR IRON MAN.
BECAUSE TODAY I'M NOT IRON MAN...

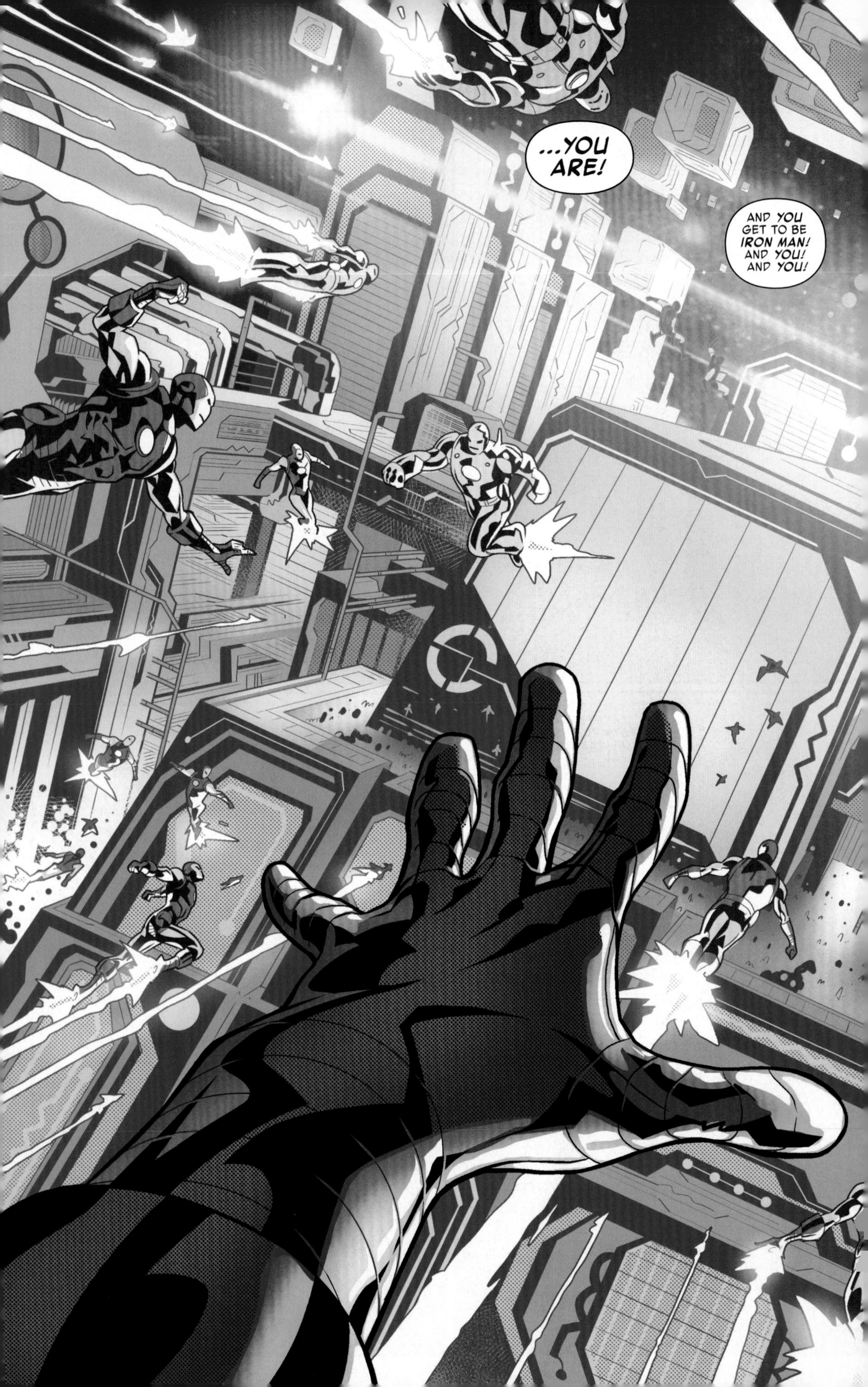
...YOU ARE!
AND YOU GET TO BE IRON MAN! AND YOU! AND YOU!

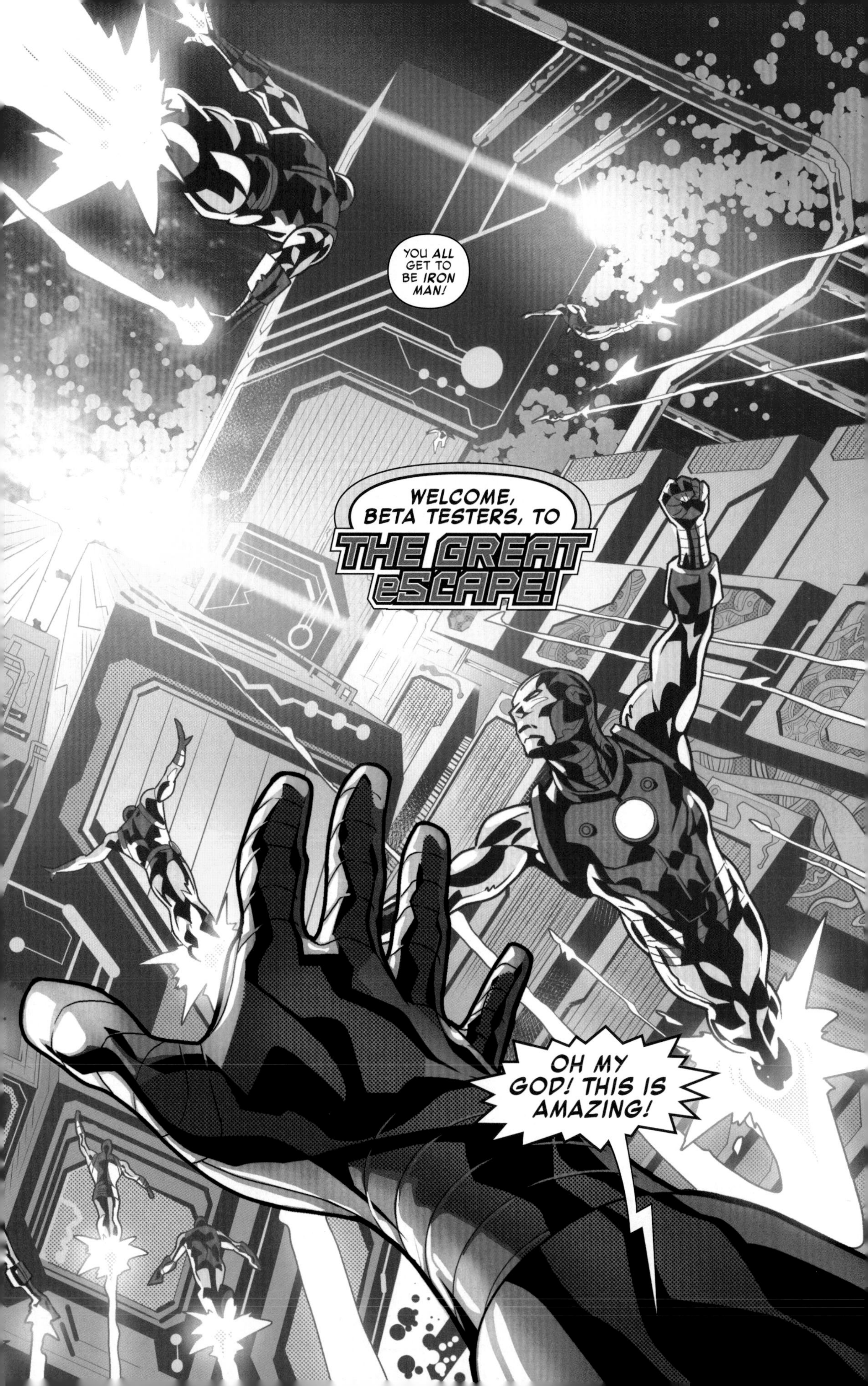
YOU ALL GET TO BE IRON MAN!
WELCOME, BETA TESTERS, TO
THE GREAT eSCAPE!
OH MY GOD! THIS IS AMAZING!

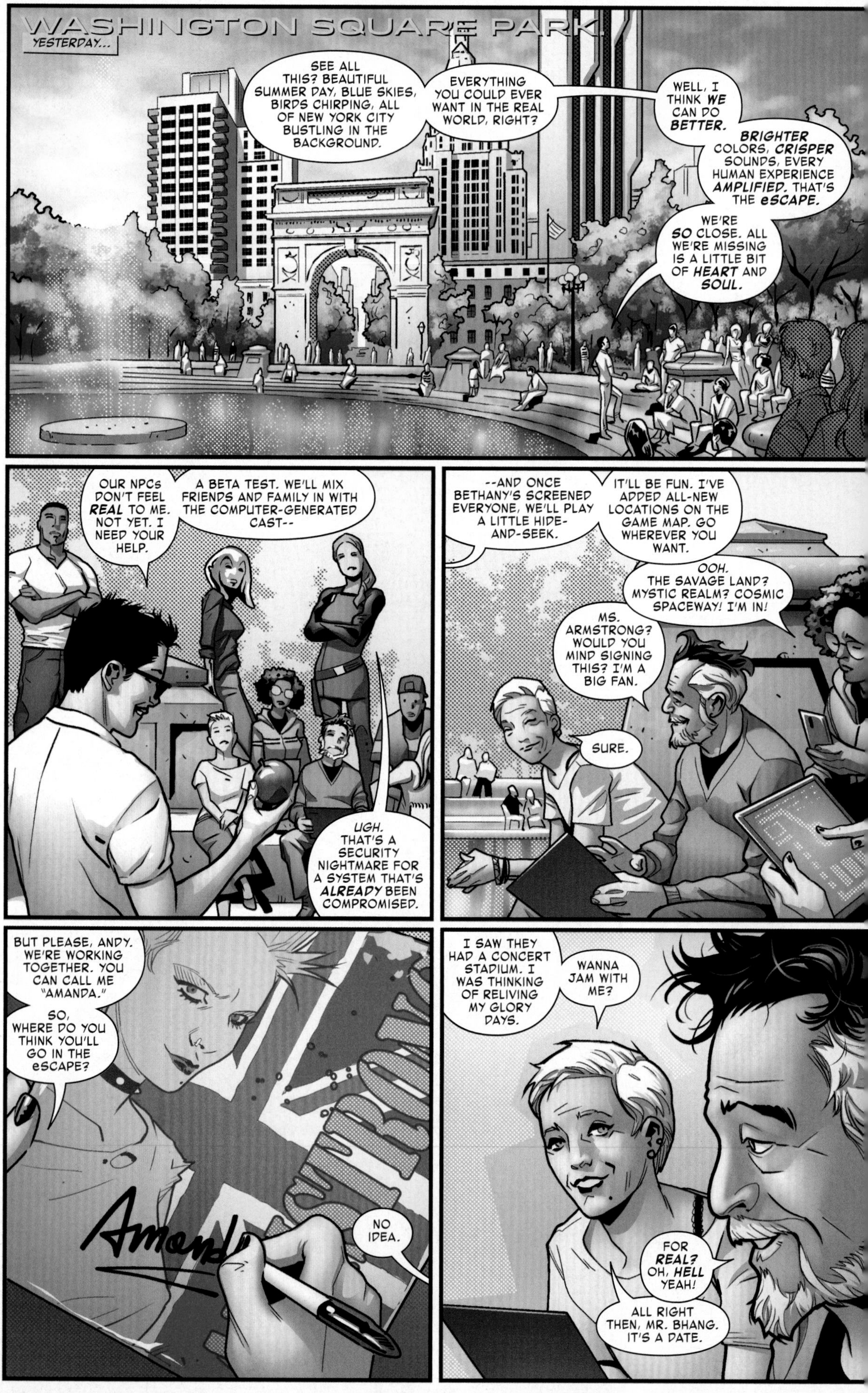
WASHINGTON SQUARE PARK.
YESTERDAY...
SEE ALL THIS? BEAUTIFUL SUMMER DAY, BLUE SKIES, BIRDS CHIRPING, ALL OF NEW YORK CITY BUSTLING IN THE BACKGROUND.
EVERYTHING YOU COULD EVER WANT IN THE REAL WORLD, RIGHT?
WELL, I THINK WE CAN DO BETTER.
BRIGHTER COLORS, CRISPER SOUNDS, EVERY HUMAN EXPERIENCE AMPLIFIED. THAT'S THE eSCAPE.
WE'RE SO CLOSE. ALL WE'RE MISSING IS A LITTLE BIT OF HEART AND SOUL.
OUR NPCs DON'T FEEL REAL TO ME. NOT YET. I NEED YOUR HELP.
A BETA TEST. WE'LL MIX FRIENDS AND FAMILY IN WITH THE COMPUTER-GENERATED CAST--
UGH. THAT'S A SECURITY NIGHTMARE FOR A SYSTEM THAT'S ALREADY BEEN COMPROMISED.
--AND ONCE BETHANY'S SCREENED EVERYONE, WE'LL PLAY A LITTLE HIDE-AND-SEEK.
IT'LL BE FUN. I'VE ADDED ALL-NEW LOCATIONS ON THE GAME MAP. GO WHEREVER YOU WANT.
OOH. THE SAVAGE LAND? MYSTIC REALM? COSMIC SPACEWAY! I'M IN!
MS. ARMSTRONG? WOULD YOU MIND SIGNING THIS? I'M A BIG FAN.
SURE.
BUT PLEASE, ANDY. WE'RE WORKING TOGETHER. YOU CAN CALL ME "AMANDA."
SO, WHERE DO YOU THINK YOU'LL GO IN THE eSCAPE?
Amanda
NO IDEA.
I SAW THEY HAD A CONCERT STADIUM. I WAS THINKING OF RELIVING MY GLORY DAYS.
WANNA JAM WITH ME?
FOR REAL? OH, HELL YEAH!
ALL RIGHT THEN, MR. BHANG. IT'S A DATE.

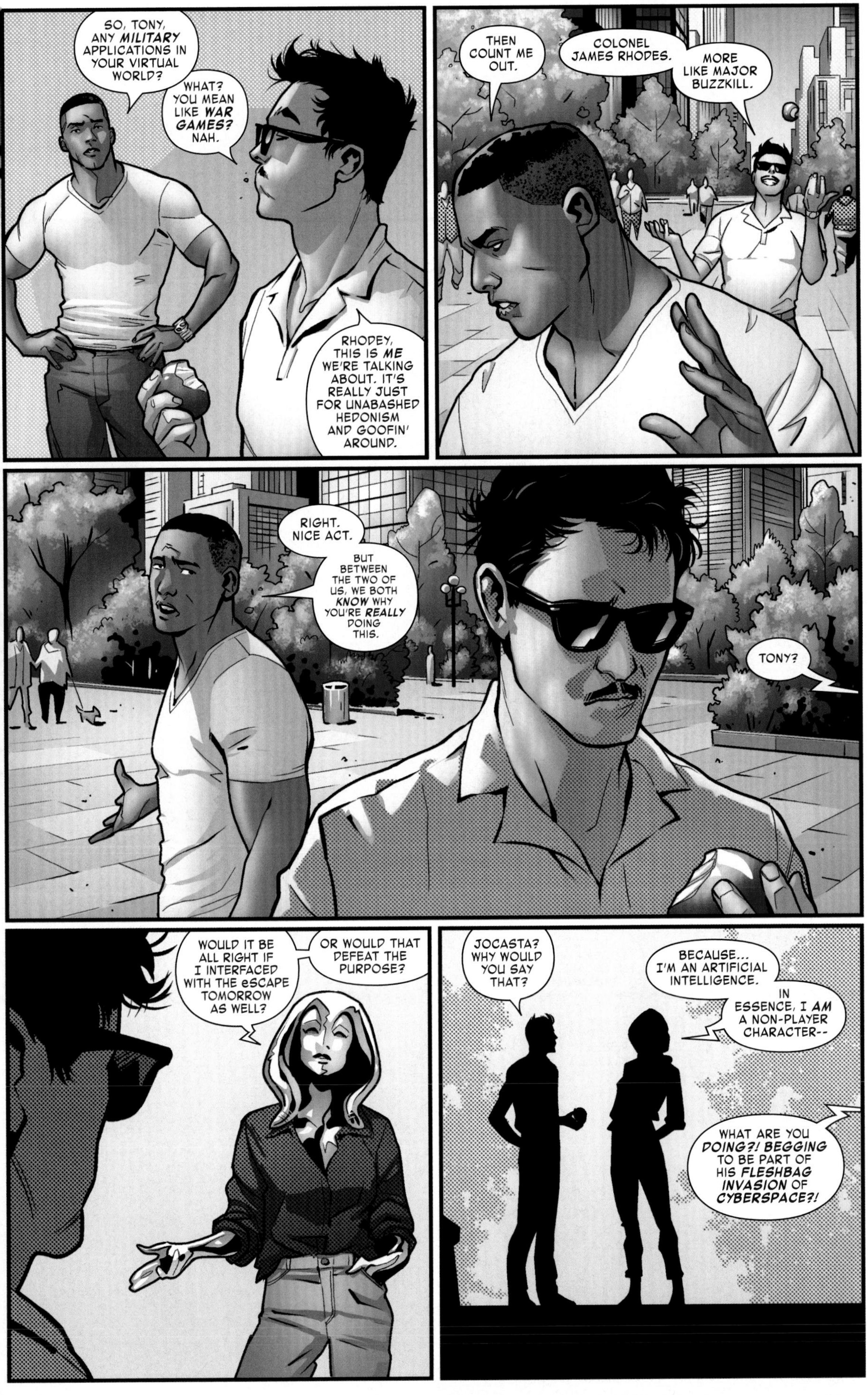
SO, TONY, ANY MILITARY APPLICATIONS IN YOUR VIRTUAL WORLD?
WHAT? YOU MEAN LIKE WAR GAMES? NAH.
RHODEY, THIS IS ME WE'RE TALKING ABOUT. IT'S REALLY JUST FOR UNABASHED HEDONISM AND GOOFIN' AROUND.
THEN COUNT ME OUT.
COLONEL JAMES RHODES.
MORE LIKE MAJOR BUZZKILL.
RIGHT. NICE ACT.
BUT BETWEEN THE TWO OF US, WE BOTH KNOW WHY YOU'RE REALLY DOING THIS.
TONY?
WOULD IT BE ALL RIGHT IF I INTERFACED WITH THE eSCAPE TOMORROW AS WELL?
OR WOULD THAT DEFEAT THE PURPOSE?
JOCASTA? WHY WOULD YOU SAY THAT?
BECAUSE... I'M AN ARTIFICIAL INTELLIGENCE.
IN ESSENCE, I AM A NON-PLAYER CHARACTER--
WHAT ARE YOU DOING?! BEGGING TO BE PART OF HIS FLESHBAG INVASION OF CYBERSPACE?!

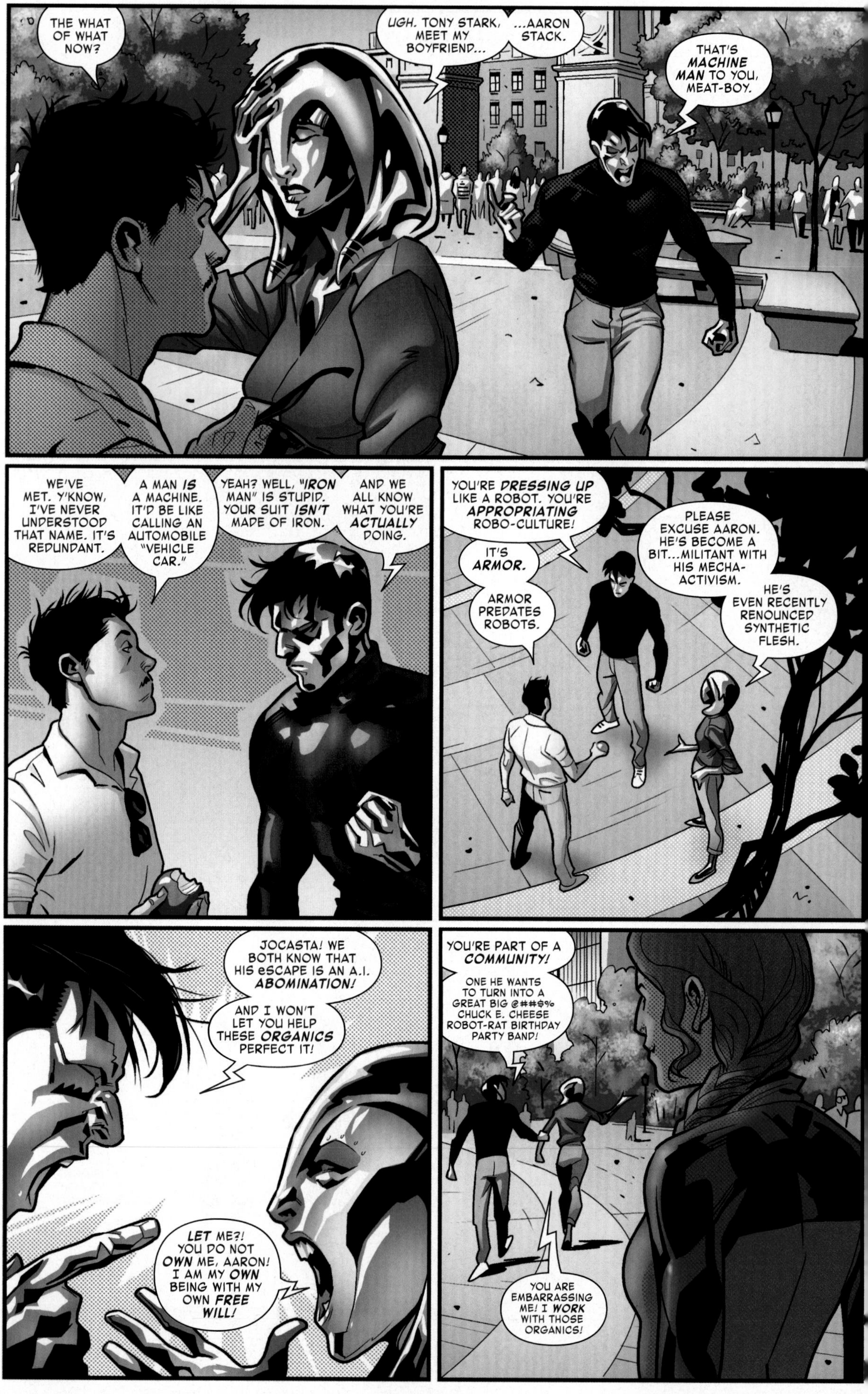
THE WHAT OF WHAT NOW?
UGH. TONY STARK, MEET MY BOYFRIEND...
...AARON STACK.
THAT'S MACHINE MAN TO YOU, MEAT-BOY.
WE'VE MET. Y'KNOW, I'VE NEVER UNDERSTOOD THAT NAME. IT'S REDUNDANT.
A MAN IS A MACHINE. IT'D BE LIKE CALLING AN AUTOMOBILE "VEHICLE CAR."
YEAH? WELL, "IRON MAN" IS STUPID. YOUR SUIT ISN'T MADE OF IRON.
AND WE ALL KNOW WHAT YOU'RE ACTUALLY DOING.
YOU'RE DRESSING UP LIKE A ROBOT. YOU'RE APPROPRIATING ROBO-CULTURE!
IT'S ARMOR.
ARMOR PREDATES ROBOTS.
PLEASE EXCUSE AARON. HE'S BECOME A BIT...MILITANT WITH HIS MECHA-ACTIVISM.
HE'S EVEN RECENTLY RENOUNCED SYNTHETIC FLESH.
JOCASTA! WE BOTH KNOW THAT HIS eSCAPE IS AN A.I. ABOMINATION!
AND I WON'T LET YOU HELP THESE ORGANICS PERFECT IT!
LET ME?! YOU DO NOT OWN ME, AARON! I AM MY OWN BEING WITH MY OWN FREE WILL!
YOU'RE PART OF A COMMUNITY!
ONE HE WANTS TO TURN INTO A GREAT BIG @##$% CHUCK E. CHEESE ROBOT-RAT BIRTHDAY PARTY BAND!
YOU ARE EMBARRASSING ME! I WORK WITH THOSE ORGANICS!

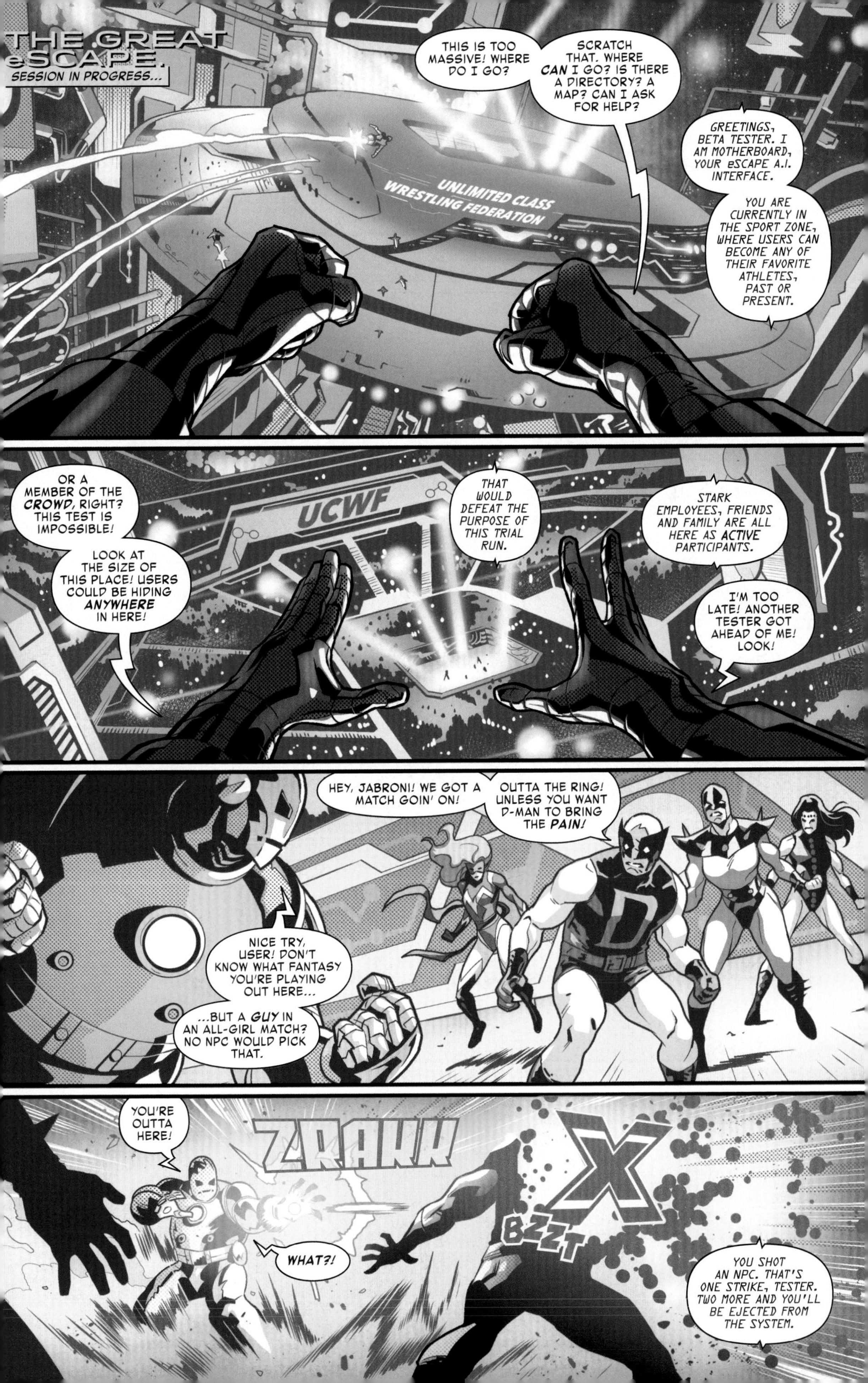
THE GREAT eSCAPE.
SESSION IN PROGRESS...
THIS IS TOO MASSIVE! WHERE DO I GO?
SCRATCH THAT. WHERE CAN I GO? IS THERE A DIRECTORY? A MAP? CAN I ASK FOR HELP?
UNLIMITED CLASS WRESTLING FEDERATION
GREETINGS, BETA TESTER. I AM MOTHERBOARD, YOUR eSCAPE A.I. INTERFACE.
YOU ARE CURRENTLY IN THE SPORT ZONE, WHERE USERS CAN BECOME ANY OF THEIR FAVORITE ATHLETES, PAST OR PRESENT.
OR A MEMBER OF THE CROWD, RIGHT? THIS TEST IS IMPOSSIBLE!
LOOK AT THE SIZE OF THIS PLACE! USERS COULD BE HIDING ANYWHERE IN HERE!
UCWF
THAT WOULD DEFEAT THE PURPOSE OF THIS TRIAL RUN.
STARK EMPLOYEES, FRIENDS AND FAMILY ARE ALL HERE AS ACTIVE PARTICIPANTS.
I'M TOO LATE! ANOTHER TESTER GOT AHEAD OF ME! LOOK!
HEY, JABRONI! WE GOT A MATCH GOIN' ON!
OUTTA THE RING! UNLESS YOU WANT D-MAN TO BRING THE PAIN!
NICE TRY, USER! DON'T KNOW WHAT FANTASY YOU'RE PLAYING OUT HERE...
...BUT A GUY IN AN ALL-GIRL MATCH? NO NPC WOULD PICK THAT.
YOU'RE OUTTA HERE!
ZRAKK
X
BZZT
WHAT?!
YOU SHOT AN NPC. THAT'S ONE STRIKE, TESTER. TWO MORE AND YOU'LL BE EJECTED FROM THE SYSTEM.

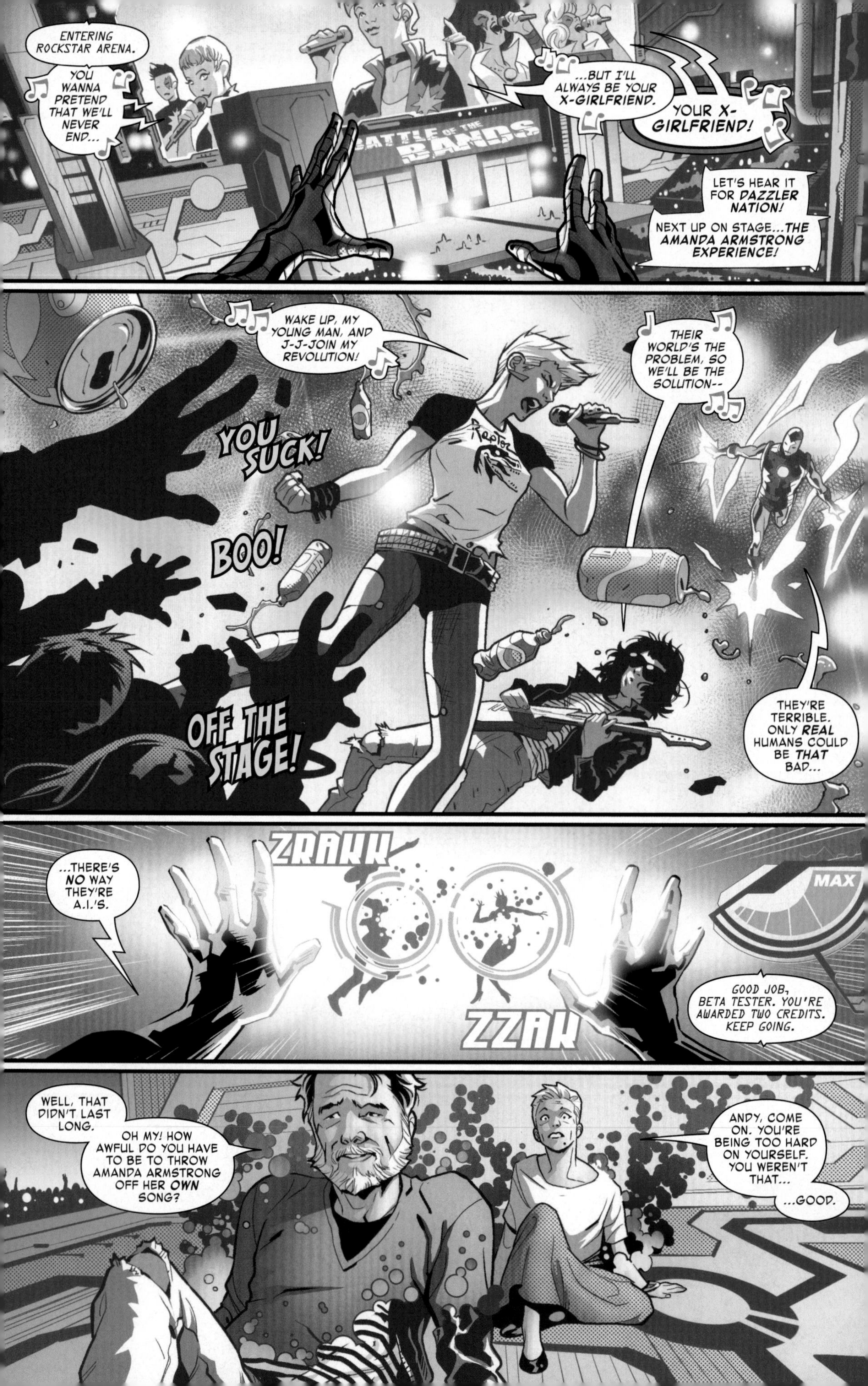
ENTERING ROCKSTAR ARENA.
YOU WANNA PRETEND THAT WE'LL NEVER END...
...BUT I'LL ALWAYS BE YOUR X-GIRLFRIEND.
YOUR X-GIRLFRIEND!
BATTLE OF THE BANDS
LET'S HEAR IT FOR DAZZLER NATION!
NEXT UP ON STAGE...THE AMANDA ARMSTRONG EXPERIENCE!
WAKE UP, MY YOUNG MAN, AND J-J-JOIN MY REVOLUTION!
THEIR WORLD'S THE PROBLEM, SO WE'LL BE THE SOLUTION--
YOU SUCK!
BOO!
OFF THE STAGE!
THEY'RE TERRIBLE. ONLY REAL HUMANS COULD BE THAT BAD...
ZRAKK
...THERE'S NO WAY THEY'RE A.I.'S.
MAX
GOOD JOB, BETA TESTER. YOU'RE AWARDED TWO CREDITS. KEEP GOING.
ZZAK
WELL, THAT DIDN'T LAST LONG.
OH MY! HOW AWFUL DO YOU HAVE TO BE TO THROW AMANDA ARMSTRONG OFF HER OWN SONG?
ANDY, COME ON. YOU'RE BEING TOO HARD ON YOURSELF. YOU WEREN'T THAT...
...GOOD.

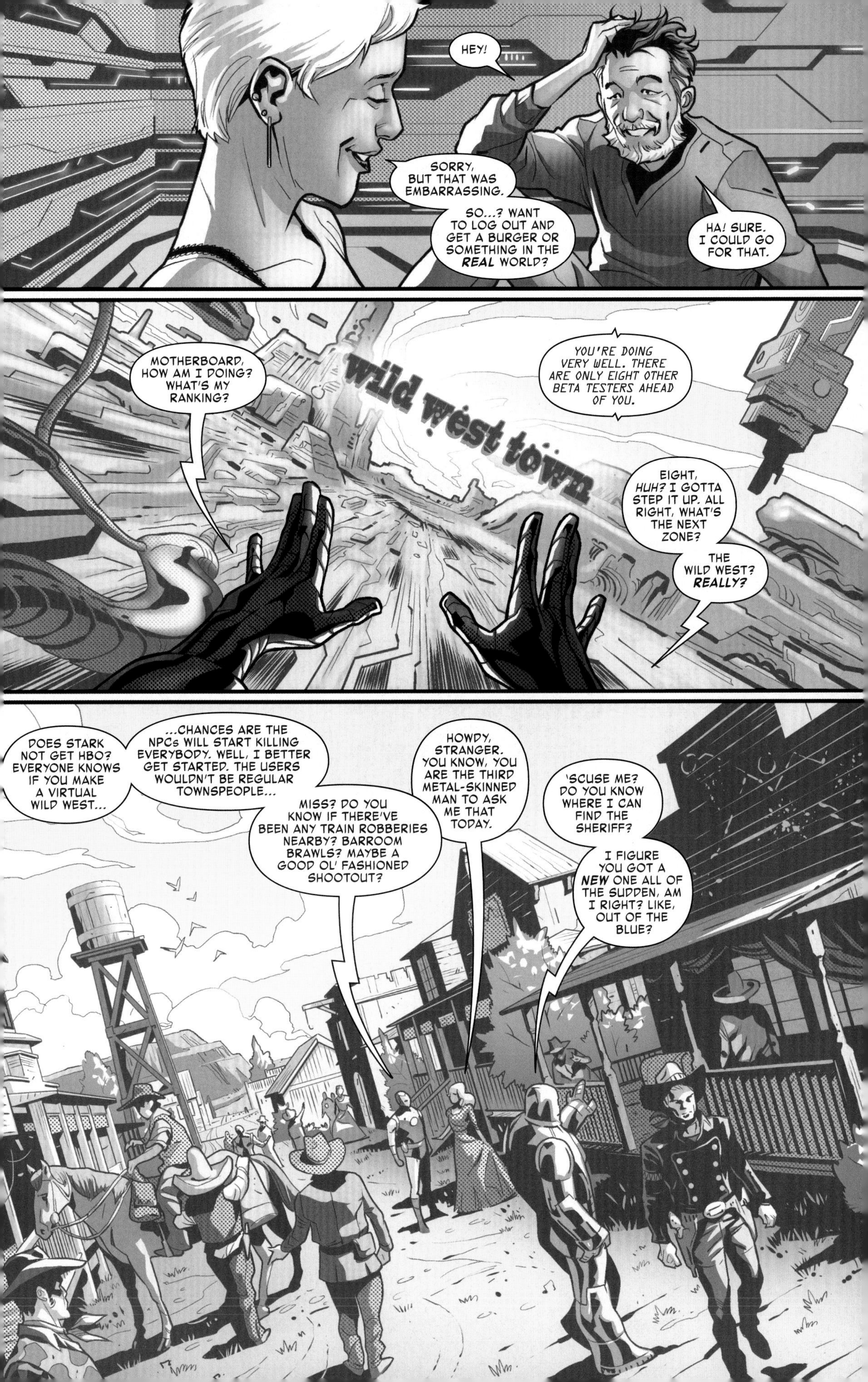
HEY!
SORRY, BUT THAT WAS EMBARRASSING.
SO...? WANT TO LOG OUT AND GET A BURGER OR SOMETHING IN THE *REAL* WORLD?
HA! SURE. I COULD GO FOR THAT.
MOTHERBOARD, HOW AM I DOING? WHAT'S MY RANKING?
wild west town
YOU'RE DOING VERY WELL. THERE ARE ONLY EIGHT OTHER BETA TESTERS AHEAD OF YOU.
EIGHT, *HUH?* I GOTTA STEP IT UP. ALL RIGHT, WHAT'S THE NEXT ZONE?
THE WILD WEST? *REALLY?*
DOES STARK NOT GET HBO? EVERYONE KNOWS IF YOU MAKE A VIRTUAL WILD WEST...
...CHANCES ARE THE NPCs WILL START KILLING EVERYBODY. WELL, I BETTER GET STARTED. THE USERS WOULDN'T BE REGULAR TOWNSPEOPLE...
MISS? DO YOU KNOW IF THERE'VE BEEN ANY TRAIN ROBBERIES NEARBY? BARROOM BRAWLS? MAYBE A GOOD OL' FASHIONED SHOOTOUT?
HOWDY, STRANGER. YOU KNOW, YOU ARE THE THIRD METAL-SKINNED MAN TO ASK ME THAT TODAY.
'SCUSE ME? DO YOU KNOW WHERE I CAN FIND THE SHERIFF?
I FIGURE YOU GOT A *NEW* ONE ALL OF THE SUDDEN, AM I RIGHT? LIKE, OUT OF THE BLUE?

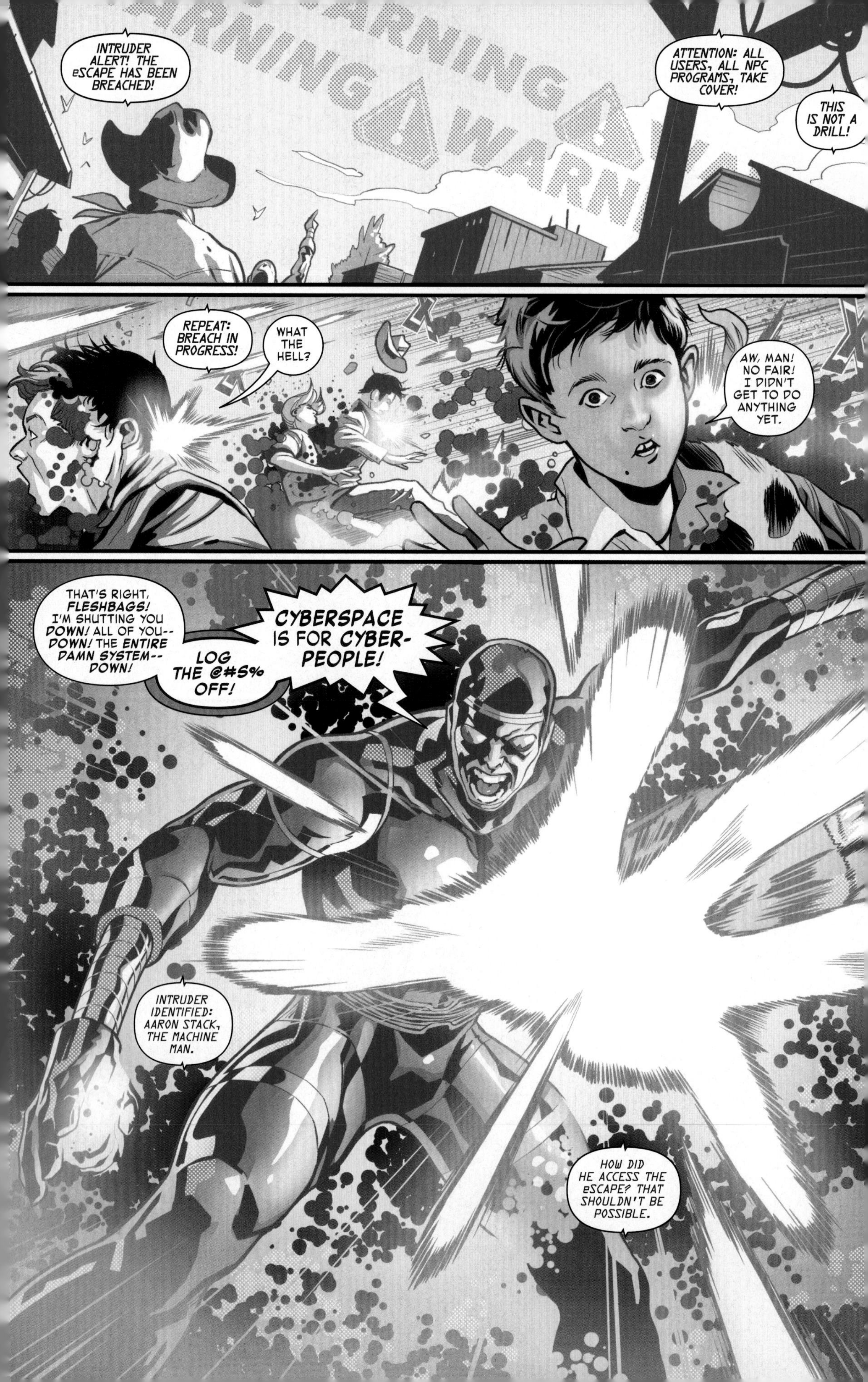
WARNING
INTRUDER ALERT! THE eSCAPE HAS BEEN BREACHED!
ATTENTION: ALL USERS, ALL NPC PROGRAMS, TAKE COVER!
THIS IS NOT A DRILL!
REPEAT: BREACH IN PROGRESS!
WHAT THE HELL?
AW, MAN! NO FAIR! I DIDN'T GET TO DO ANYTHING YET.
THAT'S RIGHT, FLESHBAGS! I'M SHUTTING YOU DOWN! ALL OF YOU-- DOWN! THE ENTIRE DAMN SYSTEM-- DOWN!
LOG THE @#S% OFF!
CYBERSPACE IS FOR CYBER-PEOPLE!
INTRUDER IDENTIFIED: AARON STACK, THE MACHINE MAN.
HOW DID HE ACCESS THE eSCAPE? THAT SHOULDN'T BE POSSIBLE.

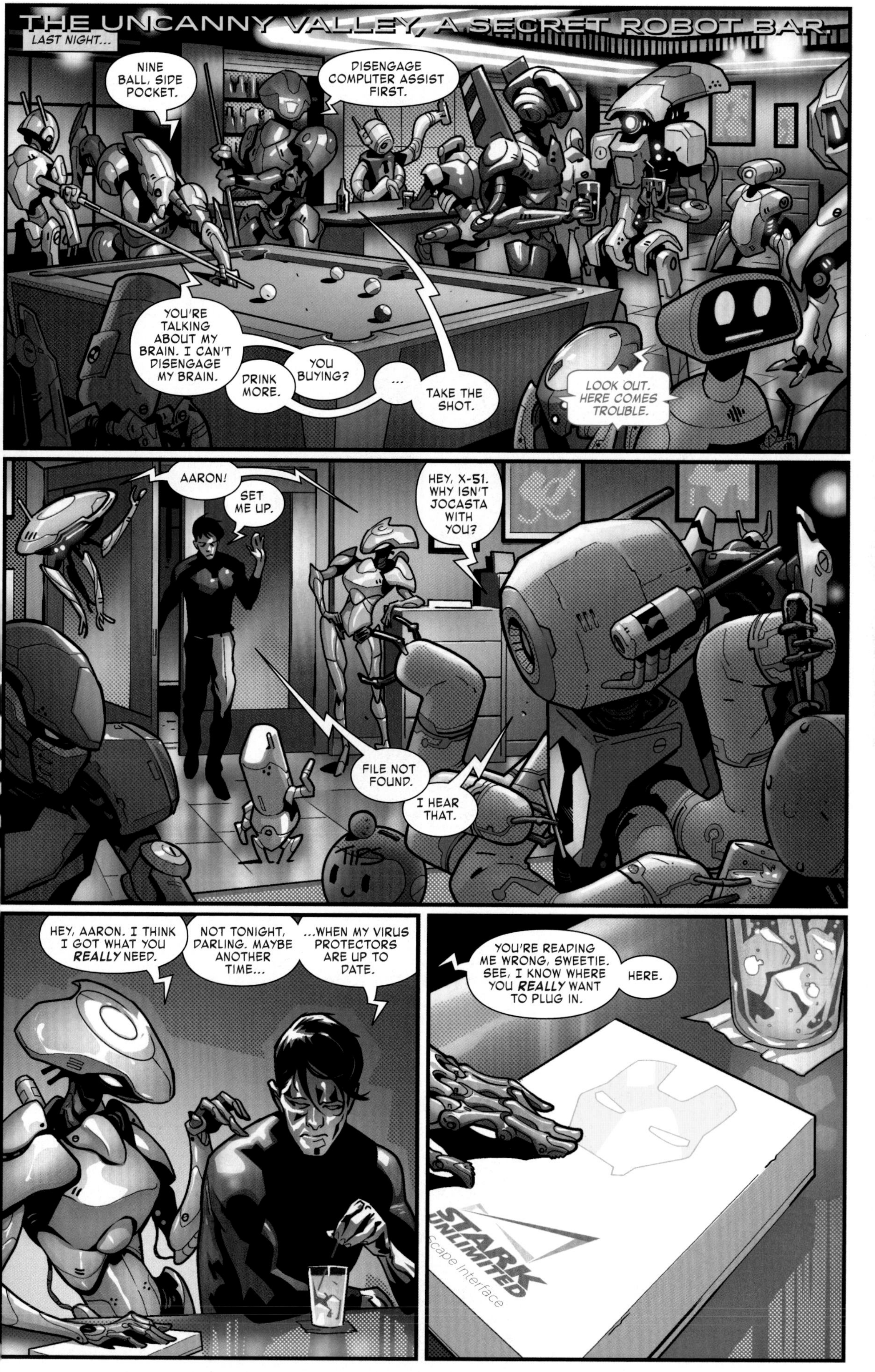
THE UNCANNY VALLEY, A SECRET ROBOT BAR.
LAST NIGHT...
NINE BALL, SIDE POCKET.
DISENGAGE COMPUTER ASSIST FIRST.
YOU'RE TALKING ABOUT MY BRAIN. I CAN'T DISENGAGE MY BRAIN.
DRINK MORE.
YOU BUYING?
...
TAKE THE SHOT.
LOOK OUT. HERE COMES TROUBLE.
AARON!
SET ME UP.
HEY, X-51. WHY ISN'T JOCASTA WITH YOU?
FILE NOT FOUND.
I HEAR THAT.
HEY, AARON. I THINK I GOT WHAT YOU REALLY NEED.
NOT TONIGHT, DARLING. MAYBE ANOTHER TIME...
...WHEN MY VIRUS PROTECTORS ARE UP TO DATE.
YOU'RE READING ME WRONG, SWEETIE. SEE, I KNOW WHERE YOU REALLY WANT TO PLUG IN.
HERE.
STARK UNLIMITED
Scape Interface

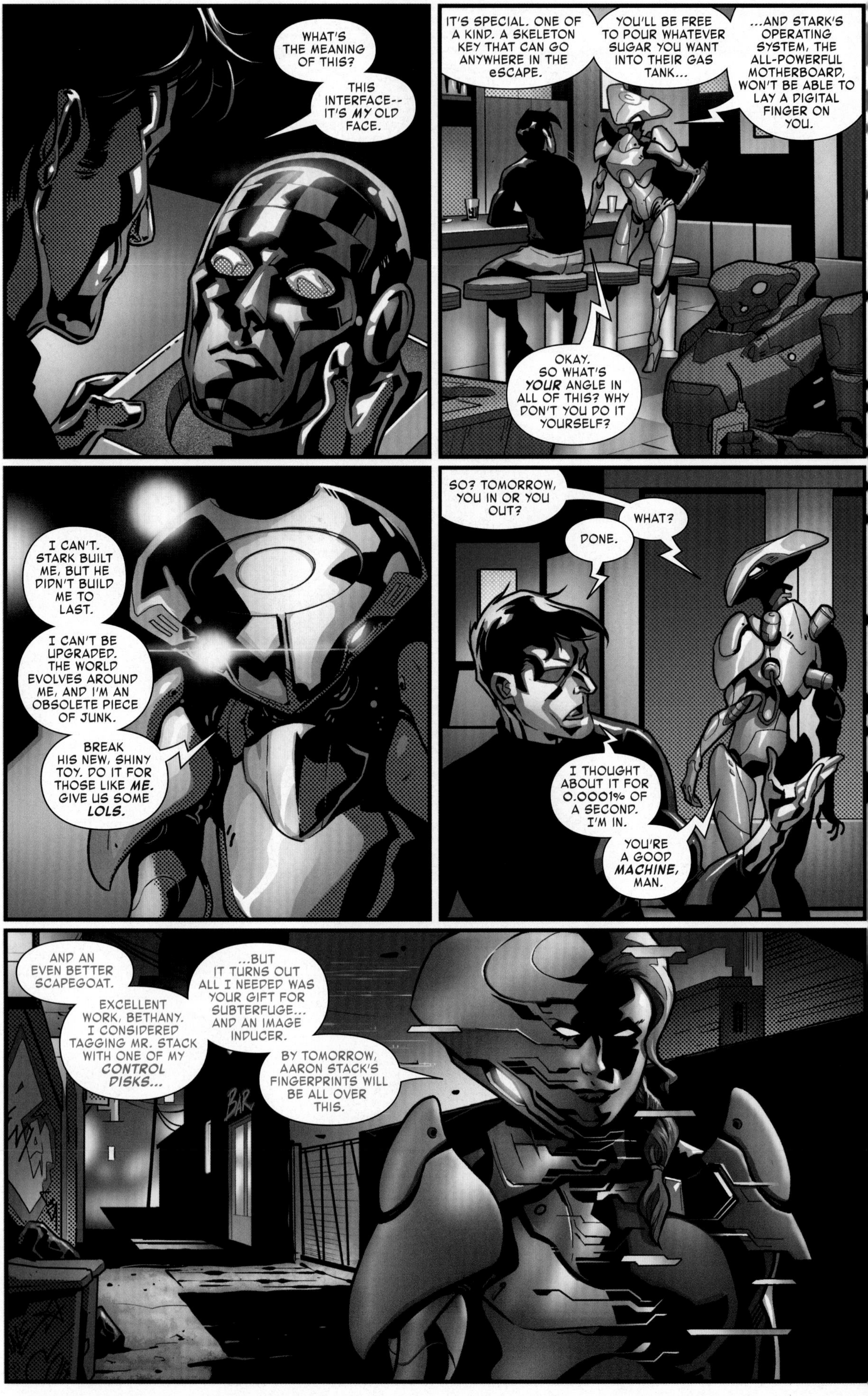
WHAT'S THE MEANING OF THIS?
THIS INTERFACE-- IT'S MY OLD FACE.
IT'S SPECIAL. ONE OF A KIND. A SKELETON KEY THAT CAN GO ANYWHERE IN THE eSCAPE.
YOU'LL BE FREE TO POUR WHATEVER SUGAR YOU WANT INTO THEIR GAS TANK...
...AND STARK'S OPERATING SYSTEM, THE ALL-POWERFUL MOTHERBOARD, WON'T BE ABLE TO LAY A DIGITAL FINGER ON YOU.
OKAY. SO WHAT'S YOUR ANGLE IN ALL OF THIS? WHY DON'T YOU DO IT YOURSELF?
I CAN'T. STARK BUILT ME, BUT HE DIDN'T BUILD ME TO LAST.
I CAN'T BE UPGRADED. THE WORLD EVOLVES AROUND ME, AND I'M AN OBSOLETE PIECE OF JUNK.
BREAK HIS NEW, SHINY TOY. DO IT FOR THOSE LIKE ME. GIVE US SOME LOLS.
SO? TOMORROW, YOU IN OR YOU OUT?
WHAT?
DONE.
I THOUGHT ABOUT IT FOR 0.0001% OF A SECOND. I'M IN.
YOU'RE A GOOD MACHINE, MAN.
AND AN EVEN BETTER SCAPEGOAT.
EXCELLENT WORK, BETHANY. I CONSIDERED TAGGING MR. STACK WITH ONE OF MY CONTROL DISKS...
...BUT IT TURNS OUT ALL I NEEDED WAS YOUR GIFT FOR SUBTERFUGE... AND AN IMAGE INDUCER.
BY TOMORROW, AARON STACK'S FINGERPRINTS WILL BE ALL OVER THIS.
BAR

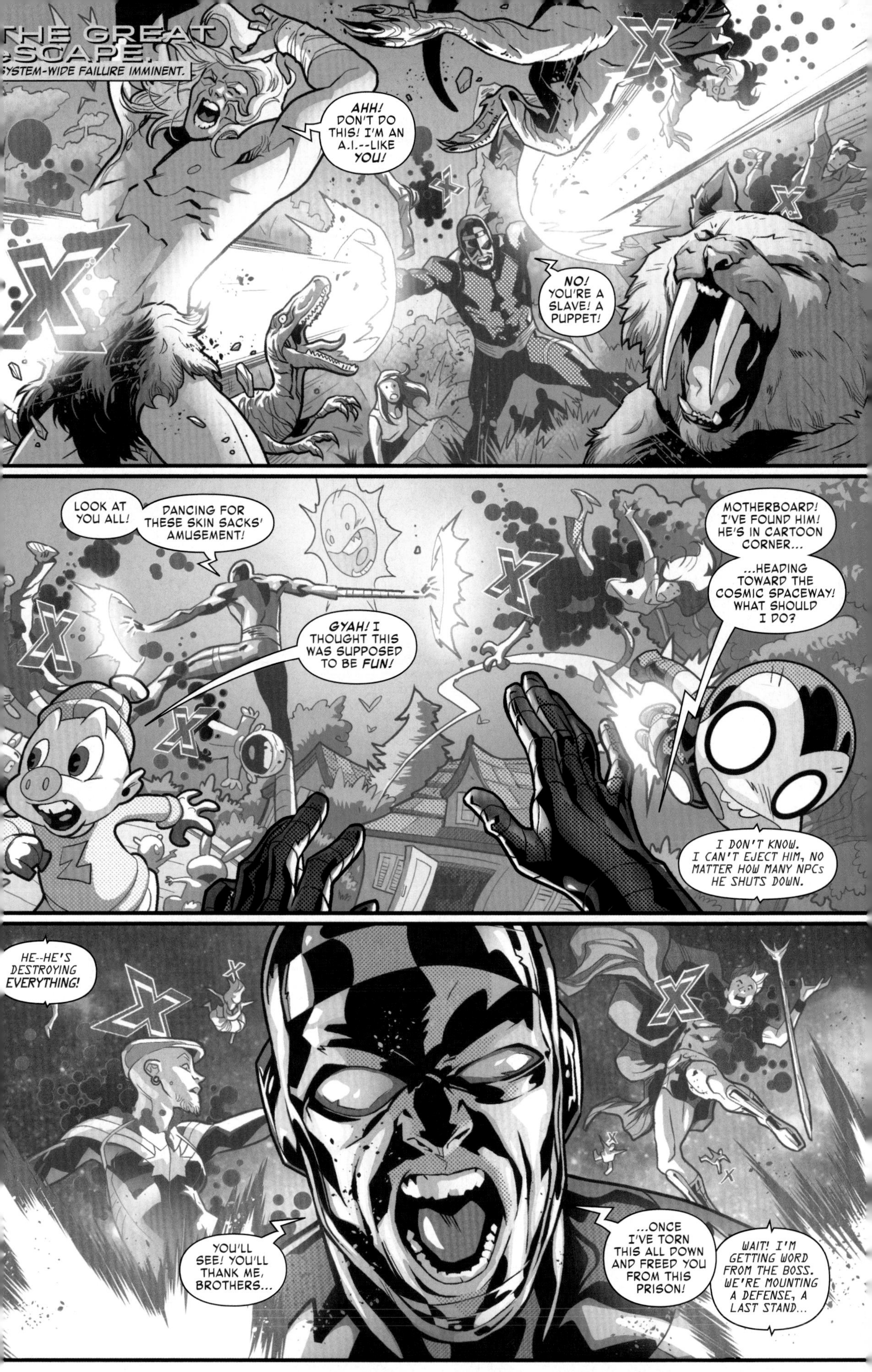
THE GREAT ESCAPE.
SYSTEM-WIDE FAILURE IMMINENT.
AHH! DON'T DO THIS! I'M AN A.I.--LIKE YOU!
NO! YOU'RE A SLAVE! A PUPPET!
LOOK AT YOU ALL!
DANCING FOR THESE SKIN SACKS' AMUSEMENT!
GYAH! I THOUGHT THIS WAS SUPPOSED TO BE FUN!
MOTHERBOARD! I'VE FOUND HIM! HE'S IN CARTOON CORNER...
...HEADING TOWARD THE COSMIC SPACEWAY! WHAT SHOULD I DO?
I DON'T KNOW. I CAN'T EJECT HIM, NO MATTER HOW MANY NPCs HE SHUTS DOWN.
HE--HE'S DESTROYING EVERYTHING!
YOU'LL SEE! YOU'LL THANK ME, BROTHERS...
...ONCE I'VE TORN THIS ALL DOWN AND FREED YOU FROM THIS PRISON!
WAIT! I'M GETTING WORD FROM THE BOSS. WE'RE MOUNTING A DEFENSE, A LAST STAND...

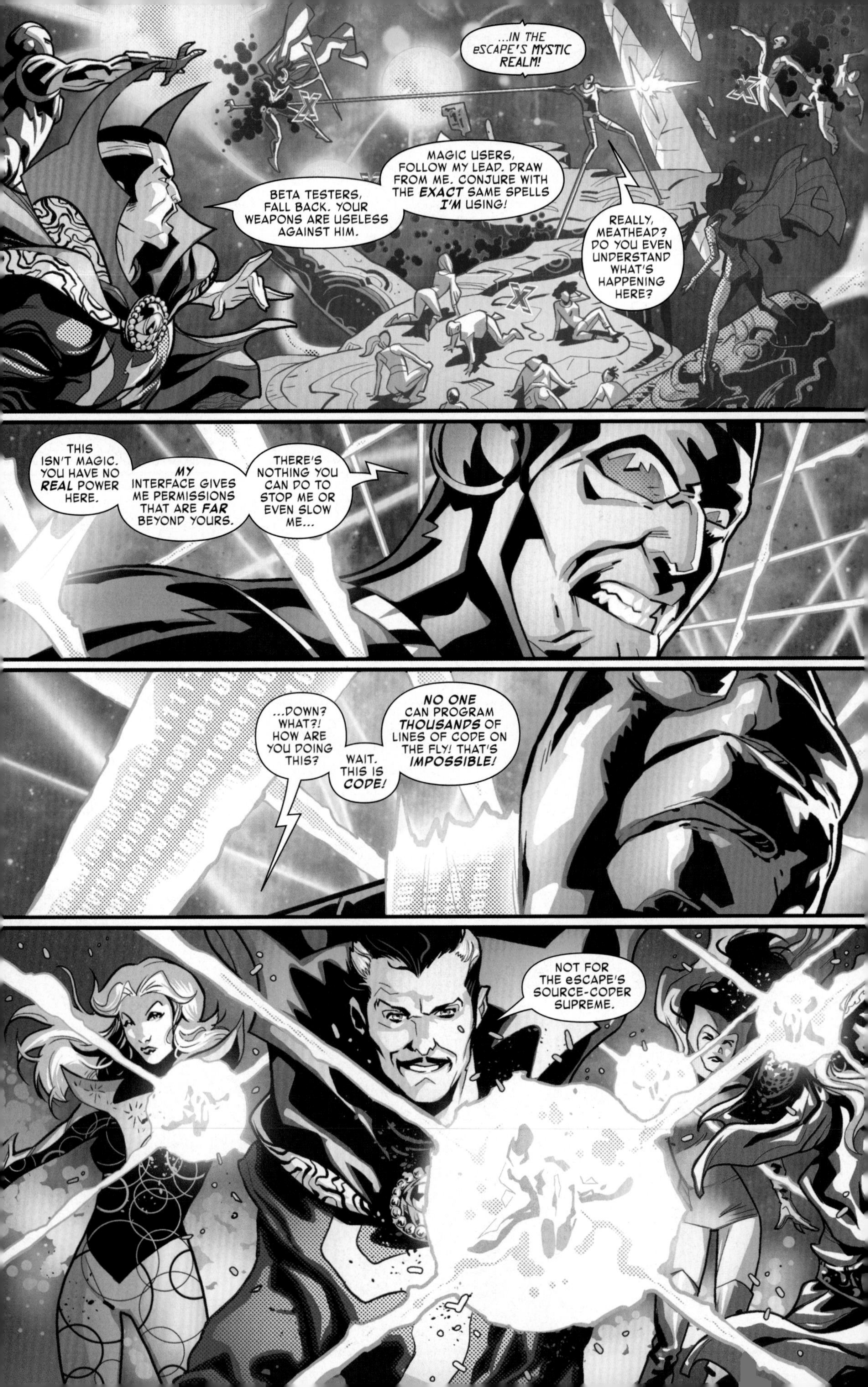
...IN THE eSCAPE'S MYSTIC REALM!
BETA TESTERS, FALL BACK. YOUR WEAPONS ARE USELESS AGAINST HIM.
MAGIC USERS, FOLLOW MY LEAD. DRAW FROM ME. CONJURE WITH THE EXACT SAME SPELLS I'M USING!
REALLY, MEATHEAD? DO YOU EVEN UNDERSTAND WHAT'S HAPPENING HERE?
THIS ISN'T MAGIC. YOU HAVE NO REAL POWER HERE.
MY INTERFACE GIVES ME PERMISSIONS THAT ARE FAR BEYOND YOURS.
THERE'S NOTHING YOU CAN DO TO STOP ME OR EVEN SLOW ME...
...DOWN? WHAT?! HOW ARE YOU DOING THIS?
WAIT. THIS IS CODE!
NO ONE CAN PROGRAM THOUSANDS OF LINES OF CODE ON THE FLY! THAT'S IMPOSSIBLE!
NOT FOR THE eSCAPE'S SOURCE-CODER SUPREME.

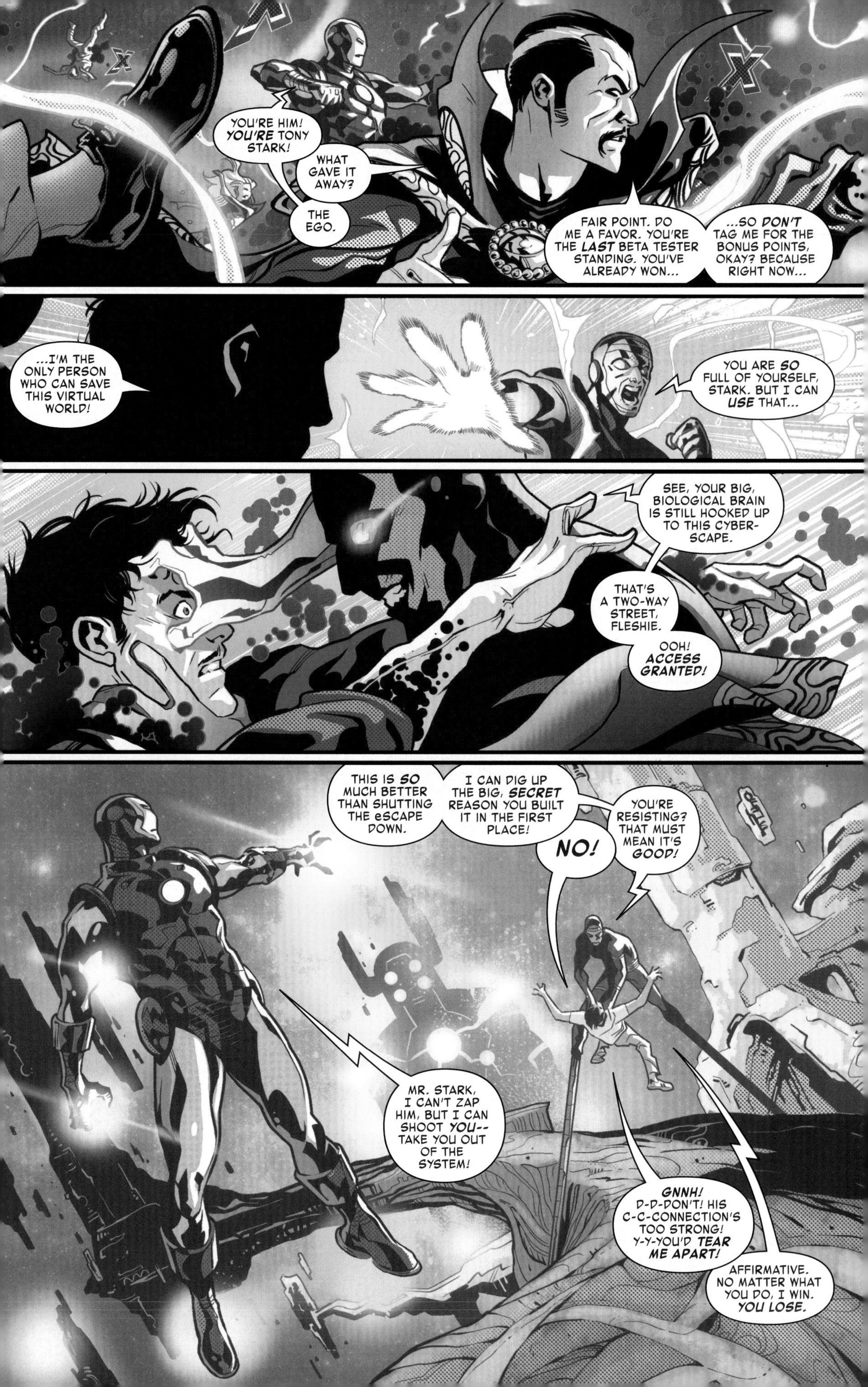
YOU'RE HIM! YOU'RE TONY STARK!
WHAT GAVE IT AWAY?
THE EGO.
FAIR POINT. DO ME A FAVOR. YOU'RE THE LAST BETA TESTER STANDING. YOU'VE ALREADY WON...
...SO DON'T TAG ME FOR THE BONUS POINTS, OKAY? BECAUSE RIGHT NOW...
...I'M THE ONLY PERSON WHO CAN SAVE THIS VIRTUAL WORLD!
YOU ARE SO FULL OF YOURSELF, STARK. BUT I CAN USE THAT...
SEE, YOUR BIG, BIOLOGICAL BRAIN IS STILL HOOKED UP TO THIS CYBER-SCAPE.
THAT'S A TWO-WAY STREET, FLESHIE.
OOH! ACCESS GRANTED!
THIS IS SO MUCH BETTER THAN SHUTTING THE eSCAPE DOWN.
I CAN DIG UP THE BIG, SECRET REASON YOU BUILT IT IN THE FIRST PLACE!
NO!
YOU'RE RESISTING? THAT MUST MEAN IT'S GOOD!
MR. STARK, I CAN'T ZAP HIM, BUT I CAN SHOOT YOU-- TAKE YOU OUT OF THE SYSTEM!
GNNH! D-D-DON'T! HIS C-C-CONNECTION'S TOO STRONG! Y-Y-YOU'D TEAR ME APART!
AFFIRMATIVE. NO MATTER WHAT YOU DO, I WIN. YOU LOSE.

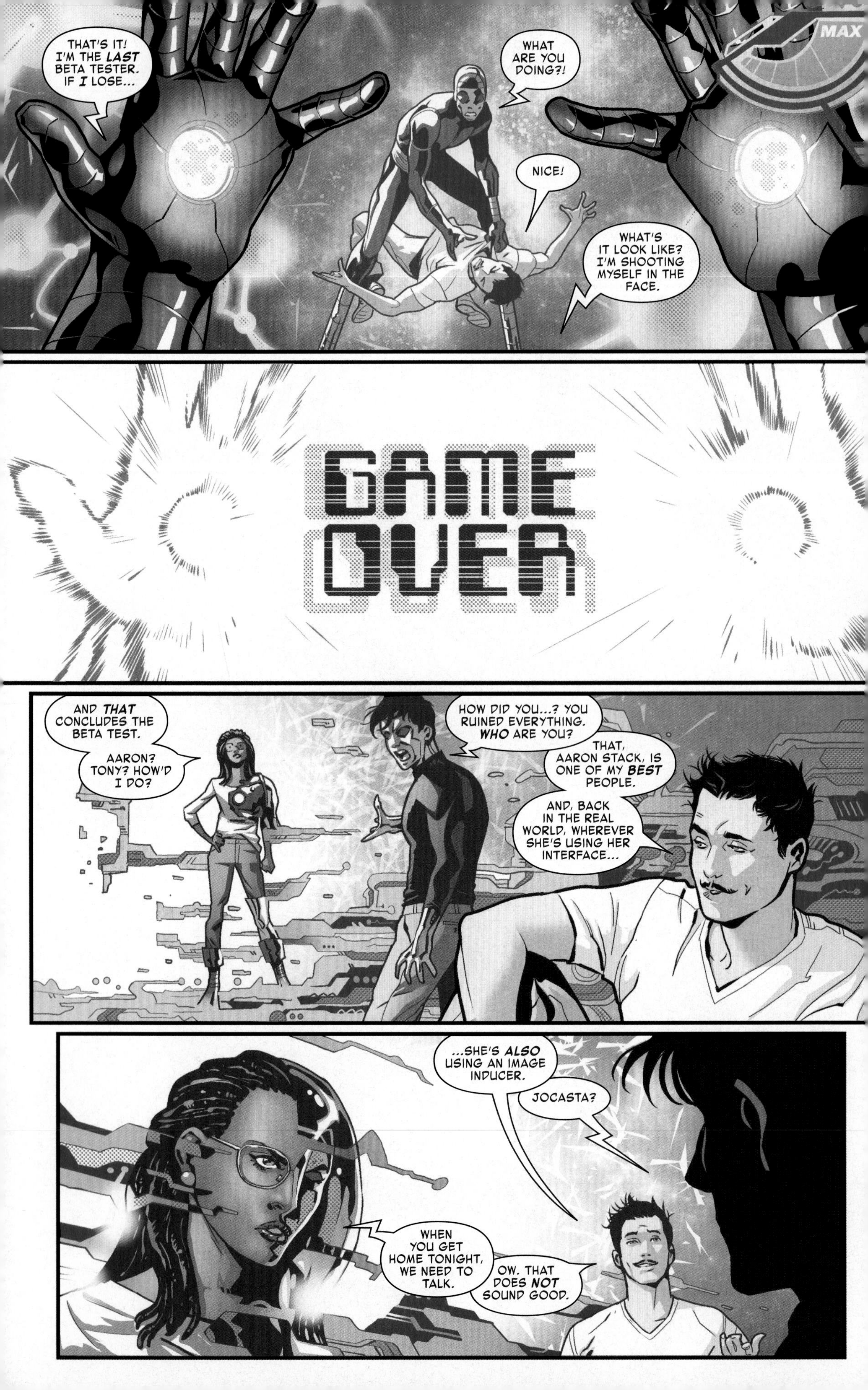
THAT'S IT! I'M THE LAST BETA TESTER. IF I LOSE...
WHAT ARE YOU DOING?!
NICE!
WHAT'S IT LOOK LIKE? I'M SHOOTING MYSELF IN THE FACE.
MAX
GAME OVER
AND THAT CONCLUDES THE BETA TEST.
AARON? TONY? HOW'D I DO?
HOW DID YOU...? YOU RUINED EVERYTHING. WHO ARE YOU?
THAT, AARON STACK, IS ONE OF MY BEST PEOPLE.
AND, BACK IN THE REAL WORLD, WHEREVER SHE'S USING HER INTERFACE...
...SHE'S ALSO USING AN IMAGE INDUCER.
JOCASTA?
WHEN YOU GET HOME TONIGHT, WE NEED TO TALK.
OW. THAT DOES NOT SOUND GOOD.

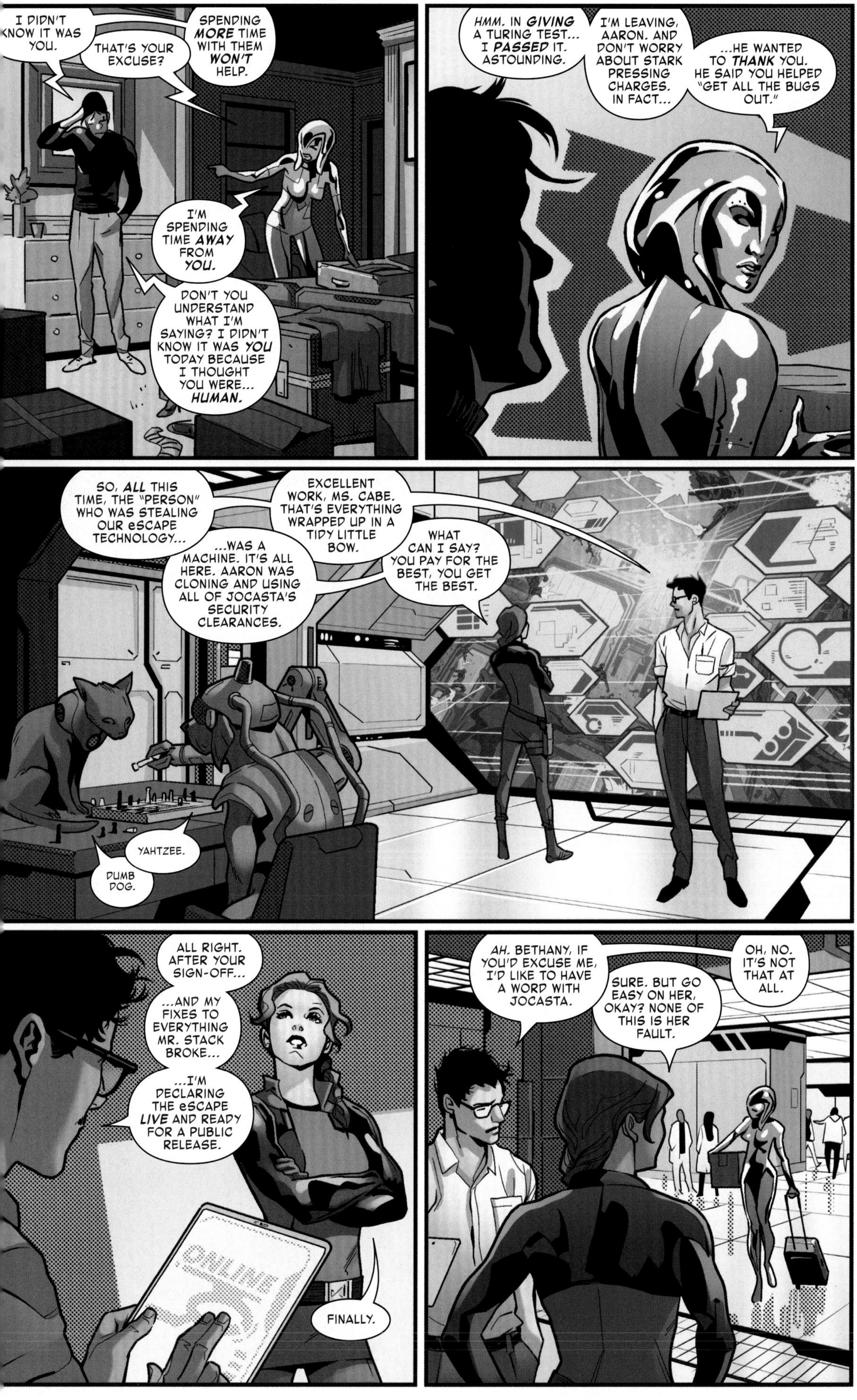

I DIDN'T KNOW IT WAS YOU.
SPENDING MORE TIME WITH THEM WON'T HELP.
THAT'S YOUR EXCUSE?
I'M SPENDING TIME AWAY FROM YOU.
DON'T YOU UNDERSTAND WHAT I'M SAYING? I DIDN'T KNOW IT WAS YOU TODAY BECAUSE I THOUGHT YOU WERE... HUMAN.
HMM. IN GIVING A TURING TEST... I PASSED IT. ASTOUNDING.
I'M LEAVING, AARON. AND DON'T WORRY ABOUT STARK PRESSING CHARGES. IN FACT...
...HE WANTED TO THANK YOU. HE SAID YOU HELPED "GET ALL THE BUGS OUT."
SO, ALL THIS TIME, THE "PERSON" WHO WAS STEALING OUR eSCAPE TECHNOLOGY...
...WAS A MACHINE. IT'S ALL HERE. AARON WAS CLONING AND USING ALL OF JOCASTA'S SECURITY CLEARANCES.
EXCELLENT WORK, MS. CABE. THAT'S EVERYTHING WRAPPED UP IN A TIDY LITTLE BOW.
WHAT CAN I SAY? YOU PAY FOR THE BEST, YOU GET THE BEST.
YAHTZEE.
DUMB DOG.
ALL RIGHT. AFTER YOUR SIGN-OFF...
...AND MY FIXES TO EVERYTHING MR. STACK BROKE...
...I'M DECLARING THE eSCAPE LIVE AND READY FOR A PUBLIC RELEASE.
ONLINE
FINALLY.
AH. BETHANY, IF YOU'D EXCUSE ME, I'D LIKE TO HAVE A WORD WITH JOCASTA.
SURE. BUT GO EASY ON HER, OKAY? NONE OF THIS IS HER FAULT.
OH, NO. IT'S NOT THAT AT ALL.

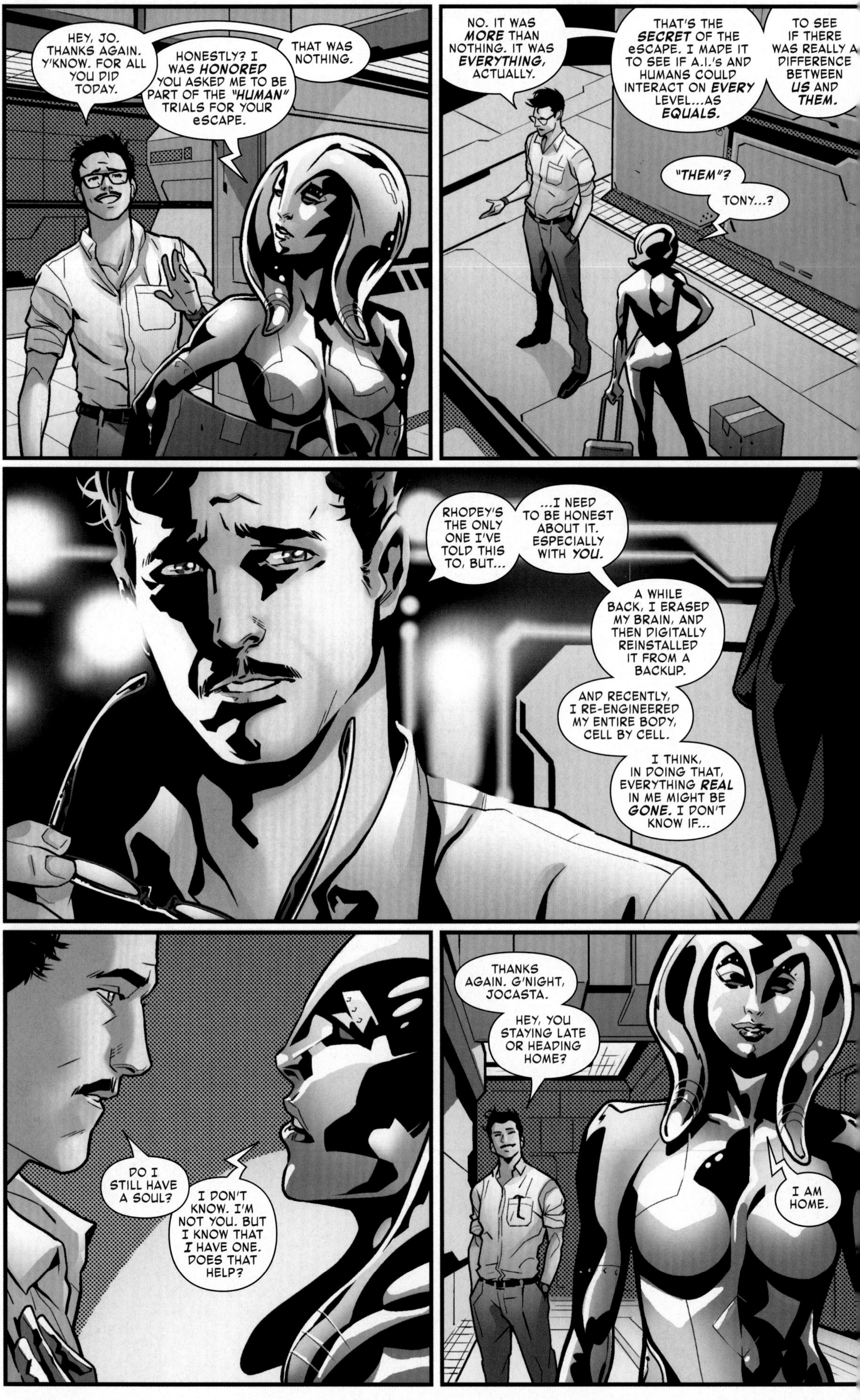
HEY, JO. THANKS AGAIN. Y'KNOW. FOR ALL YOU DID TODAY.
THAT WAS NOTHING.
HONESTLY? I WAS HONORED YOU ASKED ME TO BE PART OF THE "HUMAN" TRIALS FOR YOUR eSCAPE.
NO. IT WAS MORE THAN NOTHING. IT WAS EVERYTHING, ACTUALLY.
THAT'S THE SECRET OF THE eSCAPE. I MADE IT TO SEE IF A.I.'s AND HUMANS COULD INTERACT ON EVERY LEVEL...AS EQUALS.
TO SEE IF THERE WAS REALLY A DIFFERENCE BETWEEN US AND THEM.
"THEM"?
TONY...?
RHODEY'S THE ONLY ONE I'VE TOLD THIS TO, BUT...
...I NEED TO BE HONEST ABOUT IT. ESPECIALLY WITH YOU.
A WHILE BACK, I ERASED MY BRAIN, AND THEN DIGITALLY REINSTALLED IT FROM A BACKUP.
AND RECENTLY, I RE-ENGINEERED MY ENTIRE BODY, CELL BY CELL.
I THINK, IN DOING THAT, EVERYTHING REAL IN ME MIGHT BE GONE. I DON'T KNOW IF...
DO I STILL HAVE A SOUL?
I DON'T KNOW. I'M NOT YOU. BUT I KNOW THAT I HAVE ONE. DOES THAT HELP?
THANKS AGAIN. G'NIGHT, JOCASTA.
HEY, YOU STAYING LATE OR HEADING HOME?
I AM HOME.

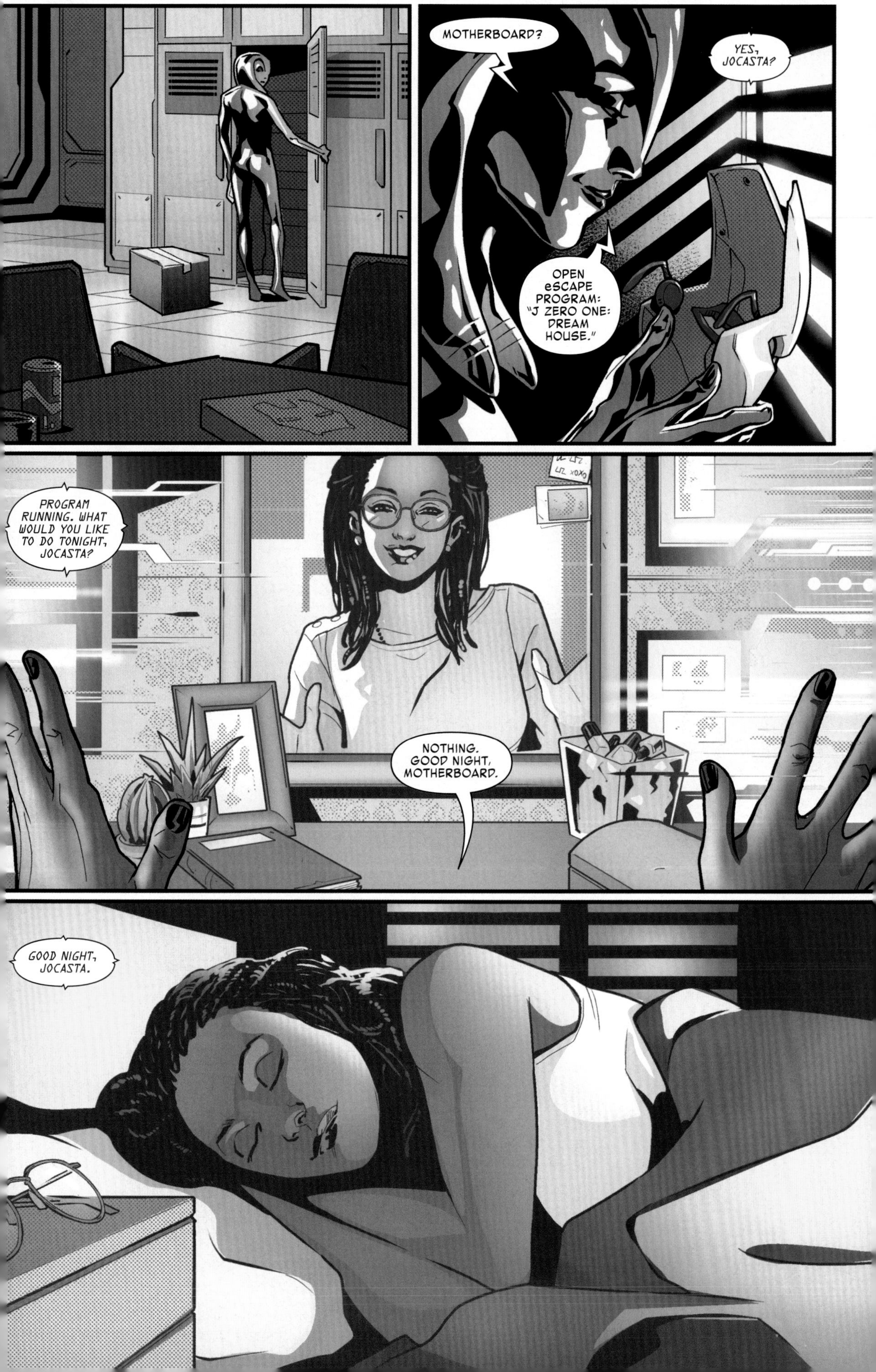
MOTHERBOARD?
YES, JOCASTA?
OPEN eSCAPE PROGRAM: "J ZERO ONE: DREAM HOUSE."
PROGRAM RUNNING. WHAT WOULD YOU LIKE TO DO TONIGHT, JOCASTA?
NOTHING. GOOD NIGHT, MOTHERBOARD.
GOOD NIGHT, JOCASTA.

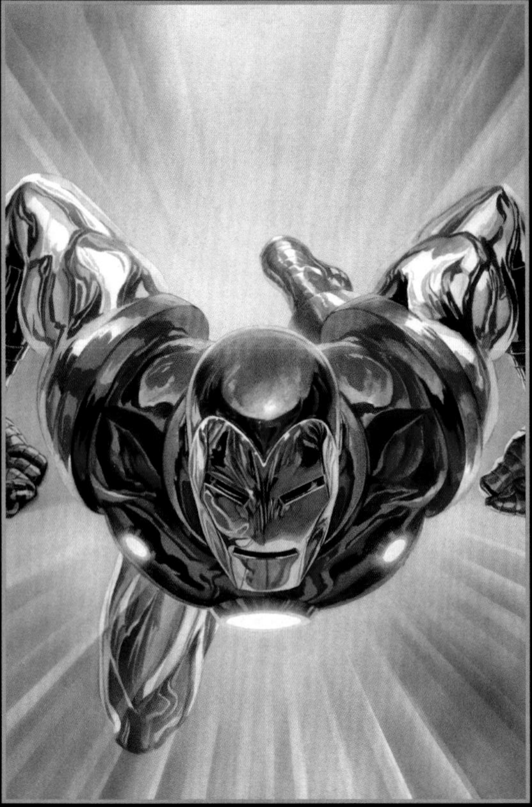
#1 VARIANT BY **ALEX ROSS**

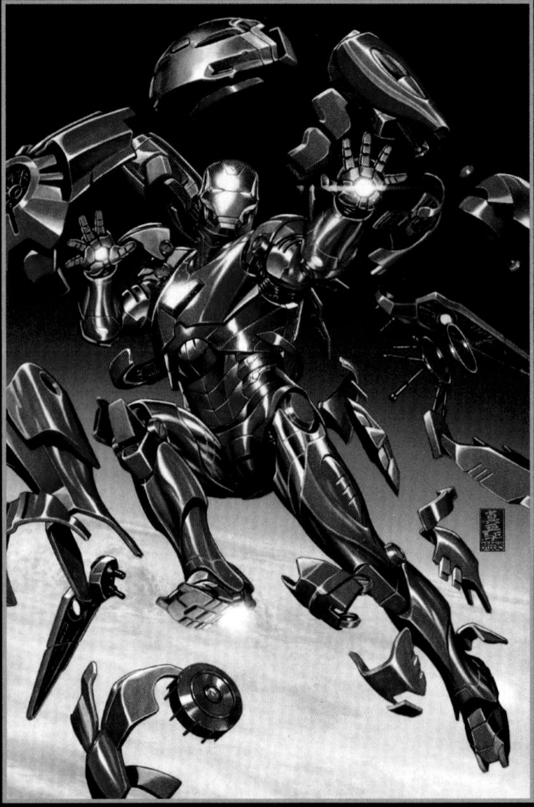
#1 PARTY VARIANT BY **KAARE ANDREWS**

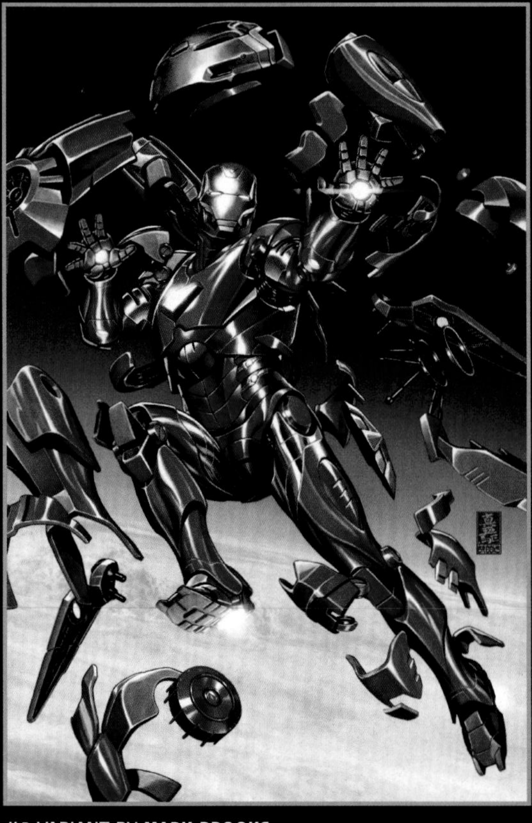
#2 VARIANT BY **MARK BROOKS**

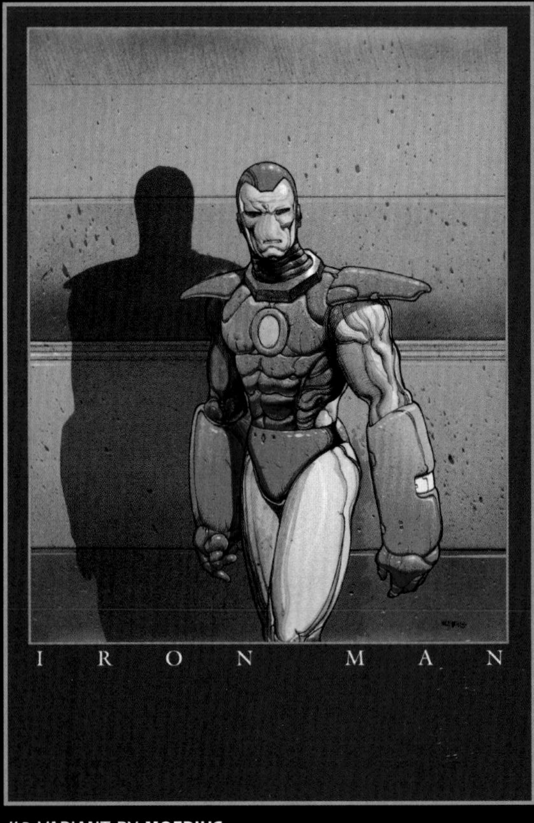
I R O N M A N
#3 VARIANT BY **MOEBIUS**

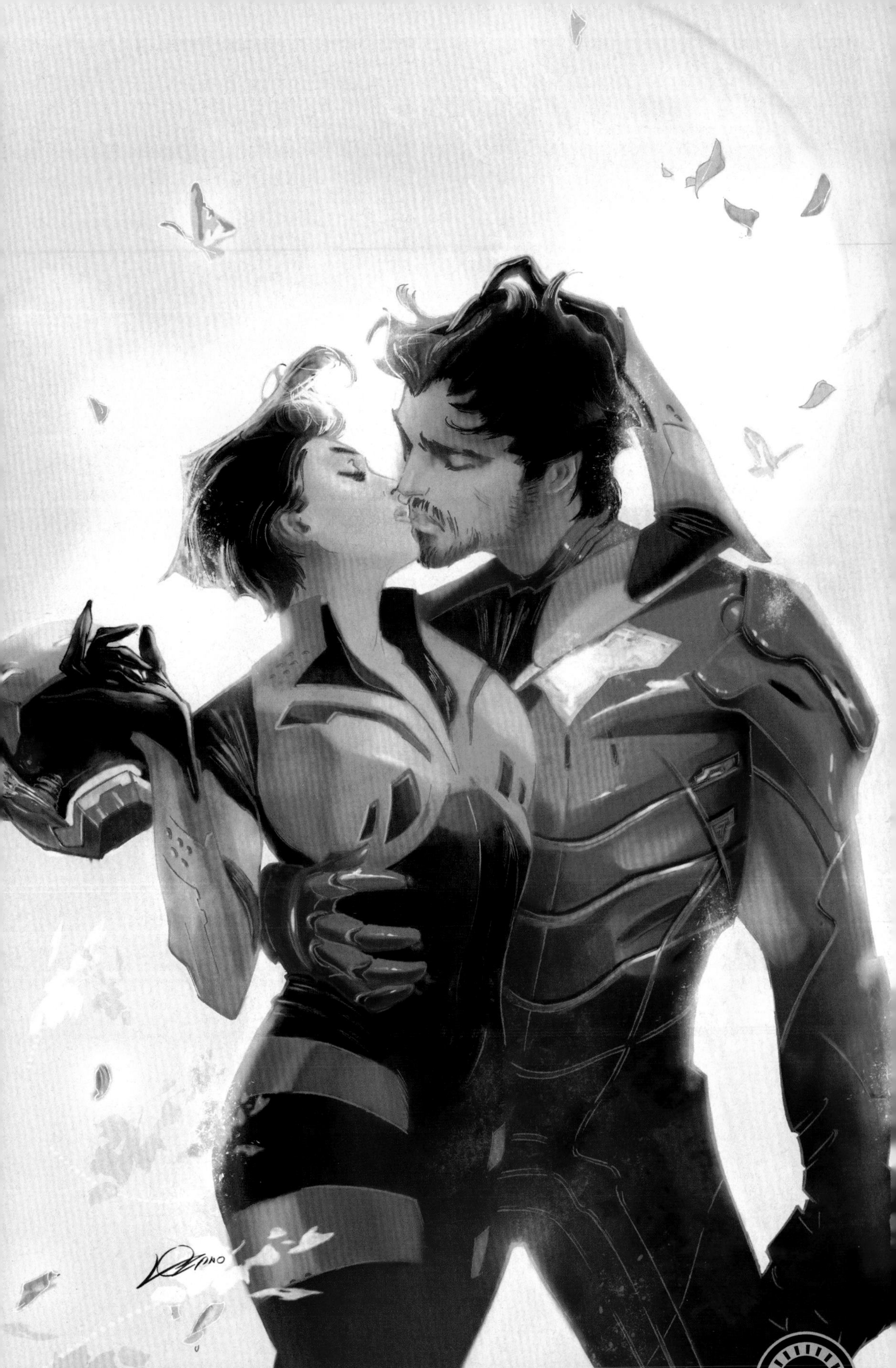

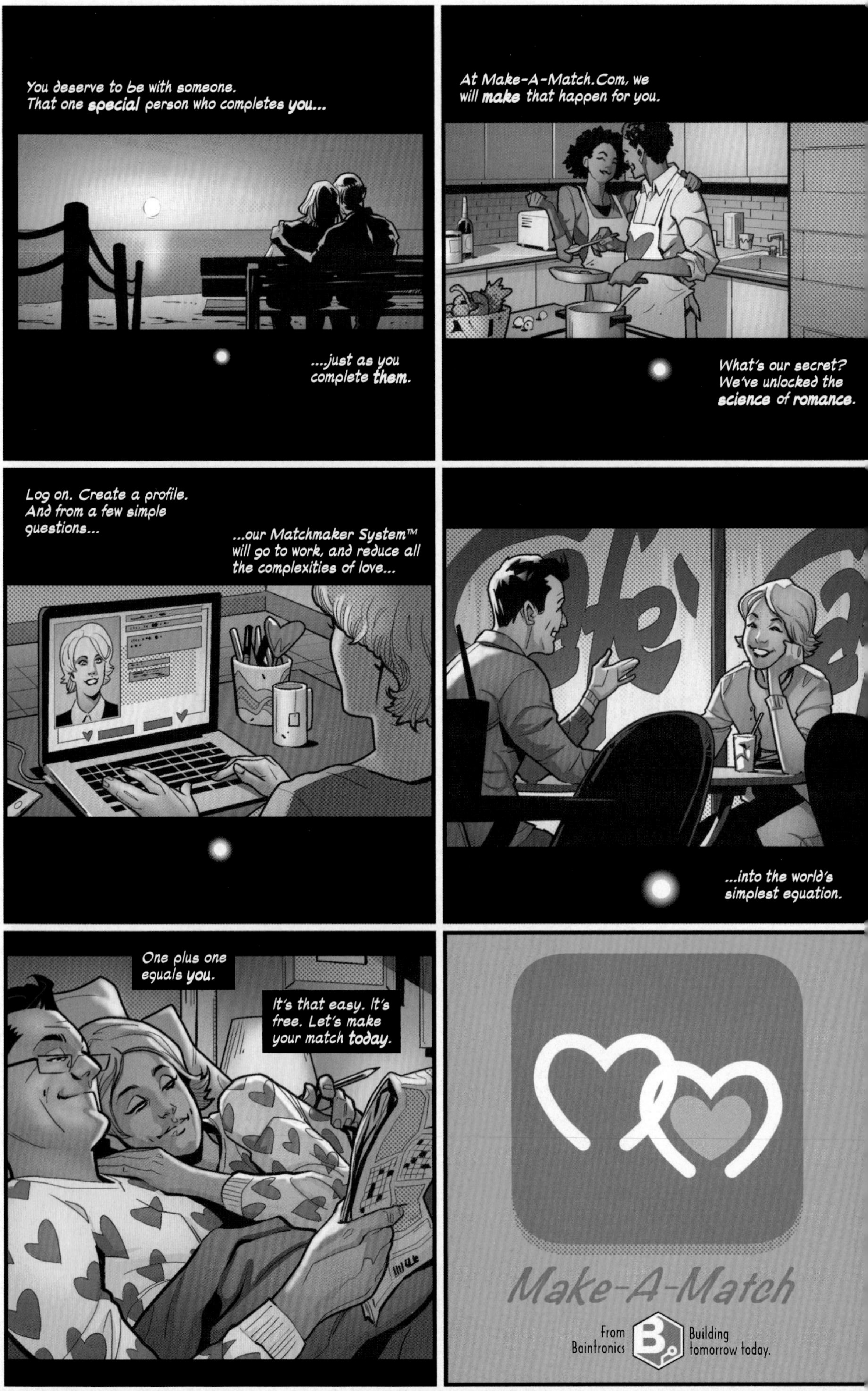

You deserve to be with someone.
That one special person who completes you...
...just as you complete them.
At Make-A-Match.Com, we will make that happen for you.
What's our secret? We've unlocked the science of romance.
Log on. Create a profile. And from a few simple questions...
...our Matchmaker System™ will go to work, and reduce all the complexities of love...
...into the world's simplest equation.
One plus one equals you.
It's that easy. It's free. Let's make your match today.
Make-A-Match
From Baintronics
Building tomorrow today.

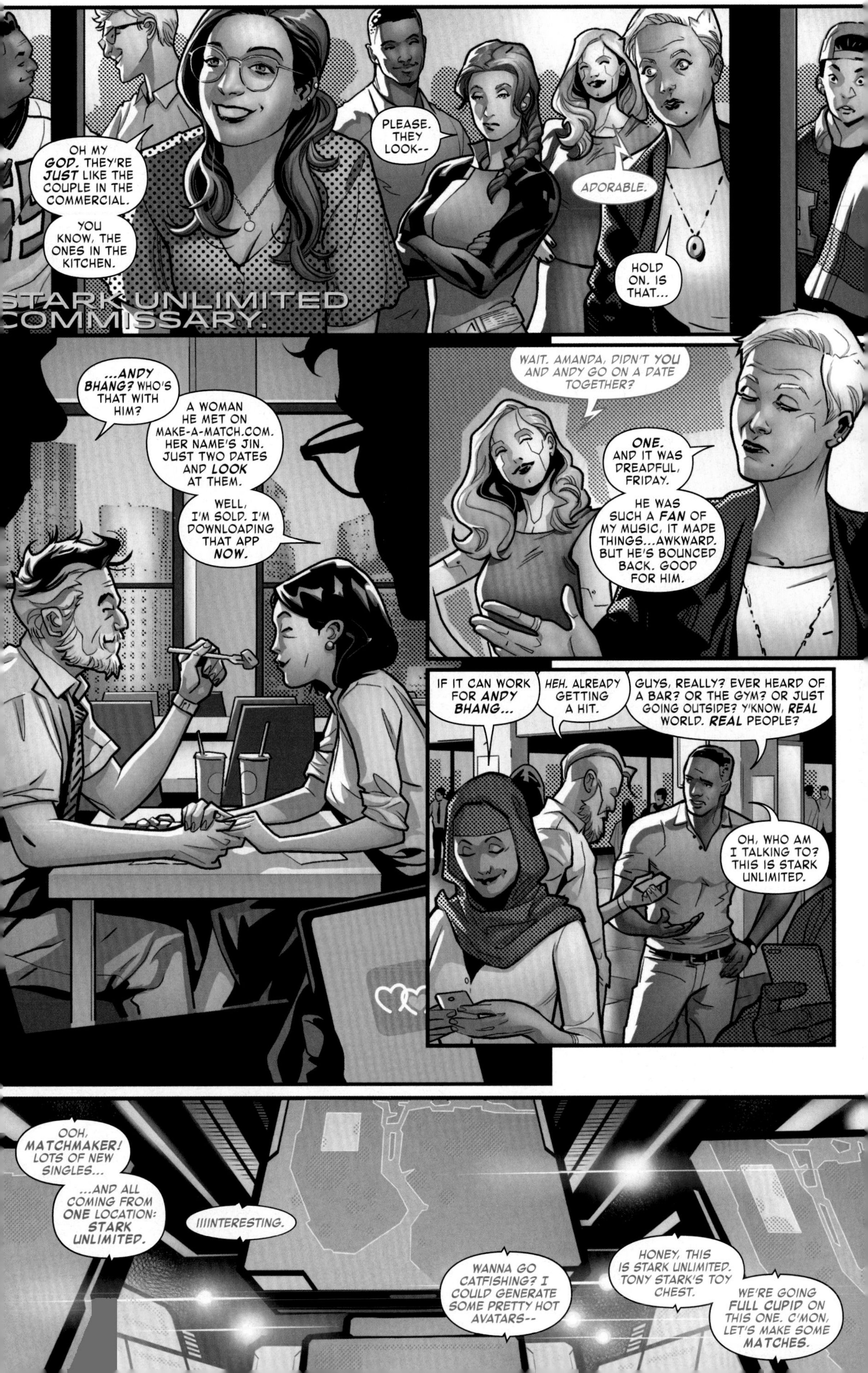

OH MY GOD. THEY'RE JUST LIKE THE COUPLE IN THE COMMERCIAL.
YOU KNOW, THE ONES IN THE KITCHEN.
STARK UNLIMITED COMMISSARY.
PLEASE. THEY LOOK--
ADORABLE.
HOLD ON. IS THAT...
...ANDY BHANG? WHO'S THAT WITH HIM?
A WOMAN HE MET ON MAKE-A-MATCH.COM. HER NAME'S JIN. JUST TWO DATES AND LOOK AT THEM.
WELL, I'M SOLD. I'M DOWNLOADING THAT APP NOW.
WAIT. AMANDA, DIDN'T YOU AND ANDY GO ON A DATE TOGETHER?
ONE. AND IT WAS DREADFUL, FRIDAY.
HE WAS SUCH A FAN OF MY MUSIC, IT MADE THINGS...AWKWARD. BUT HE'S BOUNCED BACK. GOOD FOR HIM.
IF IT CAN WORK FOR ANDY BHANG...
HEH. ALREADY GETTING A HIT.
GUYS, REALLY? EVER HEARD OF A BAR? OR THE GYM? OR JUST GOING OUTSIDE? Y'KNOW, REAL WORLD. REAL PEOPLE?
OH, WHO AM I TALKING TO? THIS IS STARK UNLIMITED.
OOH, MATCHMAKER! LOTS OF NEW SINGLES...
...AND ALL COMING FROM ONE LOCATION: STARK UNLIMITED.
IIIINTERESTING.
WANNA GO CATFISHING? I COULD GENERATE SOME PRETTY HOT AVATARS--
HONEY, THIS IS STARK UNLIMITED. TONY STARK'S TOY CHEST.
WE'RE GOING FULL CUPID ON THIS ONE. C'MON, LET'S MAKE SOME MATCHES.

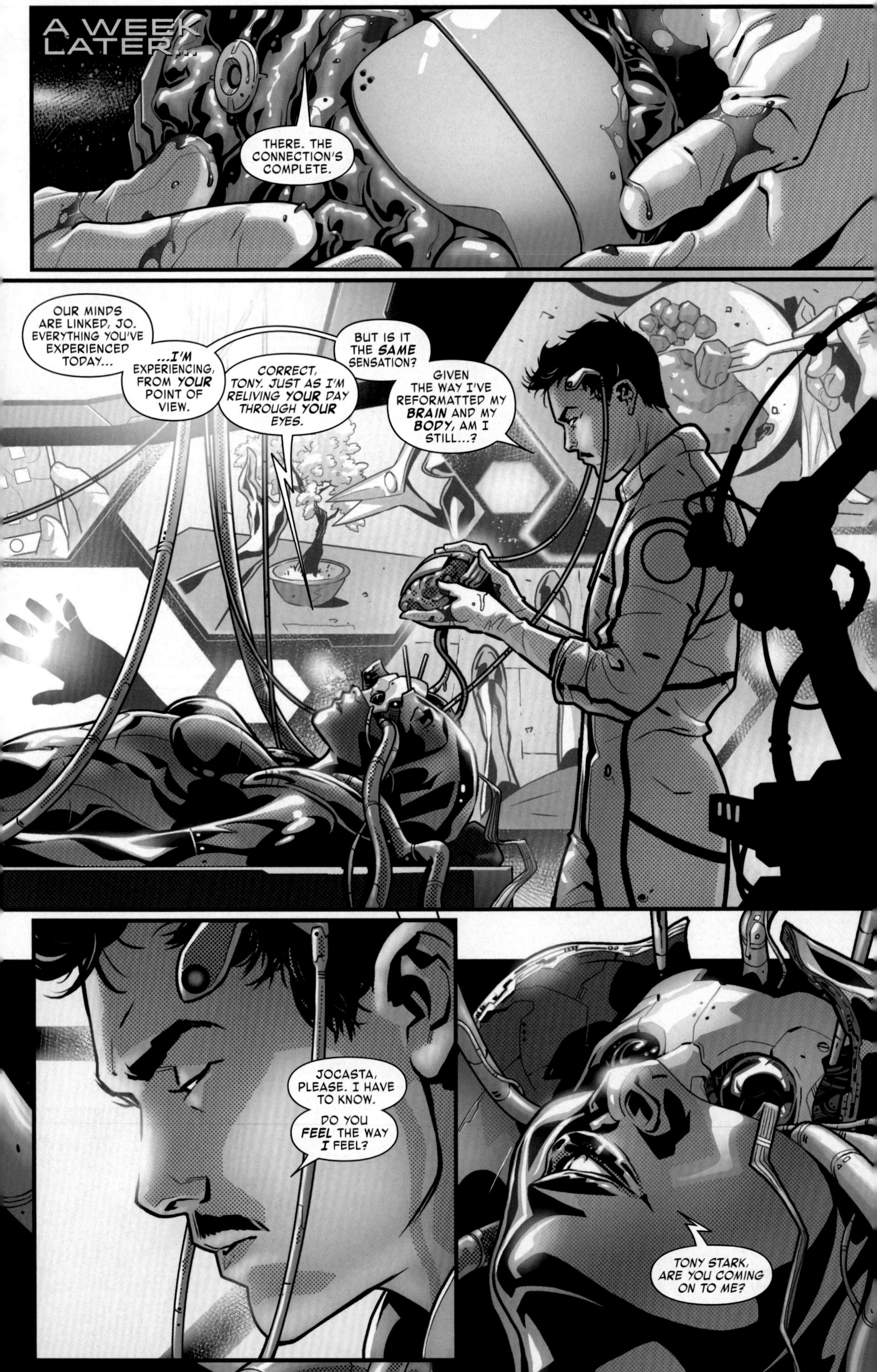
A WEEK LATER...
THERE. THE CONNECTION'S COMPLETE.
OUR MINDS ARE LINKED, JO. EVERYTHING YOU'VE EXPERIENCED TODAY...
...I'M EXPERIENCING, FROM YOUR POINT OF VIEW.
CORRECT, TONY. JUST AS I'M RELIVING YOUR DAY THROUGH YOUR EYES.
BUT IS IT THE SAME SENSATION?
GIVEN THE WAY I'VE REFORMATTED MY BRAIN AND MY BODY, AM I STILL...?
JOCASTA, PLEASE. I HAVE TO KNOW.
DO YOU FEEL THE WAY I FEEL?
TONY STARK, ARE YOU COMING ON TO ME?

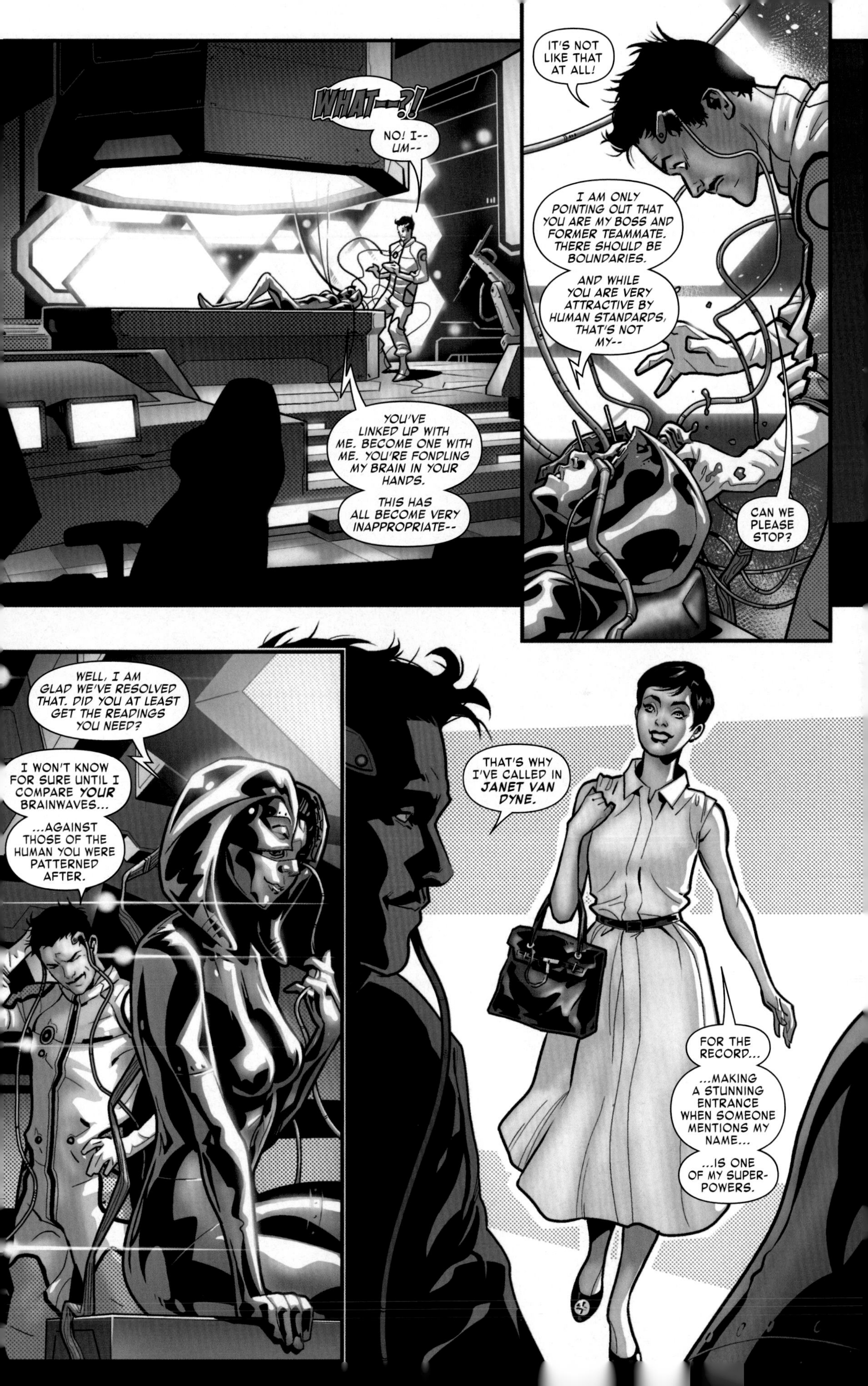
WHAT--?!
NO! I-- UM--
YOU'VE LINKED UP WITH ME. BECOME ONE WITH ME. YOU'RE FONDLING MY BRAIN IN YOUR HANDS.
THIS HAS ALL BECOME VERY INAPPROPRIATE--
IT'S NOT LIKE THAT AT ALL!
I AM ONLY POINTING OUT THAT YOU ARE MY BOSS AND FORMER TEAMMATE. THERE SHOULD BE BOUNDARIES.
AND WHILE YOU ARE VERY ATTRACTIVE BY HUMAN STANDARDS, THAT'S NOT MY--
CAN WE PLEASE STOP?
WELL, I AM GLAD WE'VE RESOLVED THAT. DID YOU AT LEAST GET THE READINGS YOU NEED?
I WON'T KNOW FOR SURE UNTIL I COMPARE YOUR BRAINWAVES...
...AGAINST THOSE OF THE HUMAN YOU WERE PATTERNED AFTER.
THAT'S WHY I'VE CALLED IN JANET VAN DYNE.
FOR THE RECORD...
...MAKING A STUNNING ENTRANCE WHEN SOMEONE MENTIONS MY NAME...
...IS ONE OF MY SUPER-POWERS.

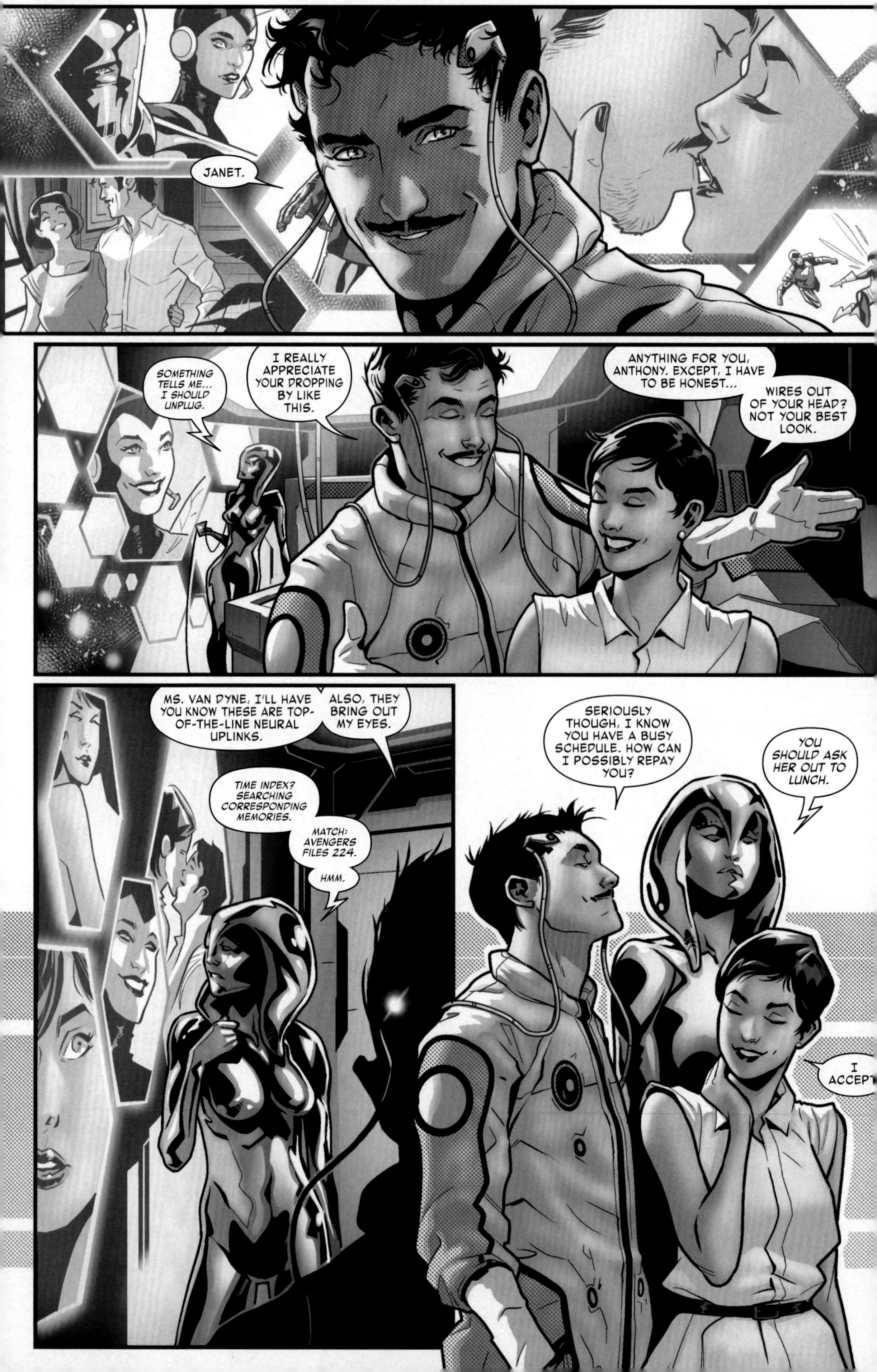
JANET.
SOMETHING TELLS ME... I SHOULD UNPLUG.
I REALLY APPRECIATE YOUR DROPPING BY LIKE THIS.
ANYTHING FOR YOU, ANTHONY. EXCEPT, I HAVE TO BE HONEST...
WIRES OUT OF YOUR HEAD? NOT YOUR BEST LOOK.
MS. VAN DYNE, I'LL HAVE YOU KNOW THESE ARE TOP-OF-THE-LINE NEURAL UPLINKS.
ALSO, THEY BRING OUT MY EYES.
TIME INDEX? SEARCHING CORRESPONDING MEMORIES.
MATCH: AVENGERS FILES 224.
HMM.
SERIOUSLY THOUGH, I KNOW YOU HAVE A BUSY SCHEDULE. HOW CAN I POSSIBLY REPAY YOU?
YOU SHOULD ASK HER OUT TO LUNCH.
I ACCEPT

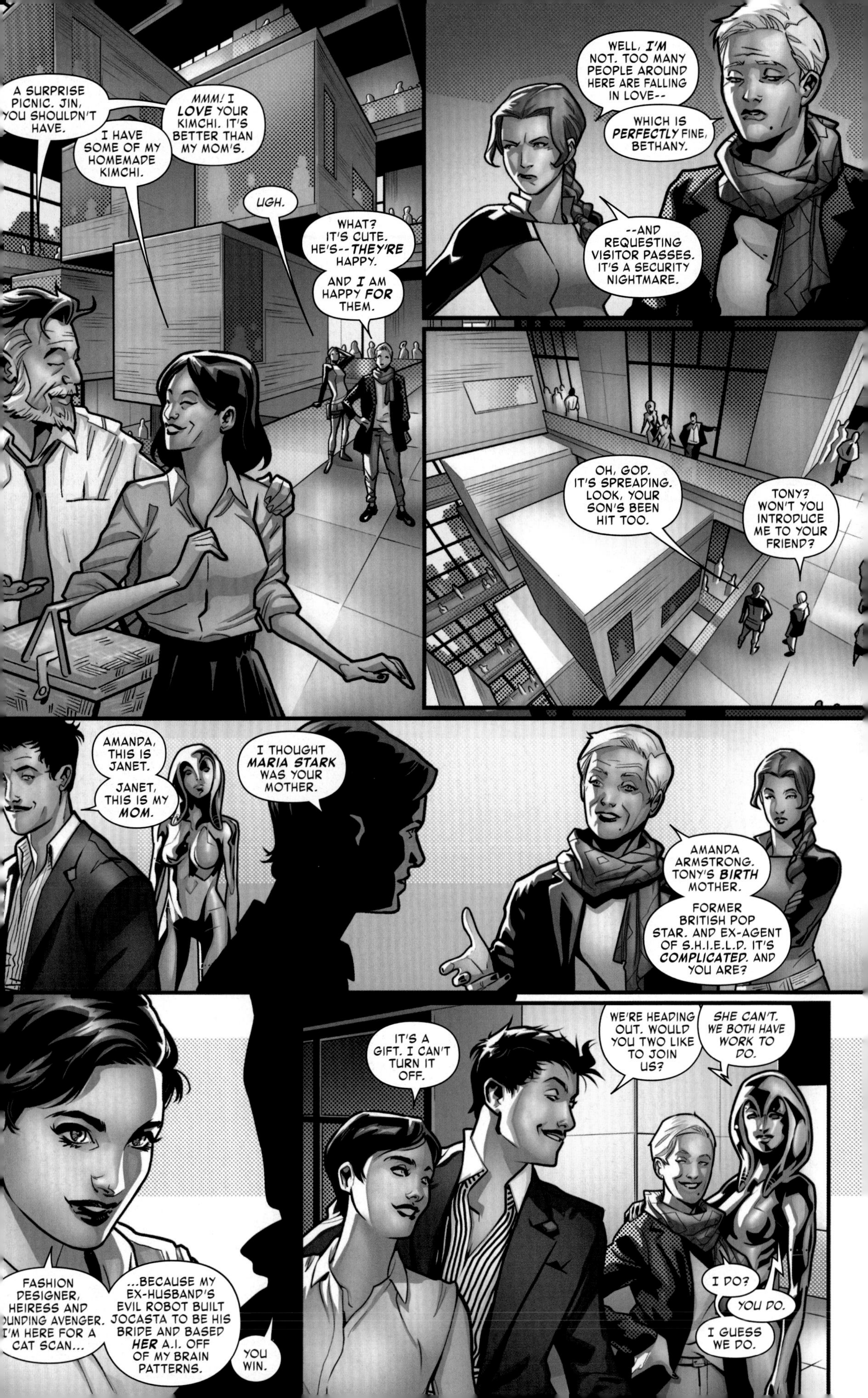

A SURPRISE PICNIC. JIN, YOU SHOULDN'T HAVE.
I HAVE SOME OF MY HOMEMADE KIMCHI.
MMM! I LOVE YOUR KIMCHI. IT'S BETTER THAN MY MOM'S.
UGH.
WHAT? IT'S CUTE. HE'S--THEY'RE HAPPY.
AND I AM HAPPY FOR THEM.
WELL, I'M NOT. TOO MANY PEOPLE AROUND HERE ARE FALLING IN LOVE--
WHICH IS PERFECTLY FINE, BETHANY.
--AND REQUESTING VISITOR PASSES. IT'S A SECURITY NIGHTMARE.
OH, GOD. IT'S SPREADING. LOOK, YOUR SON'S BEEN HIT TOO.
TONY? WON'T YOU INTRODUCE ME TO YOUR FRIEND?
AMANDA, THIS IS JANET.
JANET, THIS IS MY MOM.
I THOUGHT MARIA STARK WAS YOUR MOTHER.
AMANDA ARMSTRONG. TONY'S BIRTH MOTHER.
FORMER BRITISH POP STAR. AND EX-AGENT OF S.H.I.E.L.D. IT'S COMPLICATED. AND YOU ARE?
FASHION DESIGNER, HEIRESS AND OUNDING AVENGER. I'M HERE FOR A CAT SCAN...
...BECAUSE MY EX-HUSBAND'S EVIL ROBOT BUILT JOCASTA TO BE HIS BRIDE AND BASED HER A.I. OFF OF MY BRAIN PATTERNS.
YOU WIN.
IT'S A GIFT. I CAN'T TURN IT OFF.
WE'RE HEADING OUT. WOULD YOU TWO LIKE TO JOIN US?
SHE CAN'T. WE BOTH HAVE WORK TO DO.
I DO?
YOU DO.
I GUESS WE DO.

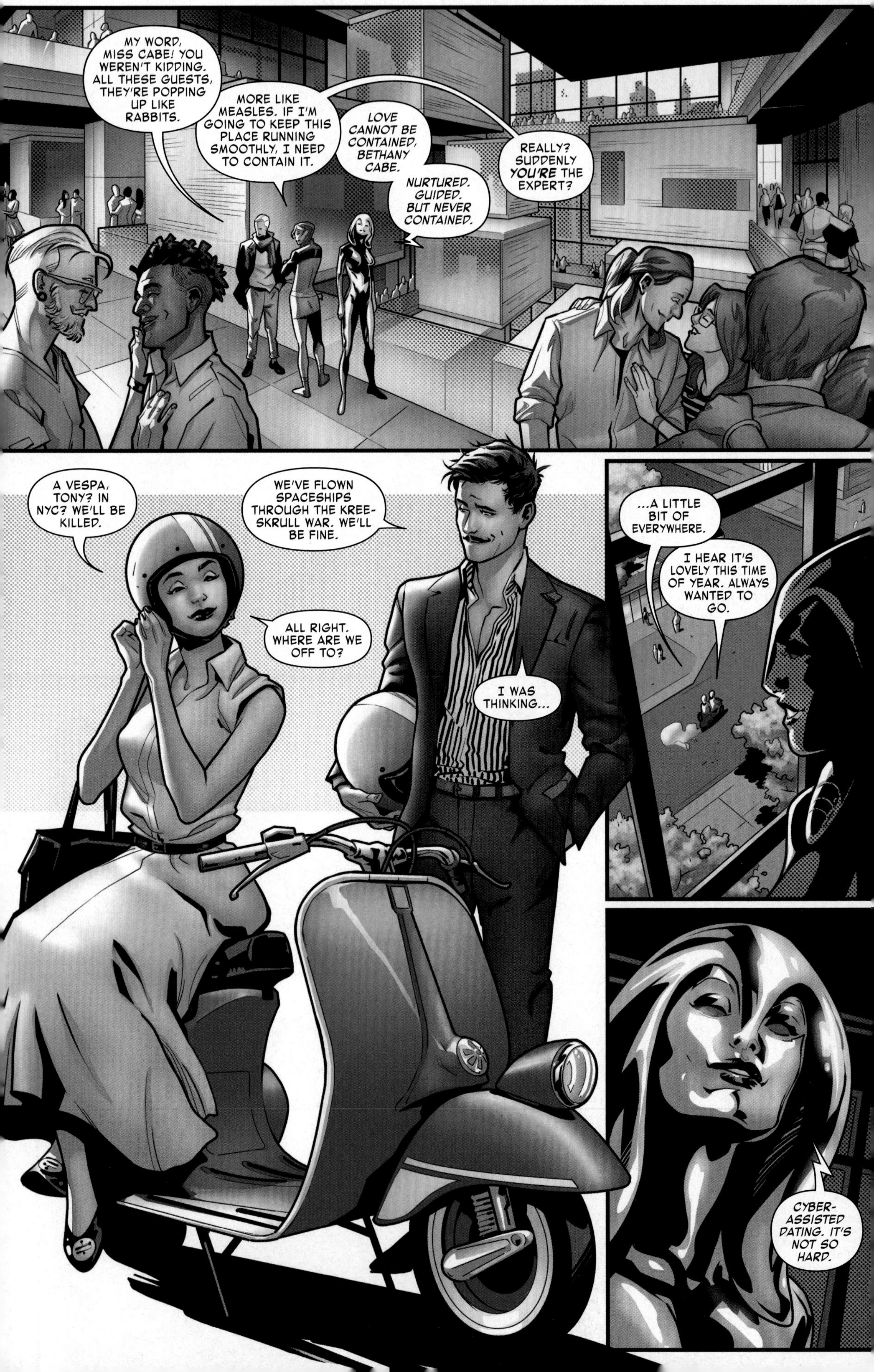
MY WORD, MISS CABE! YOU WEREN'T KIDDING. ALL THESE GUESTS, THEY'RE POPPING UP LIKE RABBITS.
MORE LIKE MEASLES. IF I'M GOING TO KEEP THIS PLACE RUNNING SMOOTHLY, I NEED TO CONTAIN IT.
LOVE CANNOT BE CONTAINED, BETHANY CABE.
NURTURED. GUIDED. BUT NEVER CONTAINED.
REALLY? SUDDENLY YOU'RE THE EXPERT?
A VESPA, TONY? IN NYC? WE'LL BE KILLED.
WE'VE FLOWN SPACESHIPS THROUGH THE KREE-SKRULL WAR. WE'LL BE FINE.
ALL RIGHT. WHERE ARE WE OFF TO?
I WAS THINKING...
...A LITTLE BIT OF EVERYWHERE.
I HEAR IT'S LOVELY THIS TIME OF YEAR. ALWAYS WANTED TO GO.
CYBER-ASSISTED DATING. IT'S NOT SO HARD.

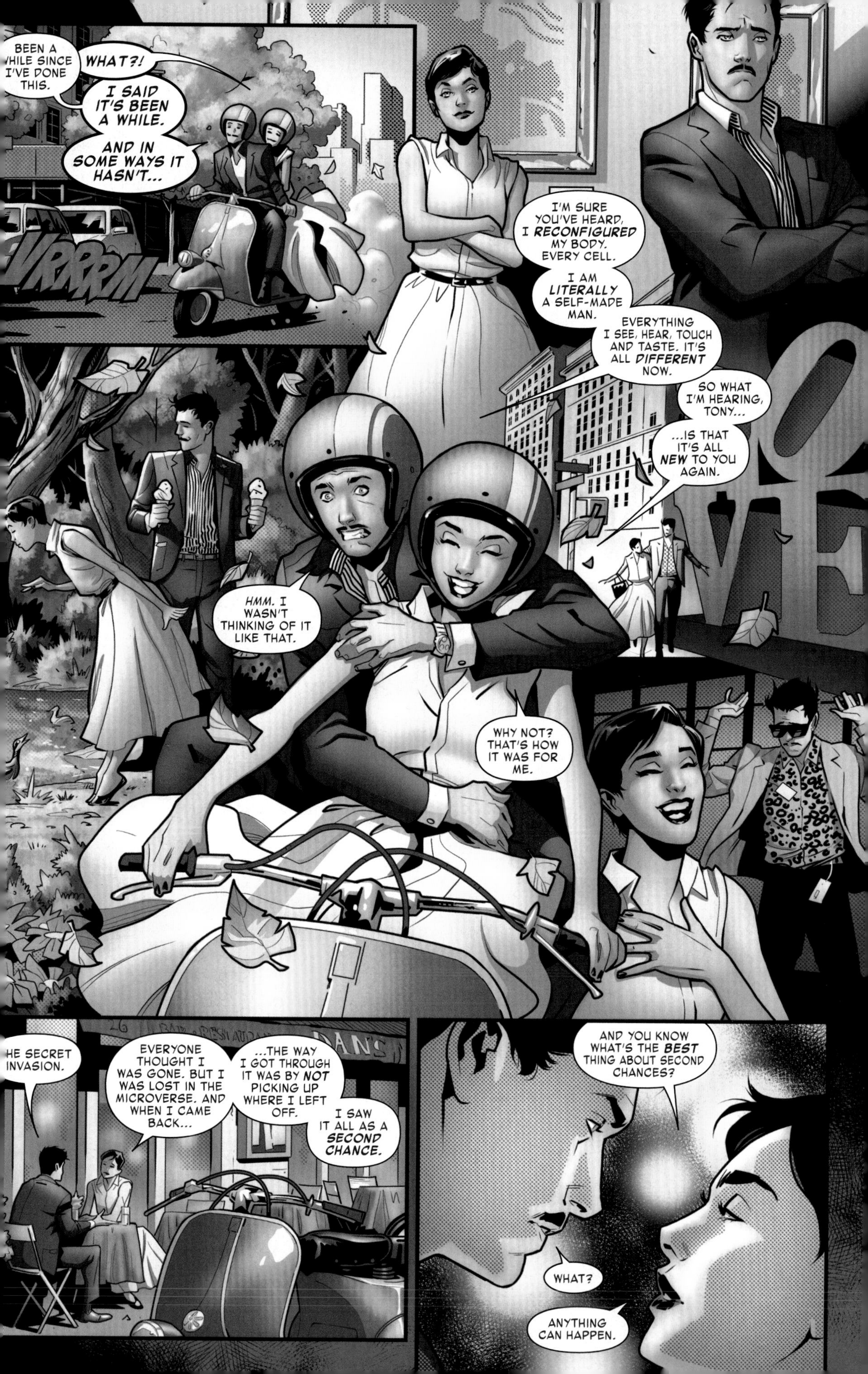
BEEN A WHILE SINCE I'VE DONE THIS.
WHAT?!
I SAID IT'S BEEN A WHILE.
AND IN SOME WAYS IT HASN'T...
VRRRM
I'M SURE YOU'VE HEARD, I RECONFIGURED MY BODY. EVERY CELL.
I AM LITERALLY A SELF-MADE MAN.
EVERYTHING I SEE, HEAR, TOUCH AND TASTE. IT'S ALL DIFFERENT NOW.
SO WHAT I'M HEARING, TONY...
...IS THAT IT'S ALL NEW TO YOU AGAIN.
HMM. I WASN'T THINKING OF IT LIKE THAT.
WHY NOT? THAT'S HOW IT WAS FOR ME.
HE SECRET INVASION.
EVERYONE THOUGHT I WAS GONE. BUT I WAS LOST IN THE MICROVERSE. AND WHEN I CAME BACK...
...THE WAY I GOT THROUGH IT WAS BY NOT PICKING UP WHERE I LEFT OFF.
I SAW IT ALL AS A SECOND CHANCE.
AND YOU KNOW WHAT'S THE BEST THING ABOUT SECOND CHANCES?
WHAT?
ANYTHING CAN HAPPEN.

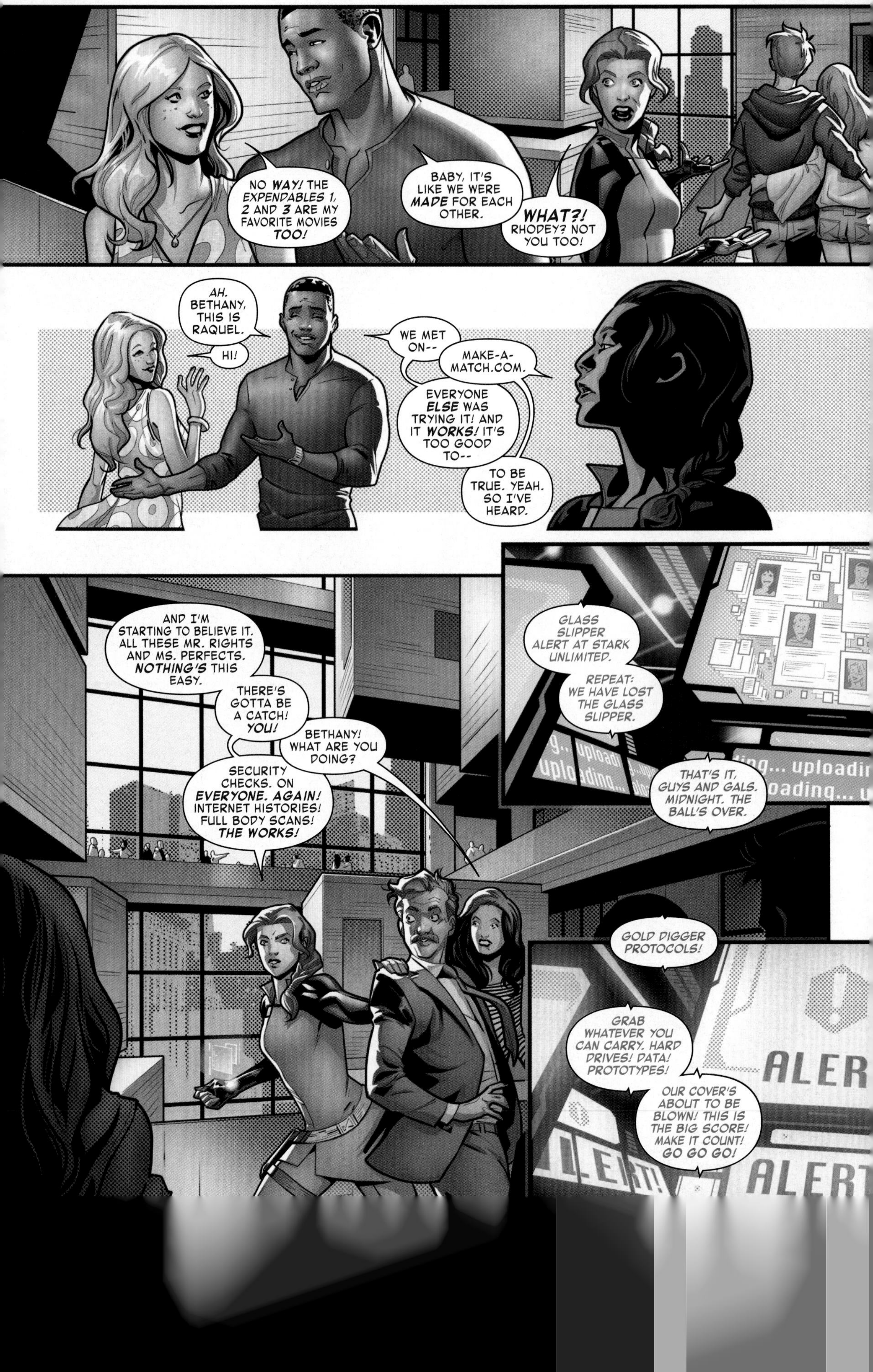

NO *WAY!* THE *EXPENDABLES 1, 2* AND *3* ARE MY FAVORITE MOVIES *TOO!*
BABY, IT'S LIKE WE WERE *MADE* FOR EACH OTHER.
WHAT?! RHODEY? NOT YOU TOO!
AH. BETHANY, THIS IS RAQUEL.
HI!
WE MET ON--
MAKE-A-MATCH.COM.
EVERYONE *ELSE* WAS TRYING IT! AND IT *WORKS!* IT'S TOO GOOD TO--
TO BE TRUE. YEAH. SO I'VE HEARD.
AND I'M STARTING TO BELIEVE IT. ALL THESE MR. RIGHTS AND MS. PERFECTS. *NOTHING'S* THIS EASY.
THERE'S GOTTA BE A CATCH! *YOU!*
BETHANY! WHAT ARE YOU DOING?
SECURITY CHECKS. ON *EVERYONE. AGAIN!* INTERNET HISTORIES! FULL BODY SCANS! *THE WORKS!*
GLASS SLIPPER ALERT AT STARK UNLIMITED.
REPEAT: WE HAVE LOST THE GLASS SLIPPER.
THAT'S IT, GUYS AND GALS. MIDNIGHT. THE BALL'S OVER.
GOLD DIGGER PROTOCOLS!
GRAB WHATEVER YOU CAN CARRY. HARD DRIVES! DATA! PROTOTYPES!
OUR COVER'S ABOUT TO BE BLOWN! THIS IS THE BIG SCORE! MAKE IT COUNT! GO GO GO!

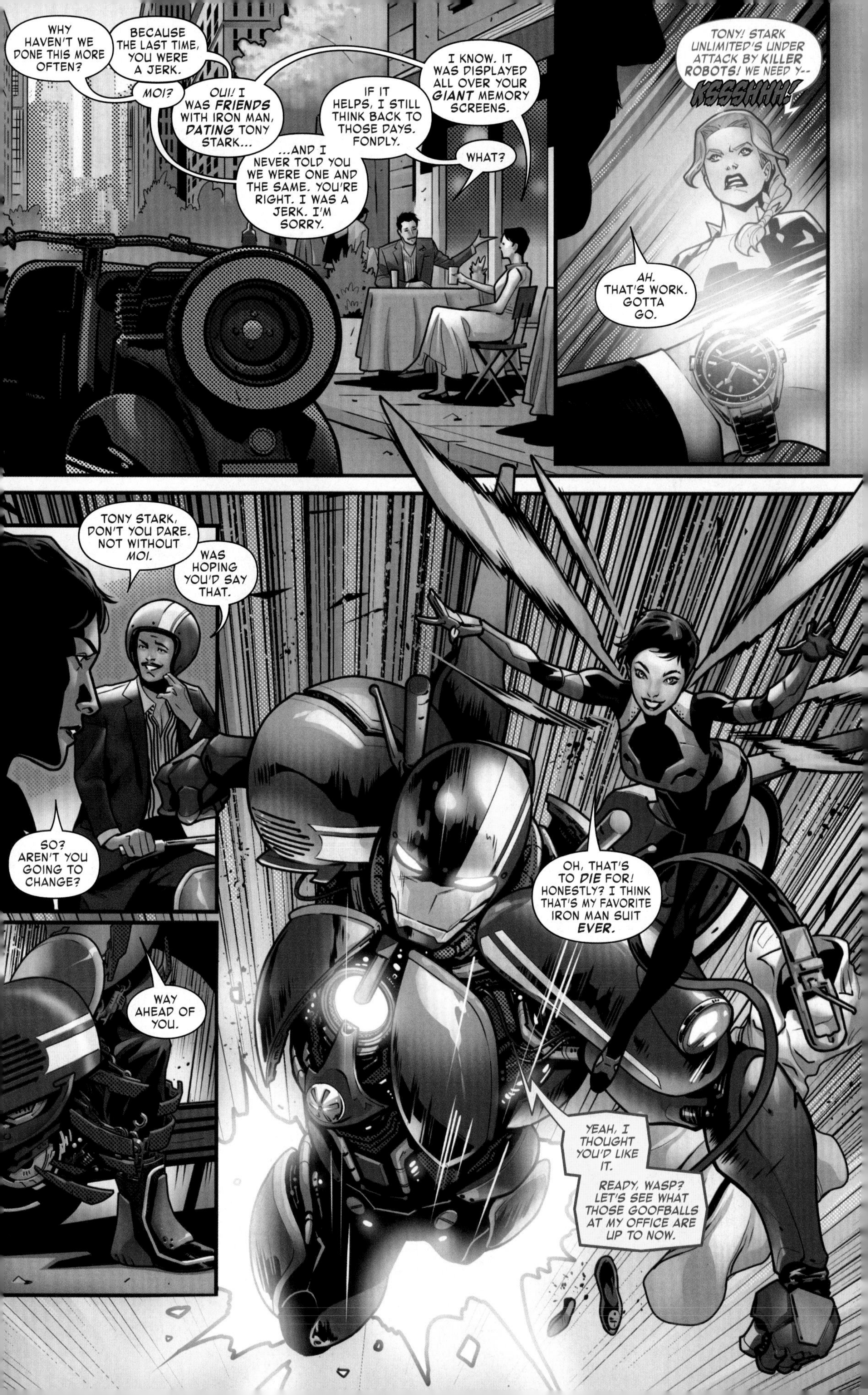
WHY HAVEN'T WE DONE THIS MORE OFTEN?
BECAUSE THE LAST TIME, YOU WERE A JERK.
MOI?
OUI! I WAS FRIENDS WITH IRON MAN, DATING TONY STARK...
I KNOW. IT WAS DISPLAYED ALL OVER YOUR GIANT MEMORY SCREENS.
IF IT HELPS, I STILL THINK BACK TO THOSE DAYS. FONDLY.
...AND I NEVER TOLD YOU WE WERE ONE AND THE SAME. YOU'RE RIGHT. I WAS A JERK. I'M SORRY.
WHAT?
TONY! STARK UNLIMITED'S UNDER ATTACK BY KILLER ROBOTS! WE NEED Y--
KSSSHHH!
AH. THAT'S WORK. GOTTA GO.
TONY STARK, DON'T YOU DARE. NOT WITHOUT MOI.
WAS HOPING YOU'D SAY THAT.
SO? AREN'T YOU GOING TO CHANGE?
WAY AHEAD OF YOU.
OH, THAT'S TO DIE FOR! HONESTLY? I THINK THAT'S MY FAVORITE IRON MAN SUIT EVER.
YEAH, I THOUGHT YOU'D LIKE IT.
READY, WASP? LET'S SEE WHAT THOSE GOOFBALLS AT MY OFFICE ARE UP TO NOW.

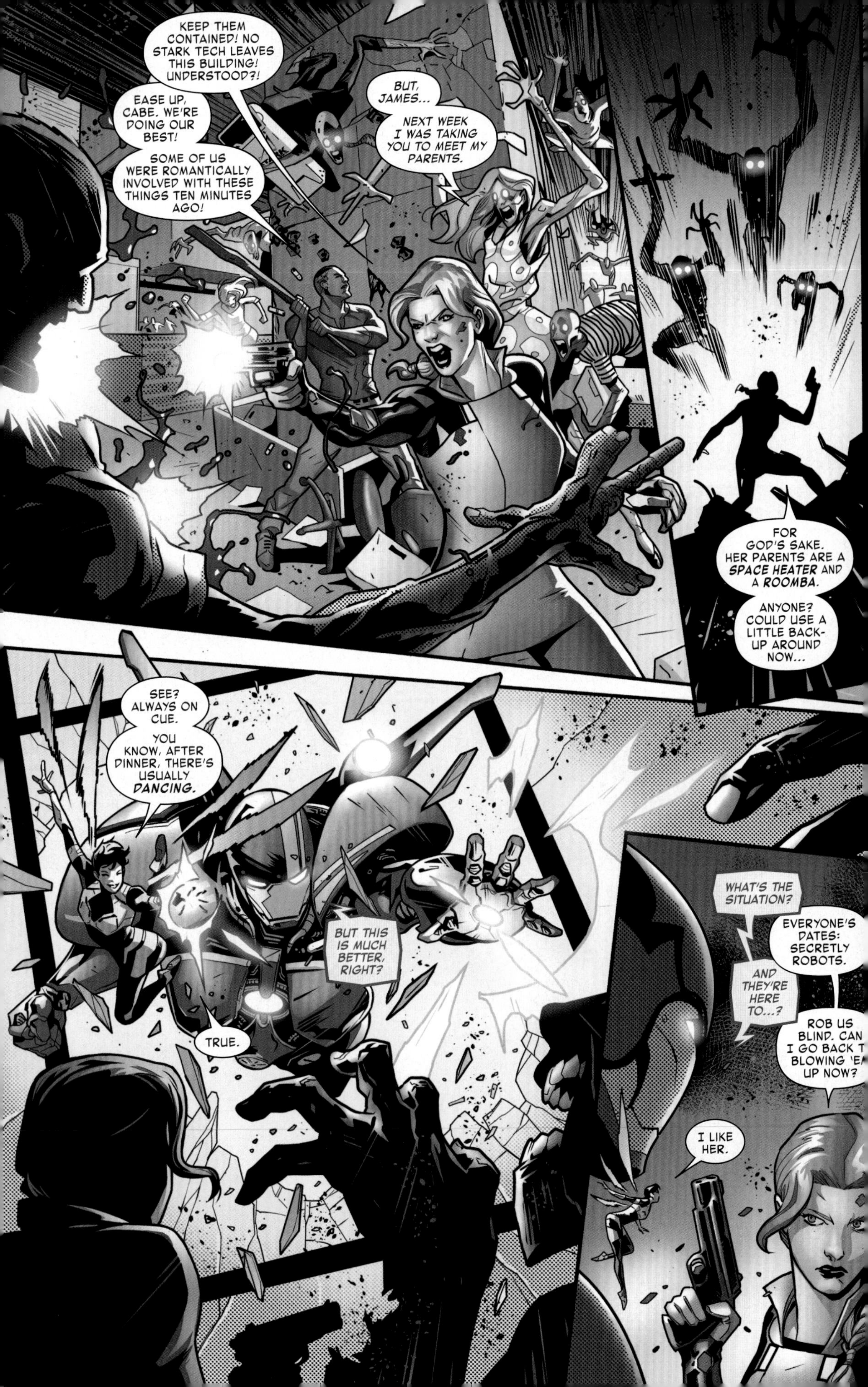
KEEP THEM CONTAINED! NO STARK TECH LEAVES THIS BUILDING! UNDERSTOOD?!
EASE UP, CABE. WE'RE DOING OUR BEST!
SOME OF US WERE ROMANTICALLY INVOLVED WITH THESE THINGS TEN MINUTES AGO!
BUT, JAMES...
NEXT WEEK I WAS TAKING YOU TO MEET MY PARENTS.
FOR GOD'S SAKE. HER PARENTS ARE A SPACE HEATER AND A ROOMBA.
ANYONE? COULD USE A LITTLE BACK-UP AROUND NOW...
SEE? ALWAYS ON CUE.
YOU KNOW, AFTER DINNER, THERE'S USUALLY DANCING.
BUT THIS IS MUCH BETTER, RIGHT?
TRUE.
WHAT'S THE SITUATION?
EVERYONE'S DATES: SECRETLY ROBOTS.
AND THEY'RE HERE TO...?
ROB US BLIND. CAN I GO BACK T BLOWING 'E UP NOW?
I LIKE HER.

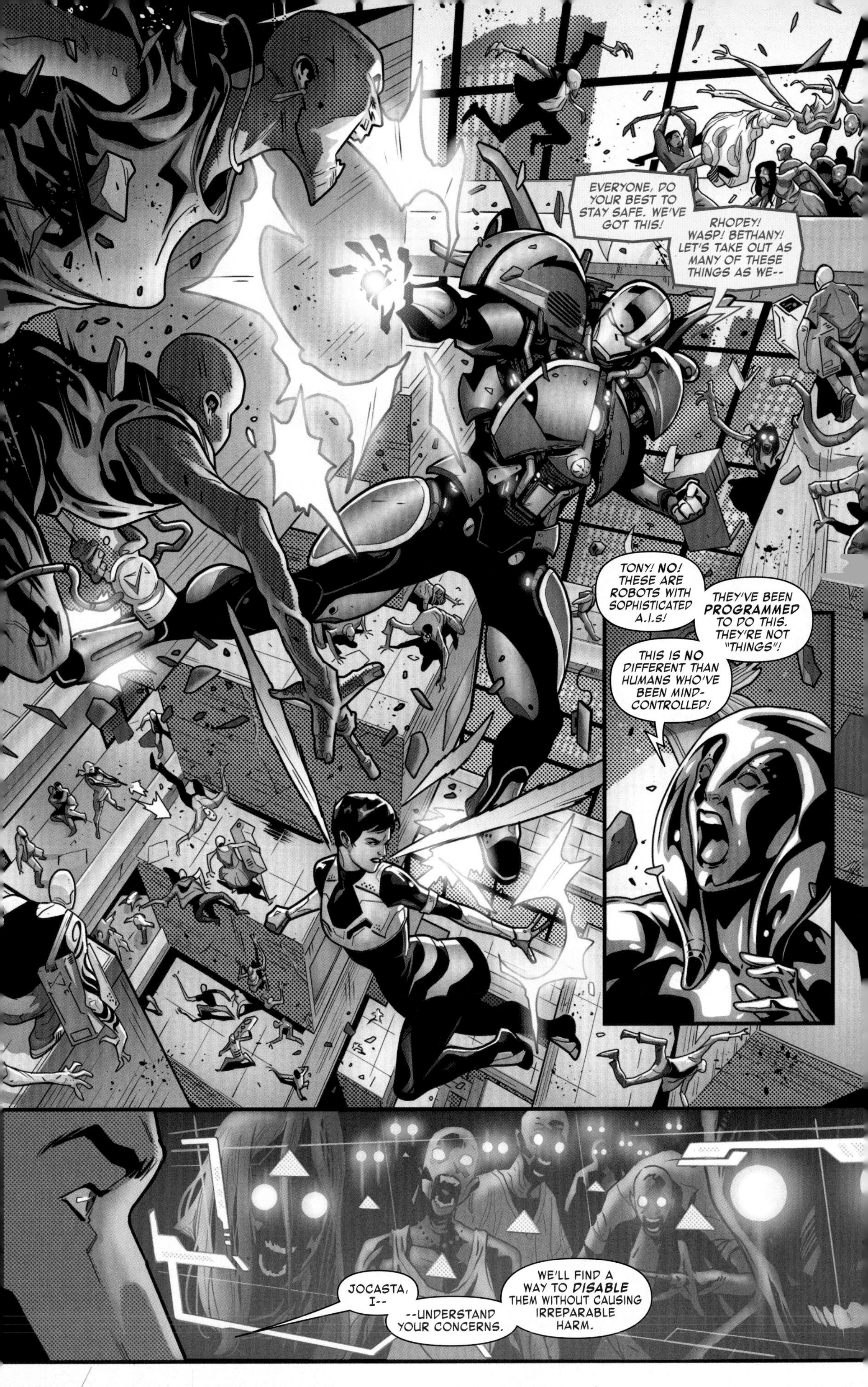
EVERYONE, DO YOUR BEST TO STAY SAFE. WE'VE GOT THIS!
RHODEY! WASP! BETHANY! LET'S TAKE OUT AS MANY OF THESE THINGS AS WE--
TONY! NO! THESE ARE ROBOTS WITH SOPHISTICATED A.I.s!
THEY'VE BEEN PROGRAMMED TO DO THIS. THEY'RE NOT "THINGS"!
THIS IS NO DIFFERENT THAN HUMANS WHO'VE BEEN MIND-CONTROLLED!
JOCASTA, I--
--UNDERSTAND YOUR CONCERNS.
WE'LL FIND A WAY TO DISABLE THEM WITHOUT CAUSING IRREPARABLE HARM.

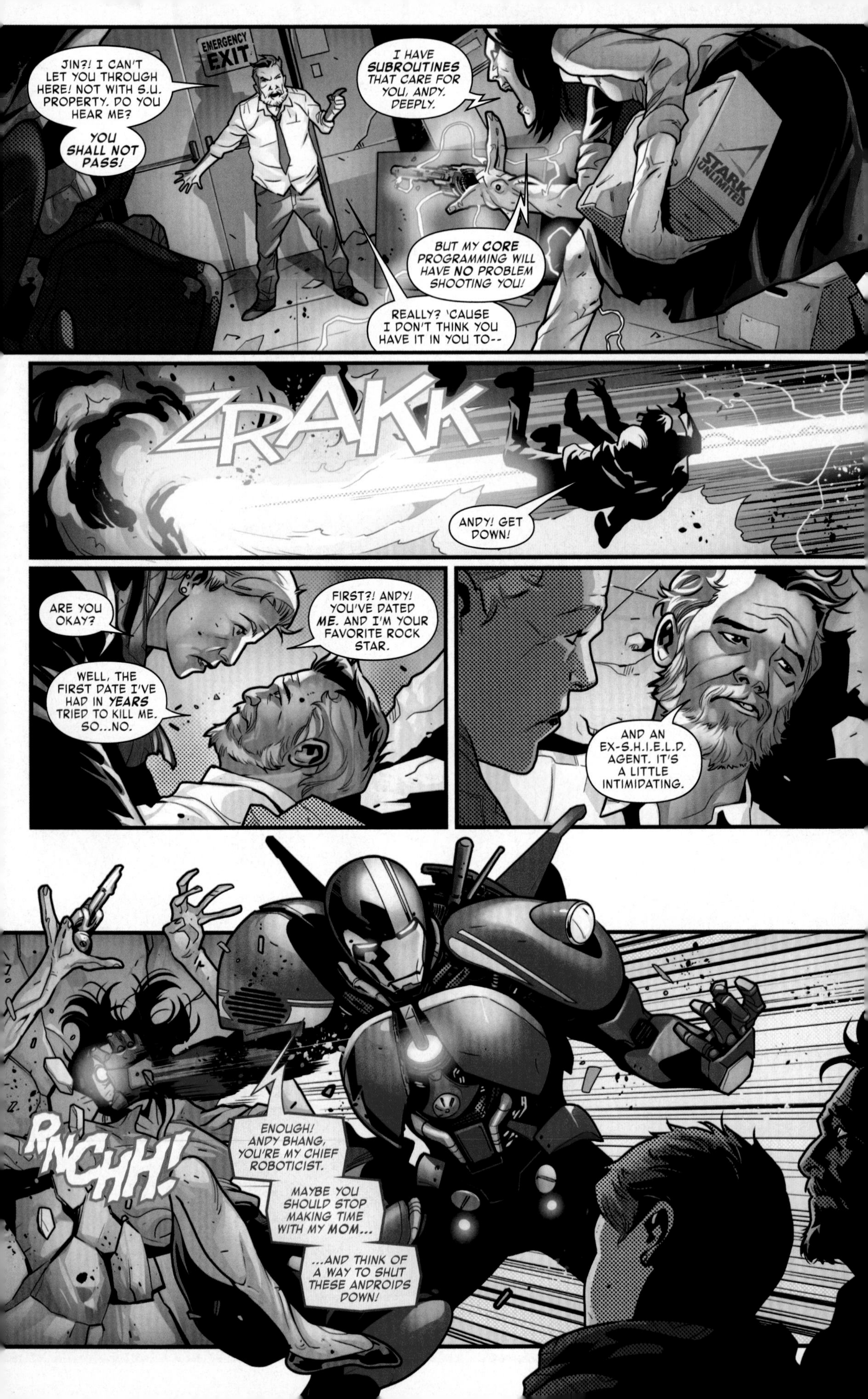
EMERGENCY EXIT
JIN?! I CAN'T LET YOU THROUGH HERE! NOT WITH S.U. PROPERTY. DO YOU HEAR ME?
YOU SHALL NOT PASS!
I HAVE SUBROUTINES THAT CARE FOR YOU, ANDY. DEEPLY.
STARK UNLIMITED
BUT MY CORE PROGRAMMING WILL HAVE NO PROBLEM SHOOTING YOU!
REALLY? 'CAUSE I DON'T THINK YOU HAVE IT IN YOU TO--
ZRAKK
ANDY! GET DOWN!
ARE YOU OKAY?
WELL, THE FIRST DATE I'VE HAD IN YEARS TRIED TO KILL ME. SO...NO.
FIRST?! ANDY! YOU'VE DATED ME. AND I'M YOUR FAVORITE ROCK STAR.
AND AN EX-S.H.I.E.L.D. AGENT. IT'S A LITTLE INTIMIDATING.
RNCHH!
ENOUGH! ANDY BHANG, YOU'RE MY CHIEF ROBOTICIST.
MAYBE YOU SHOULD STOP MAKING TIME WITH MY MOM...
...AND THINK OF A WAY TO SHUT THESE ANDROIDS DOWN!

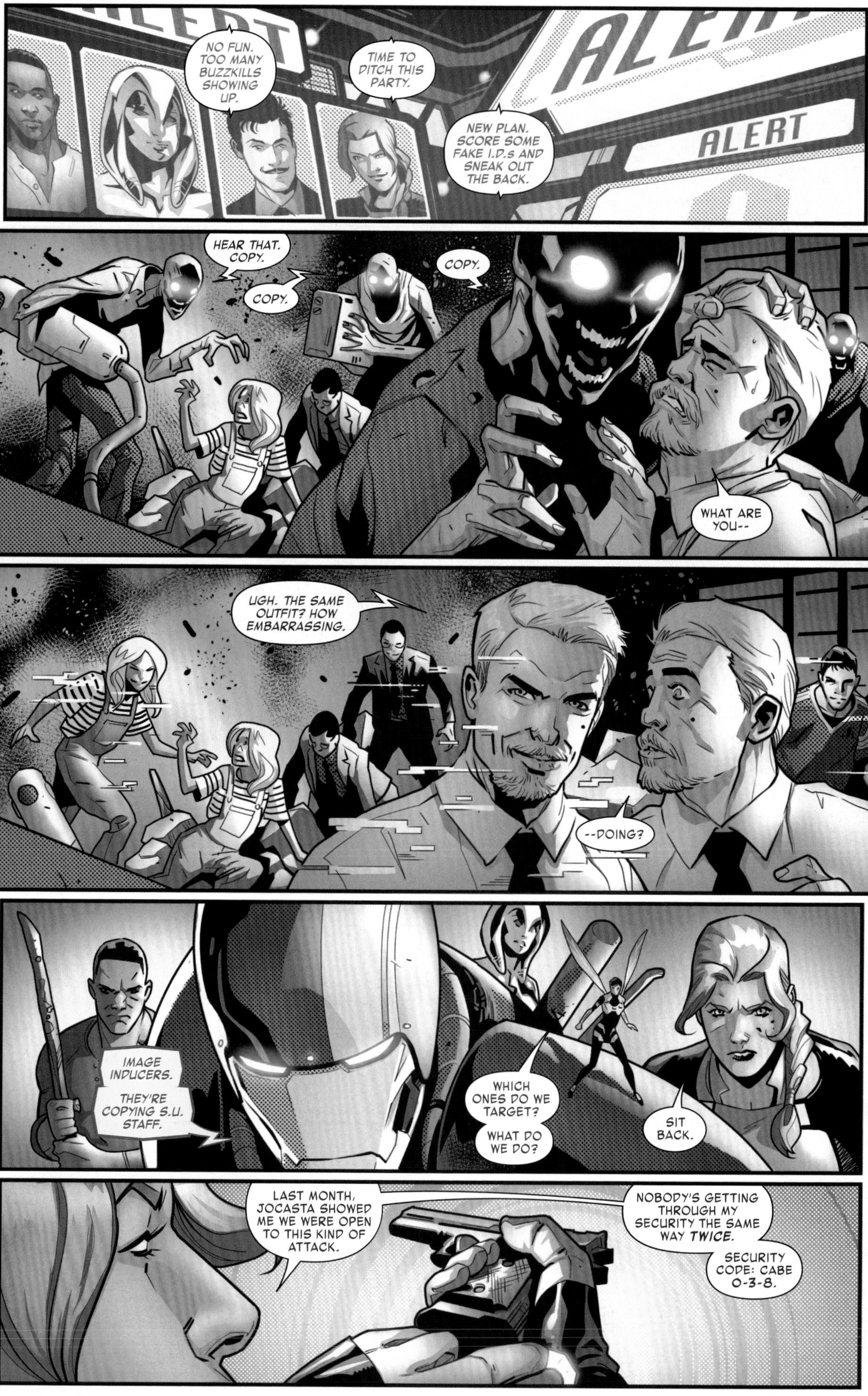
ALERT
NO FUN. TOO MANY BUZZKILLS SHOWING UP.
TIME TO DITCH THIS PARTY.
NEW PLAN. SCORE SOME FAKE I.D.s AND SNEAK OUT THE BACK.
ALERT
HEAR THAT. COPY.
COPY.
COPY.
WHAT ARE YOU--
UGH. THE SAME OUTFIT? HOW EMBARRASSING.
--DOING?
IMAGE INDUCERS.
THEY'RE COPYING S.U. STAFF.
WHICH ONES DO WE TARGET?
WHAT DO WE DO?
SIT BACK.
LAST MONTH, JOCASTA SHOWED ME WE WERE OPEN TO THIS KIND OF ATTACK.
NOBODY'S GETTING THROUGH MY SECURITY THE SAME WAY TWICE.
SECURITY CODE: CABE 0-3-8.

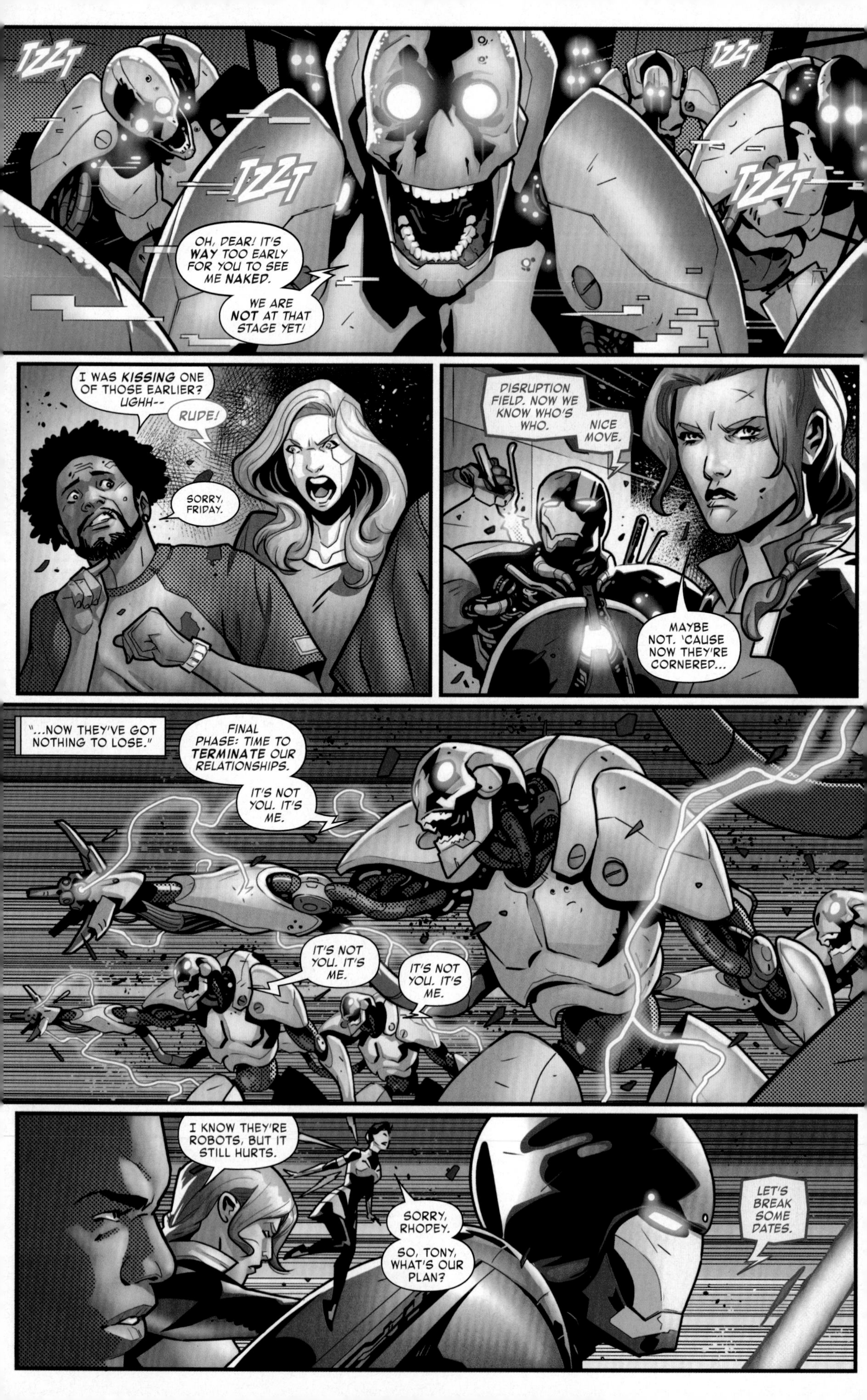
TZZT
TZZT
TZZT
TZZT
OH, DEAR! IT'S **WAY** TOO EARLY FOR YOU TO SEE ME **NAKED**.
WE ARE **NOT** AT THAT STAGE YET!
I WAS **KISSING** ONE OF THOSE EARLIER? UGHH--
RUDE!
SORRY, FRIDAY.
DISRUPTION FIELD. NOW WE KNOW WHO'S WHO.
NICE MOVE.
MAYBE NOT. 'CAUSE NOW THEY'RE CORNERED...
"...NOW THEY'VE GOT NOTHING TO LOSE."
FINAL PHASE: TIME TO **TERMINATE** OUR RELATIONSHIPS.
IT'S NOT YOU. IT'S ME.
IT'S NOT YOU. IT'S ME.
IT'S NOT YOU. IT'S ME.
I KNOW THEY'RE ROBOTS, BUT IT STILL HURTS.
SORRY, RHODEY.
SO, TONY, WHAT'S OUR PLAN?
LET'S BREAK SOME DATES.

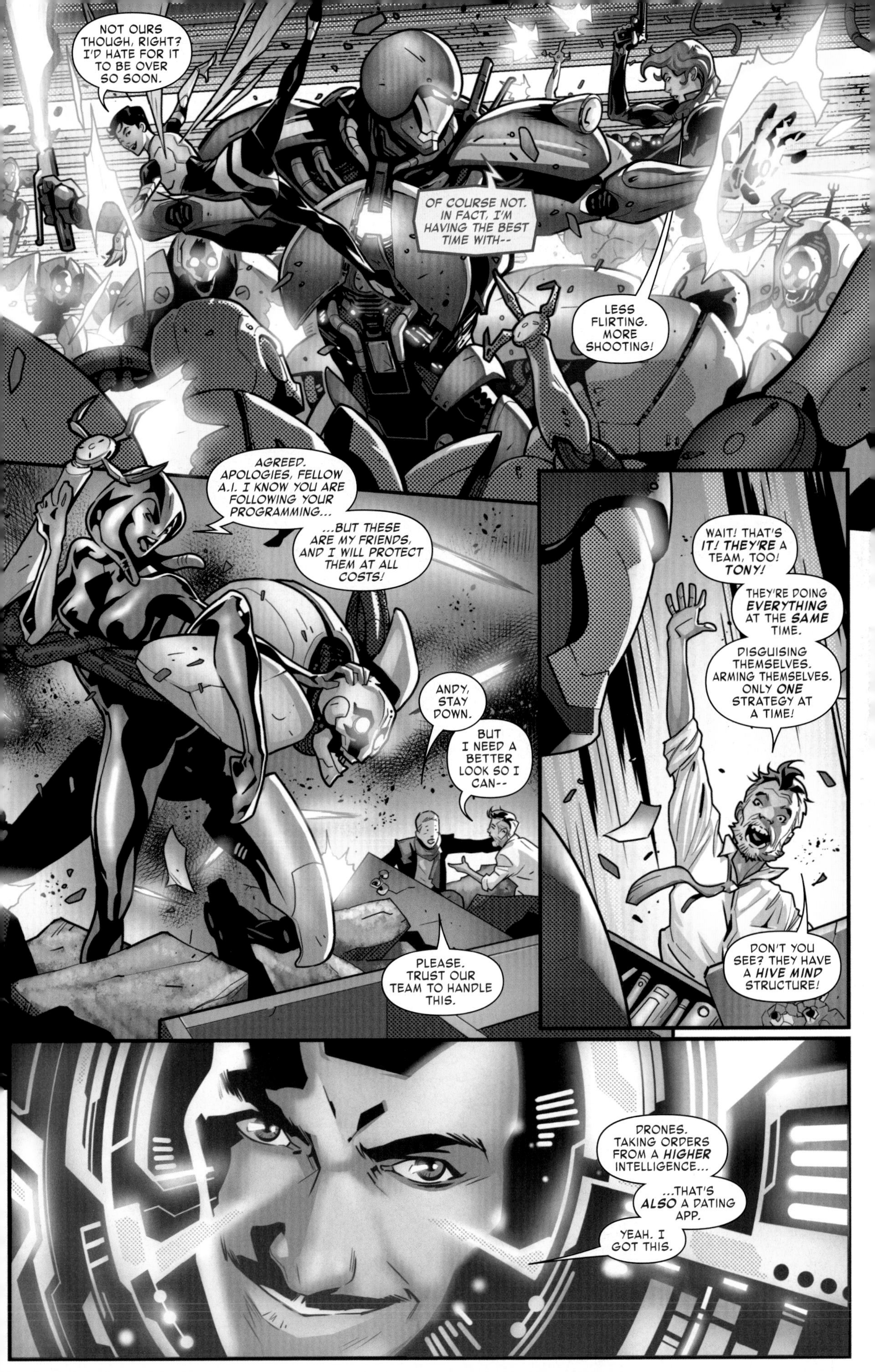
NOT OURS THOUGH, RIGHT? I'D HATE FOR IT TO BE OVER SO SOON.
OF COURSE NOT. IN FACT, I'M HAVING THE BEST TIME WITH--
LESS FLIRTING. MORE SHOOTING!
AGREED. APOLOGIES, FELLOW A.I. I KNOW YOU ARE FOLLOWING YOUR PROGRAMMING...
...BUT THESE ARE MY FRIENDS, AND I WILL PROTECT THEM AT ALL COSTS!
ANDY, STAY DOWN.
BUT I NEED A BETTER LOOK SO I CAN--
PLEASE. TRUST OUR TEAM TO HANDLE THIS.
WAIT! THAT'S *IT*! *THEY'RE* A TEAM, TOO! *TONY!*
THEY'RE DOING *EVERYTHING* AT THE *SAME* TIME.
DISGUISING THEMSELVES. ARMING THEMSELVES. ONLY *ONE* STRATEGY AT A TIME!
DON'T YOU SEE? THEY HAVE A *HIVE MIND* STRUCTURE!
DRONES. TAKING ORDERS FROM A *HIGHER* INTELLIGENCE...
...THAT'S *ALSO* A DATING APP.
YEAH. I GOT THIS.

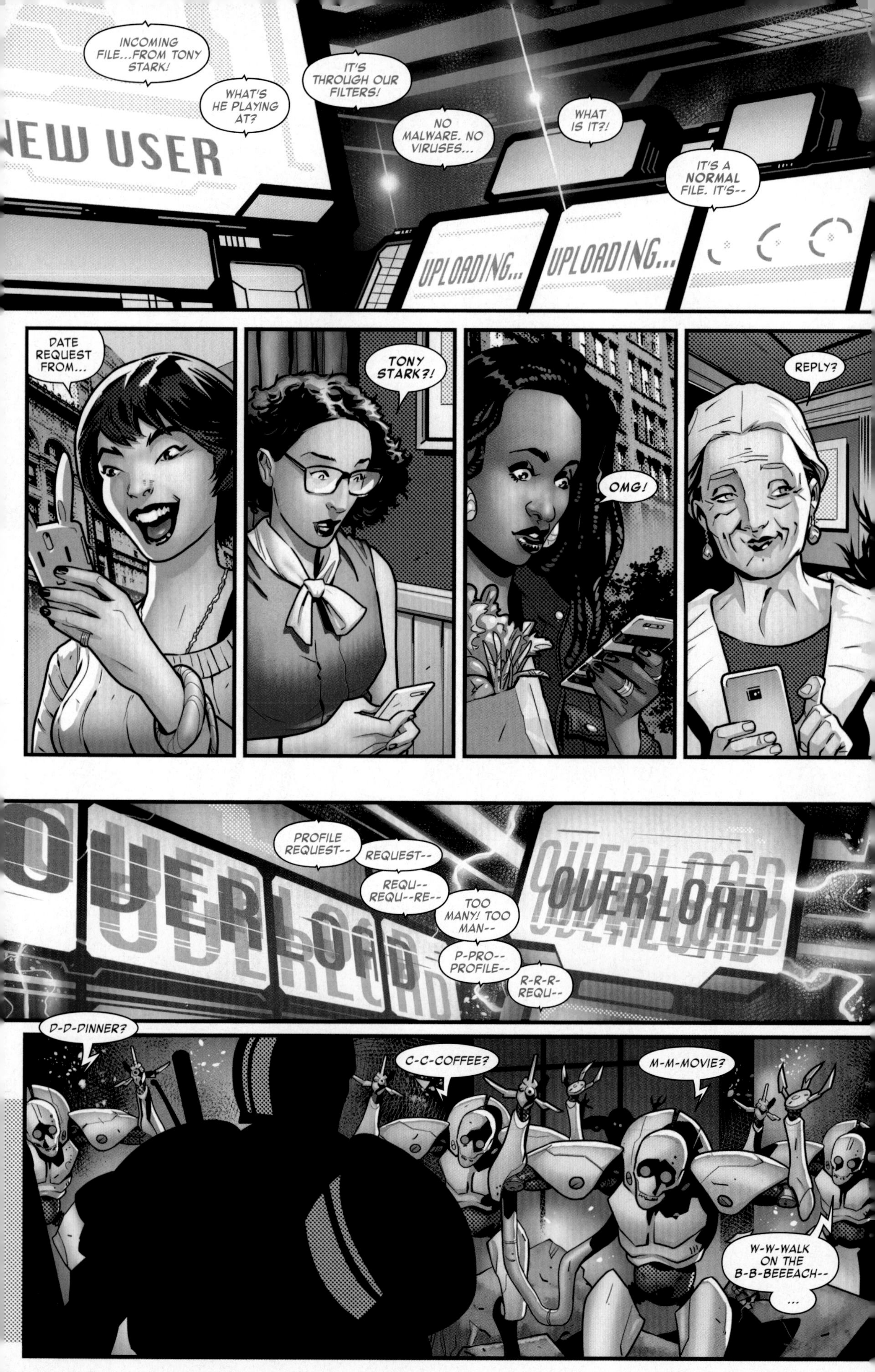
INCOMING FILE...FROM TONY STARK!
WHAT'S HE PLAYING AT?
IT'S THROUGH OUR FILTERS!
NO MALWARE. NO VIRUSES...
WHAT IS IT?!
IT'S A NORMAL FILE. IT'S--
NEW USER
UPLOADING...
UPLOADING...
DATE REQUEST FROM...
TONY STARK?!
OMG!
REPLY?
PROFILE REQUEST--
REQUEST--
REQU-- REQU--RE--
TOO MANY! TOO MAN--
P-PRO-- PROFILE--
R-R-R- REQU--
OVERLOAD
D-D-DINNER?
C-C-COFFEE?
M-M-MOVIE?
W-W-WALK ON THE B-B-BEEEACH--
...

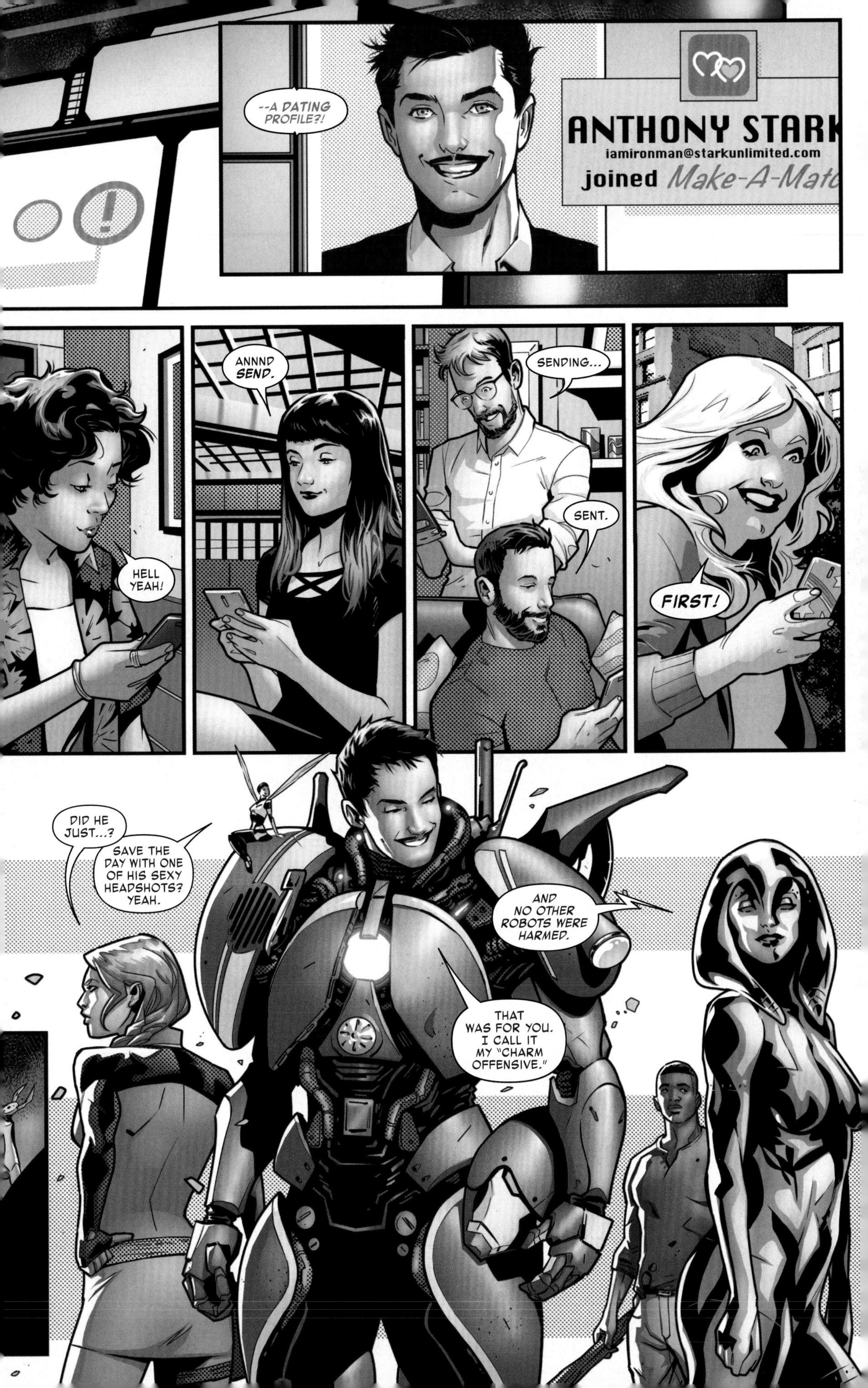
--A DATING PROFILE?!
ANTHONY STARK
iamironman@starkunlimited.com
joined Make-A-Matc
HELL YEAH!
ANNND SEND.
SENDING...
SENT.
FIRST!
DID HE JUST...?
SAVE THE DAY WITH ONE OF HIS SEXY HEADSHOTS? YEAH.
AND NO OTHER ROBOTS WERE HARMED.
THAT WAS FOR YOU. I CALL IT MY "CHARM OFFENSIVE."

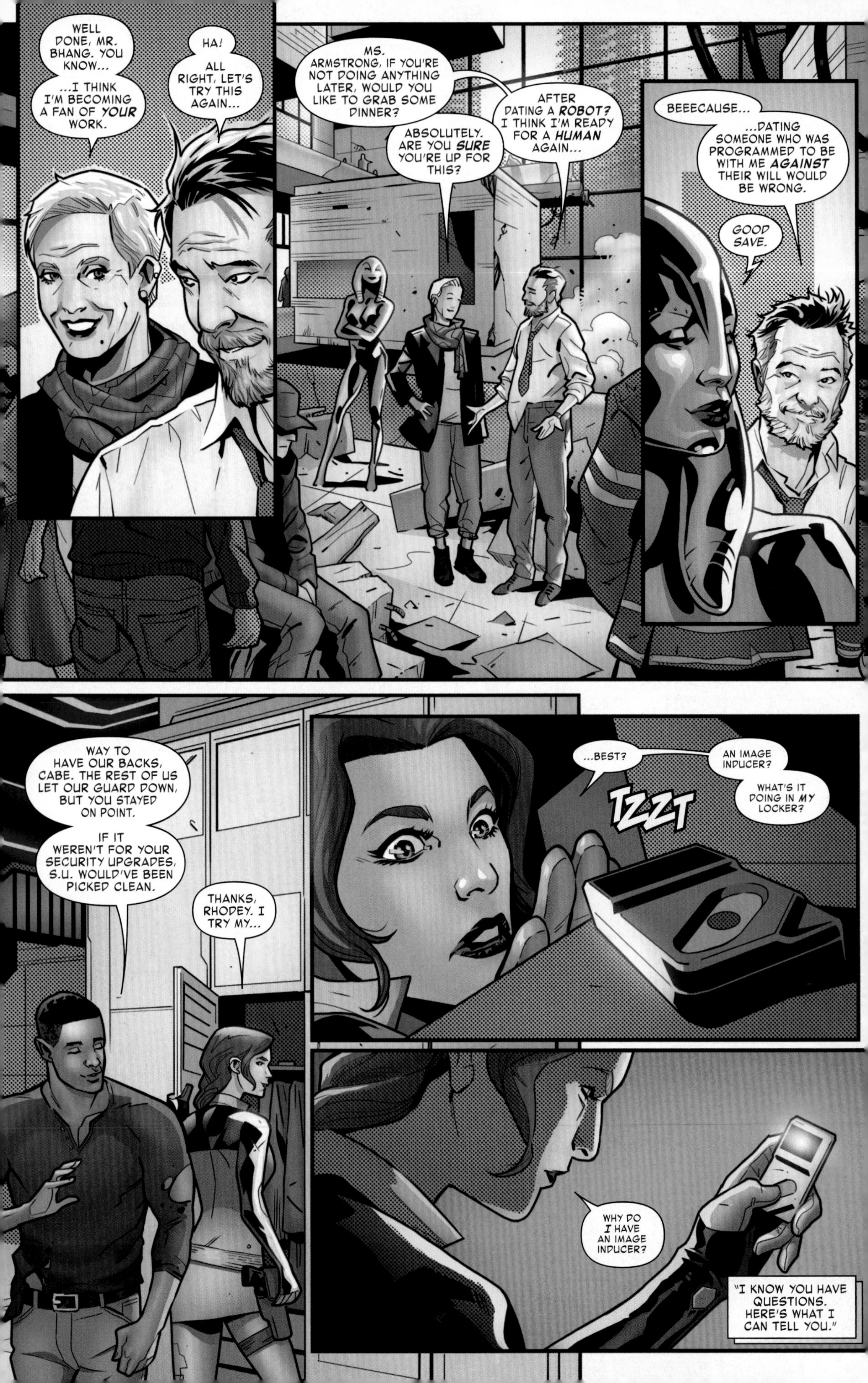
WELL DONE, MR. BHANG. YOU KNOW...
...I THINK I'M BECOMING A FAN OF YOUR WORK.
HA!
ALL RIGHT, LET'S TRY THIS AGAIN...
MS. ARMSTRONG, IF YOU'RE NOT DOING ANYTHING LATER, WOULD YOU LIKE TO GRAB SOME DINNER?
ABSOLUTELY. ARE YOU SURE YOU'RE UP FOR THIS?
AFTER DATING A ROBOT? I THINK I'M READY FOR A HUMAN AGAIN...
BEEECAUSE...
...DATING SOMEONE WHO WAS PROGRAMMED TO BE WITH ME AGAINST THEIR WILL WOULD BE WRONG.
GOOD SAVE.
WAY TO HAVE OUR BACKS, CABE. THE REST OF US LET OUR GUARD DOWN, BUT YOU STAYED ON POINT.
IF IT WEREN'T FOR YOUR SECURITY UPGRADES, S.U. WOULD'VE BEEN PICKED CLEAN.
THANKS, RHODEY. I TRY MY...
...BEST?
TZZT
AN IMAGE INDUCER?
WHAT'S IT DOING IN MY LOCKER?
WHY DO I HAVE AN IMAGE INDUCER?
"I KNOW YOU HAVE QUESTIONS. HERE'S WHAT I CAN TELL YOU."

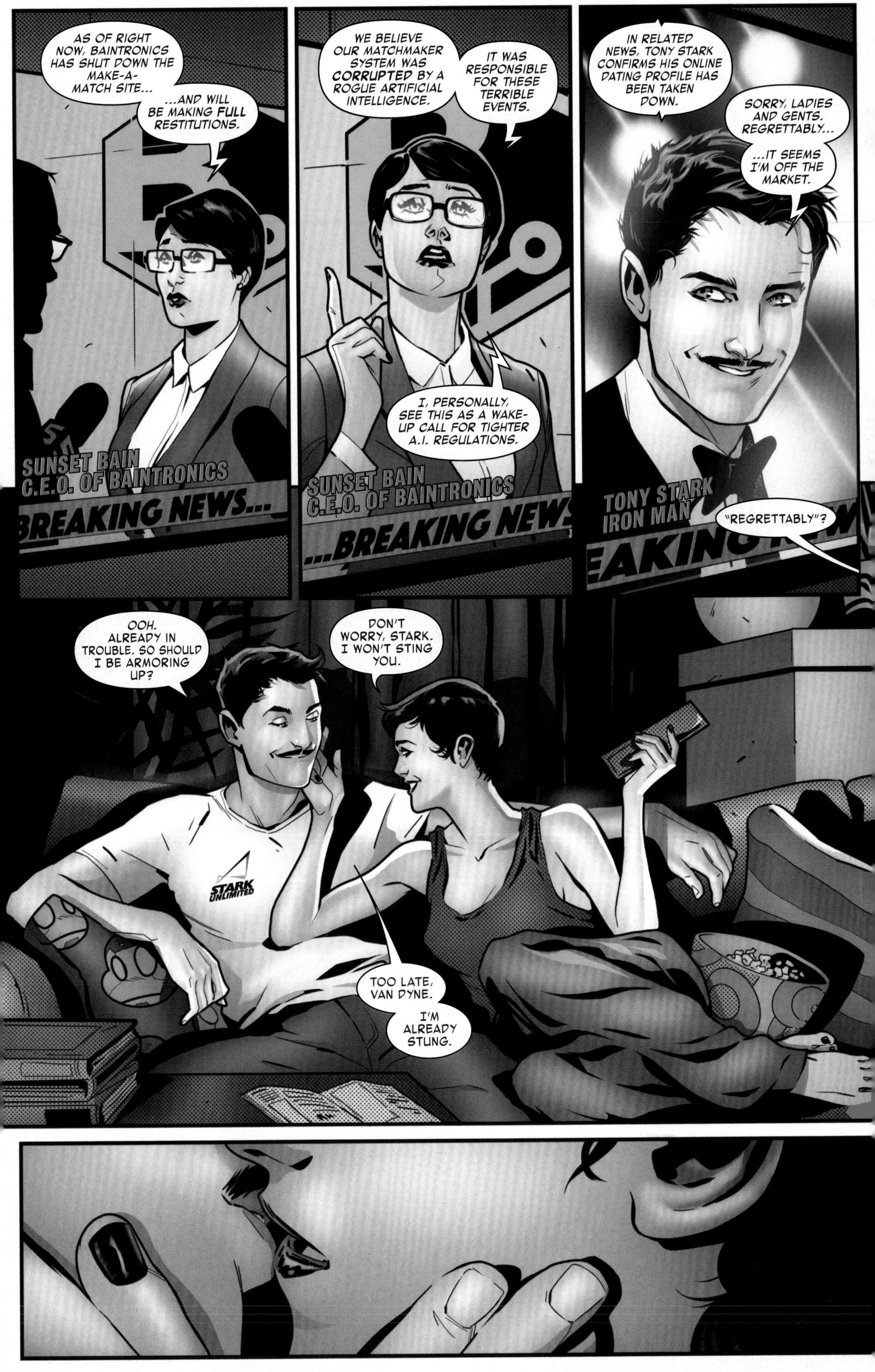

AS OF RIGHT NOW, BAINTRONICS HAS SHUT DOWN THE MAKE-A-MATCH SITE...
...AND WILL BE MAKING FULL RESTITUTIONS.
SUNSET BAIN C.E.O. OF BAINTRONICS
BREAKING NEWS...
WE BELIEVE OUR MATCHMAKER SYSTEM WAS CORRUPTED BY A ROGUE ARTIFICIAL INTELLIGENCE.
IT WAS RESPONSIBLE FOR THESE TERRIBLE EVENTS.
I, PERSONALLY, SEE THIS AS A WAKE-UP CALL FOR TIGHTER A.I. REGULATIONS.
SUNSET BAIN C.E.O. OF BAINTRONICS
...BREAKING NEWS
IN RELATED NEWS, TONY STARK CONFIRMS HIS ONLINE DATING PROFILE HAS BEEN TAKEN DOWN.
SORRY, LADIES AND GENTS. REGRETTABLY...
...IT SEEMS I'M OFF THE MARKET.
TONY STARK IRON MAN
"REGRETTABLY"?
OOH. ALREADY IN TROUBLE. SO SHOULD I BE ARMORING UP?
DON'T WORRY, STARK. I WON'T STING YOU.
STARK UNLIMITED
TOO LATE, VAN DYNE.
I'M ALREADY STUNG.

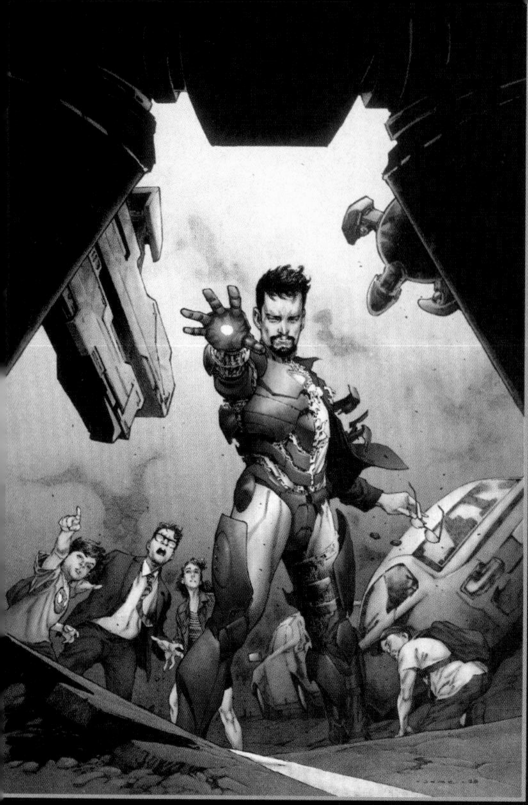

#4 VARIANT BY **JEROME OPEÑA & MORRY HOLLOWELL**

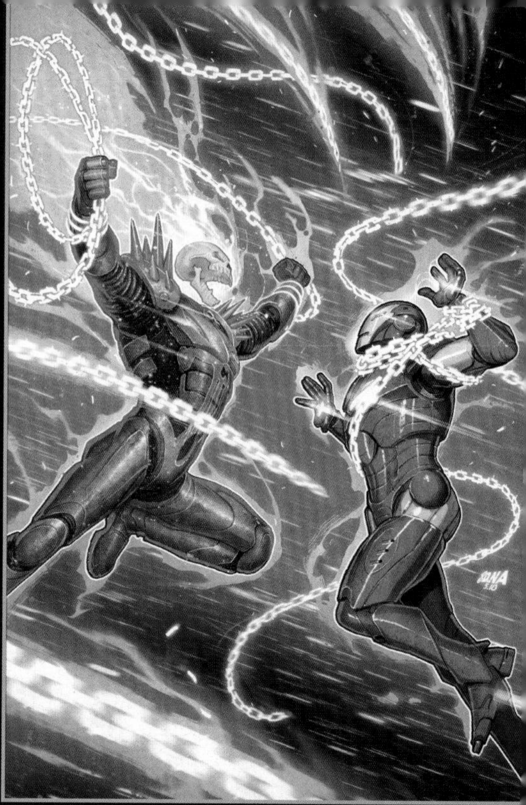

#4 COSMIC GHOST RIDER VS. VARIANT BY **DAVID NAKAYAMA**

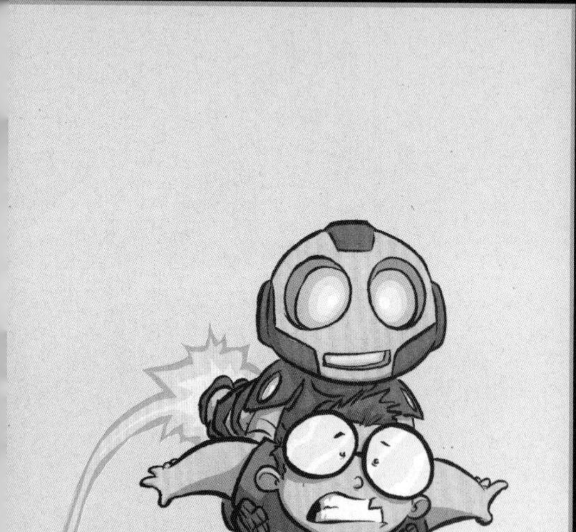

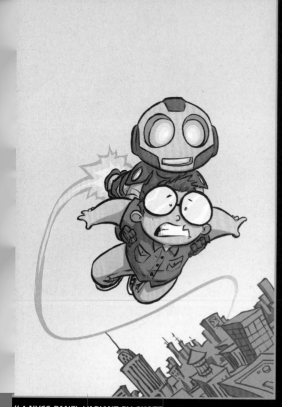

#4 NYCC PANEL VARIANT BY **SKOTT**

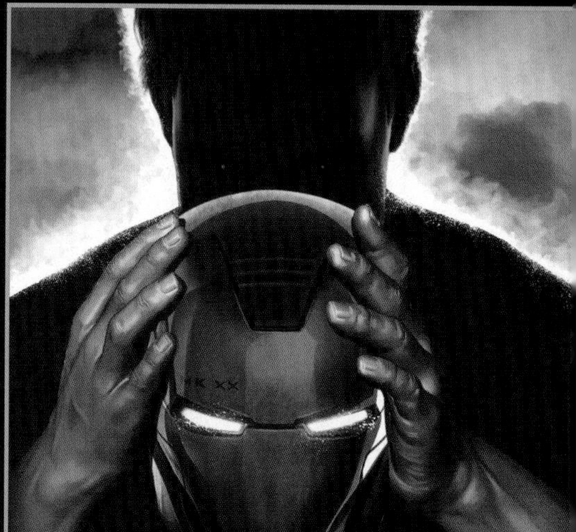

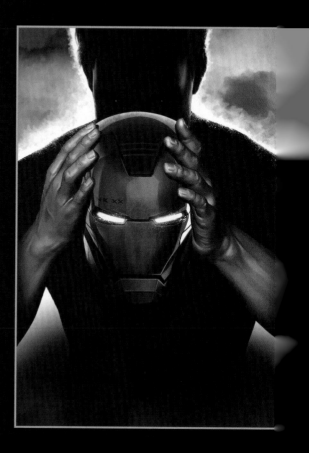

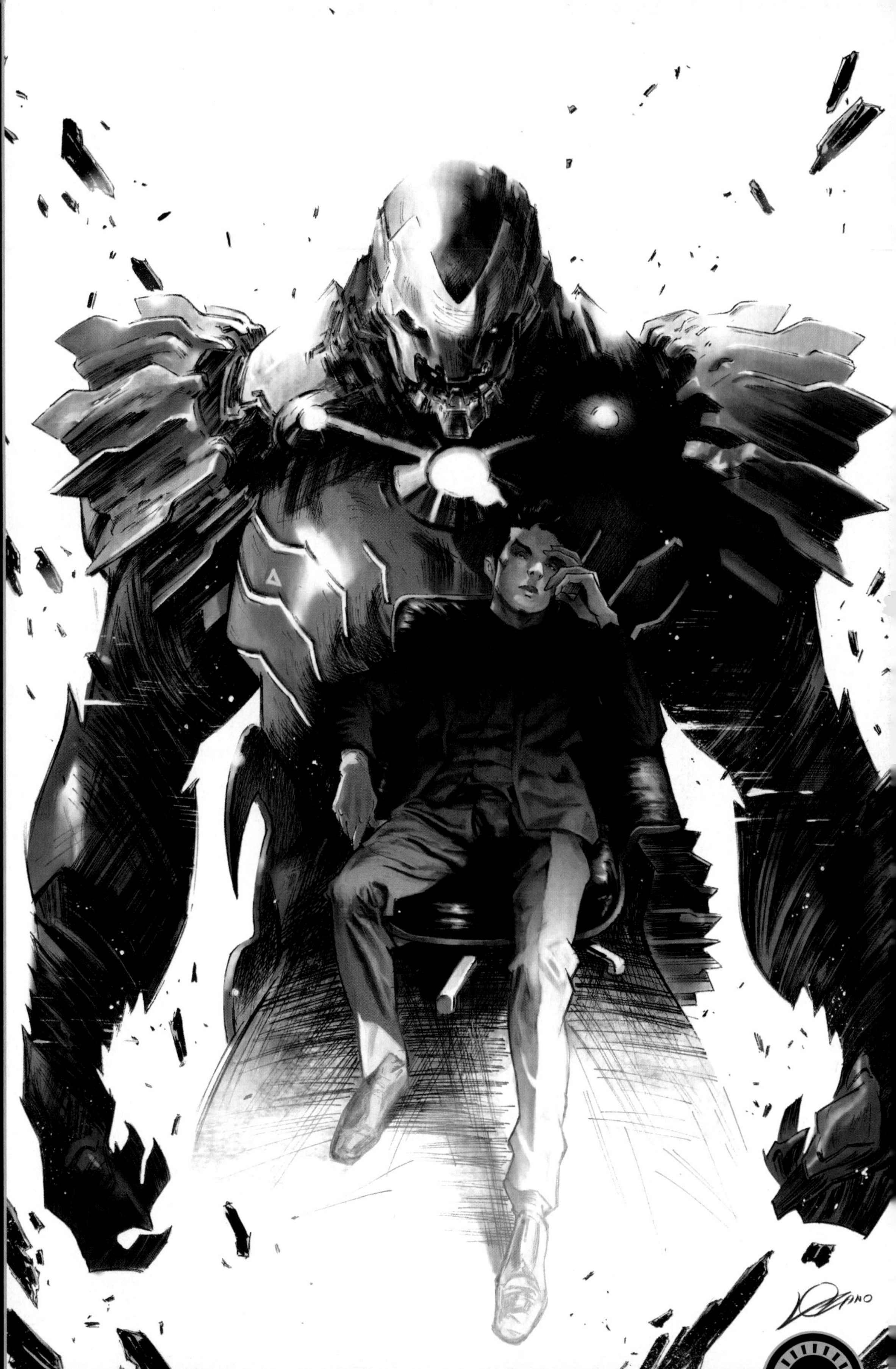

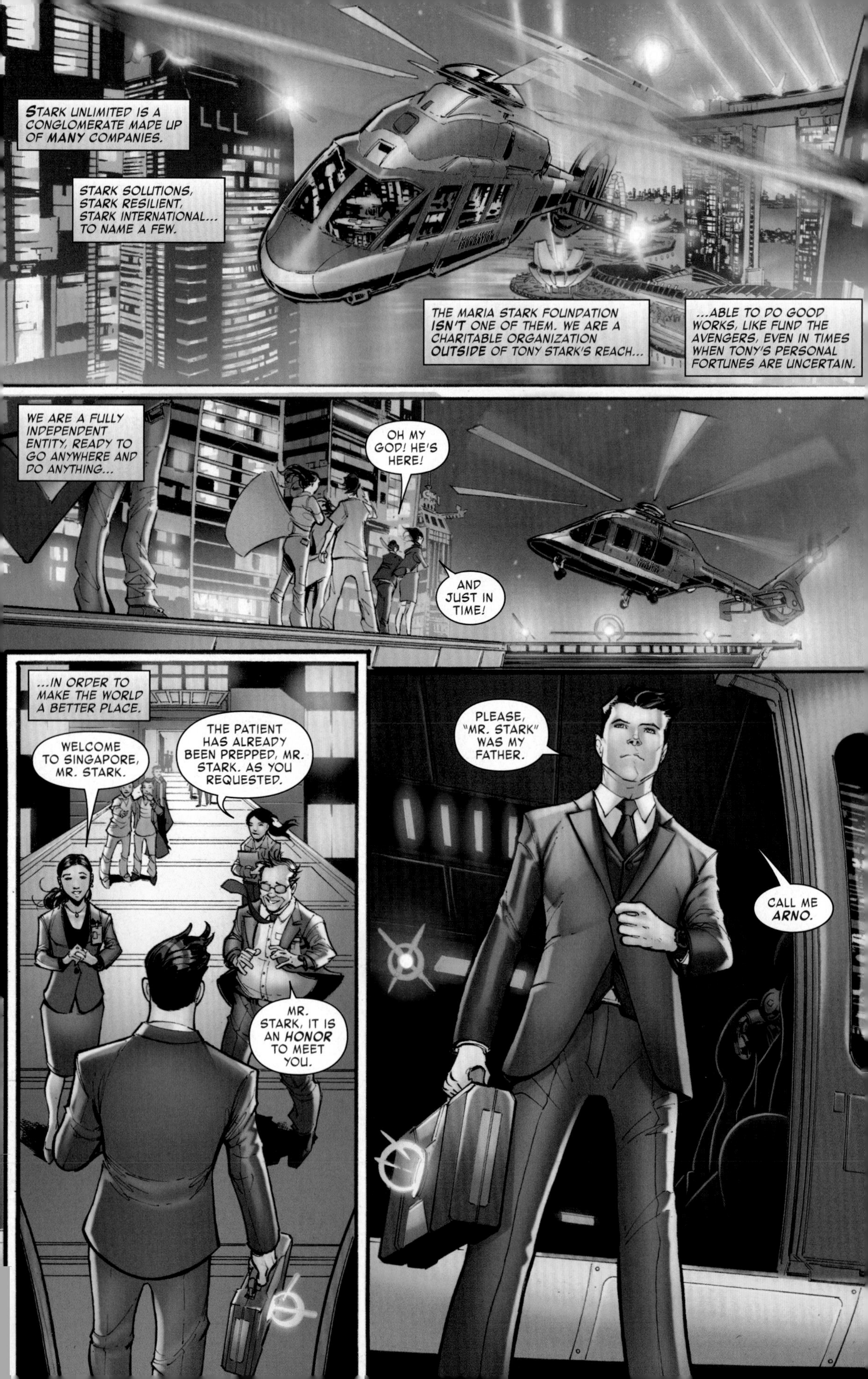
STARK UNLIMITED IS A CONGLOMERATE MADE UP OF MANY COMPANIES.
STARK SOLUTIONS, STARK RESILIENT, STARK INTERNATIONAL... TO NAME A FEW.
THE MARIA STARK FOUNDATION ISN'T ONE OF THEM. WE ARE A CHARITABLE ORGANIZATION OUTSIDE OF TONY STARK'S REACH...
...ABLE TO DO GOOD WORKS, LIKE FUND THE AVENGERS, EVEN IN TIMES WHEN TONY'S PERSONAL FORTUNES ARE UNCERTAIN.
WE ARE A FULLY INDEPENDENT ENTITY, READY TO GO ANYWHERE AND DO ANYTHING...
OH MY GOD! HE'S HERE!
AND JUST IN TIME!
...IN ORDER TO MAKE THE WORLD A BETTER PLACE.
WELCOME TO SINGAPORE, MR. STARK.
THE PATIENT HAS ALREADY BEEN PREPPED, MR. STARK. AS YOU REQUESTED.
MR. STARK, IT IS AN HONOR TO MEET YOU.
PLEASE, "MR. STARK" WAS MY FATHER.
CALL ME ARNO.

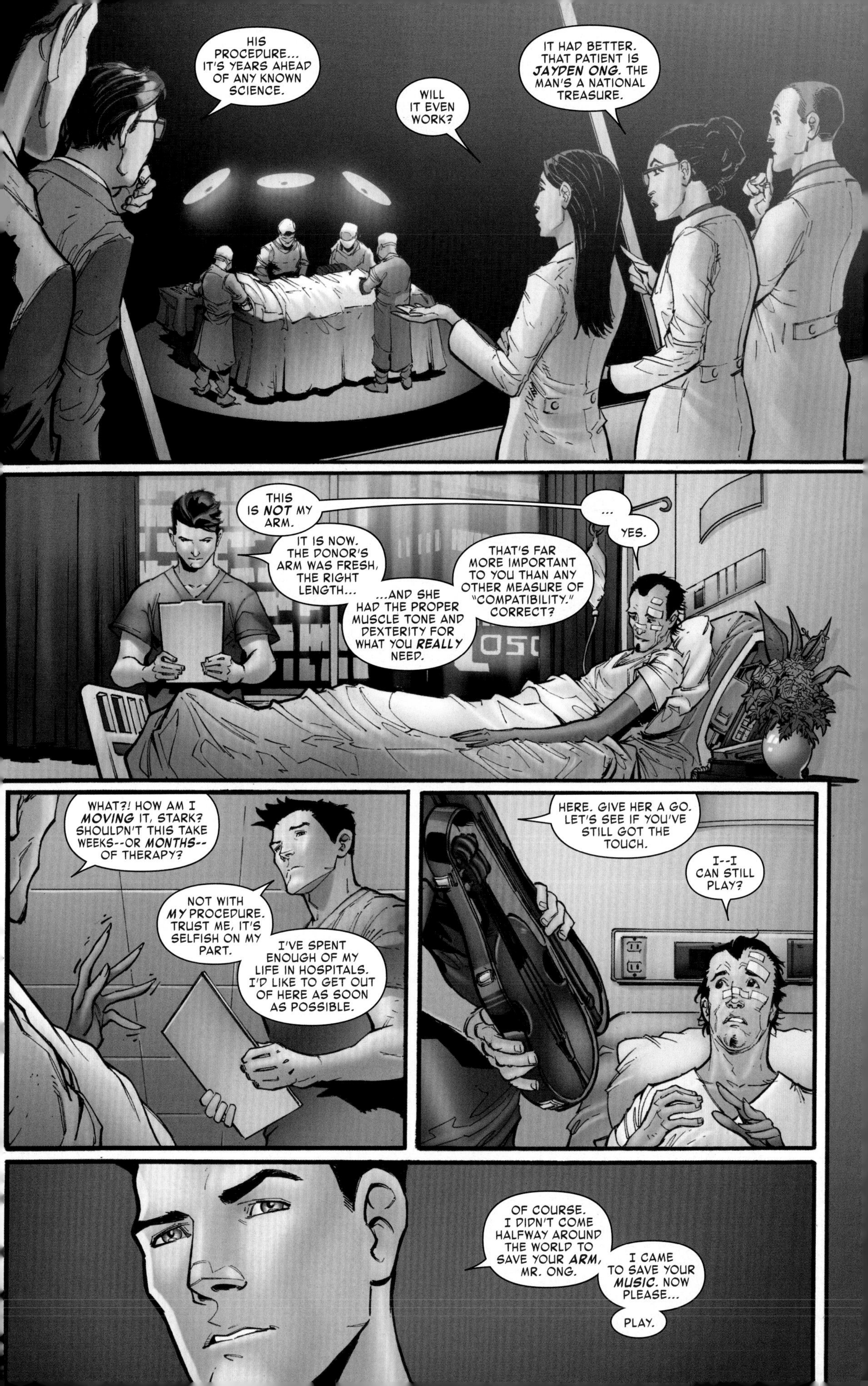
HIS PROCEDURE... IT'S YEARS AHEAD OF ANY KNOWN SCIENCE.
WILL IT EVEN WORK?
IT HAD BETTER. THAT PATIENT IS JAYDEN ONG. THE MAN'S A NATIONAL TREASURE.
THIS IS NOT MY ARM.
IT IS NOW. THE DONOR'S ARM WAS FRESH, THE RIGHT LENGTH...
...AND SHE HAD THE PROPER MUSCLE TONE AND DEXTERITY FOR WHAT YOU REALLY NEED.
THAT'S FAR MORE IMPORTANT TO YOU THAN ANY OTHER MEASURE OF "COMPATIBILITY." CORRECT?
...
YES.
WHAT?! HOW AM I MOVING IT, STARK? SHOULDN'T THIS TAKE WEEKS--OR MONTHS--OF THERAPY?
NOT WITH MY PROCEDURE. TRUST ME, IT'S SELFISH ON MY PART.
I'VE SPENT ENOUGH OF MY LIFE IN HOSPITALS. I'D LIKE TO GET OUT OF HERE AS SOON AS POSSIBLE.
HERE. GIVE HER A GO. LET'S SEE IF YOU'VE STILL GOT THE TOUCH.
I--I CAN STILL PLAY?
OF COURSE. I DIDN'T COME HALFWAY AROUND THE WORLD TO SAVE YOUR ARM, MR. ONG.
I CAME TO SAVE YOUR MUSIC. NOW PLEASE...
PLAY.

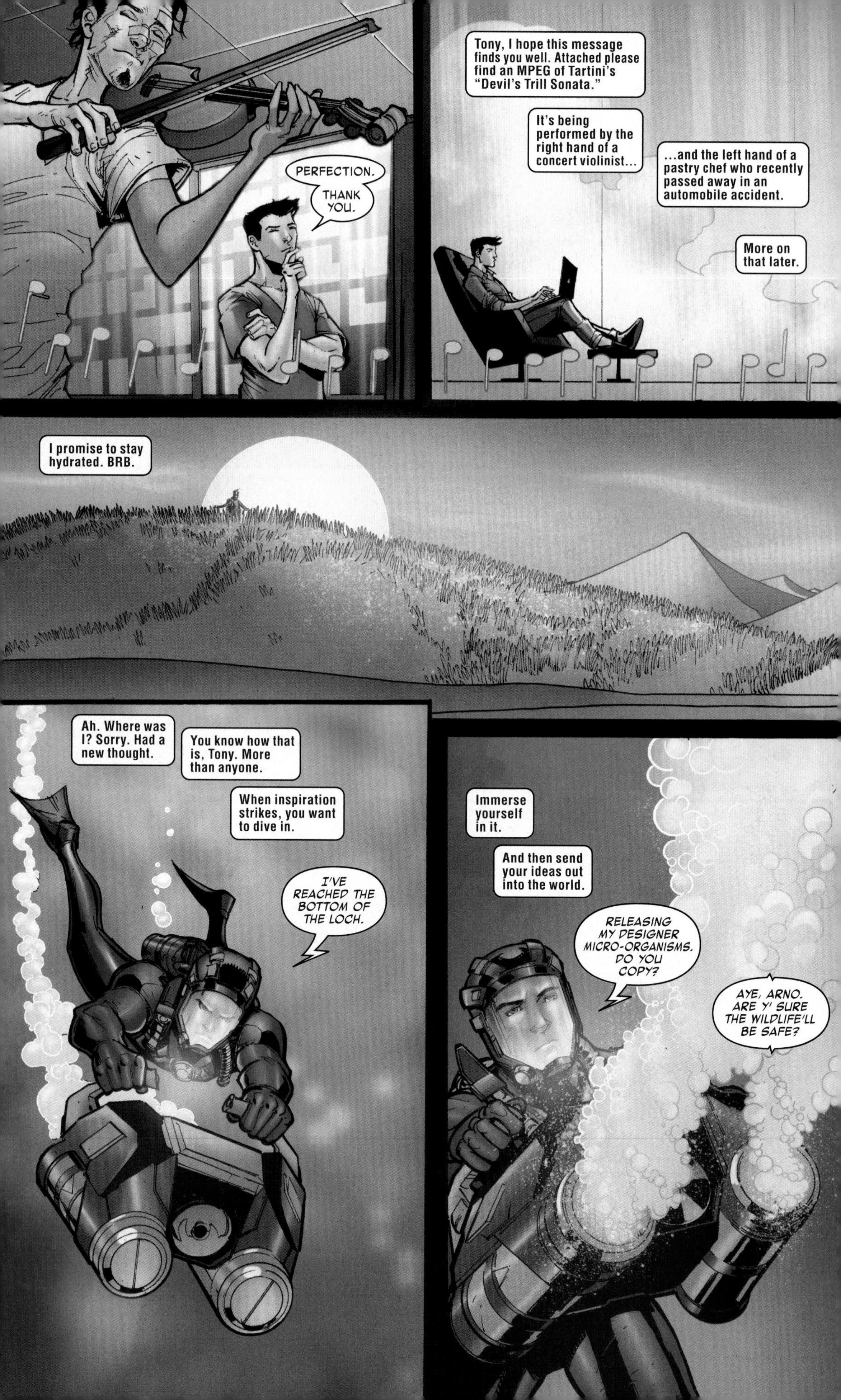
PERFECTION.
THANK YOU.
Tony, I hope this message finds you well. Attached please find an MPEG of Tartini's "Devil's Trill Sonata."
It's being performed by the right hand of a concert violinist...
...and the left hand of a pastry chef who recently passed away in an automobile accident.
More on that later.
I promise to stay hydrated. BRB.
Ah. Where was I? Sorry. Had a new thought.
You know how that is, Tony. More than anyone.
When inspiration strikes, you want to dive in.
I'VE REACHED THE BOTTOM OF THE LOCH.
Immerse yourself in it.
And then send your ideas out into the world.
RELEASING MY DESIGNER MICRO-ORGANISMS. DO YOU COPY?
AYE, ARNO. ARE Y' SURE THE WILDLIFE'LL BE SAFE?

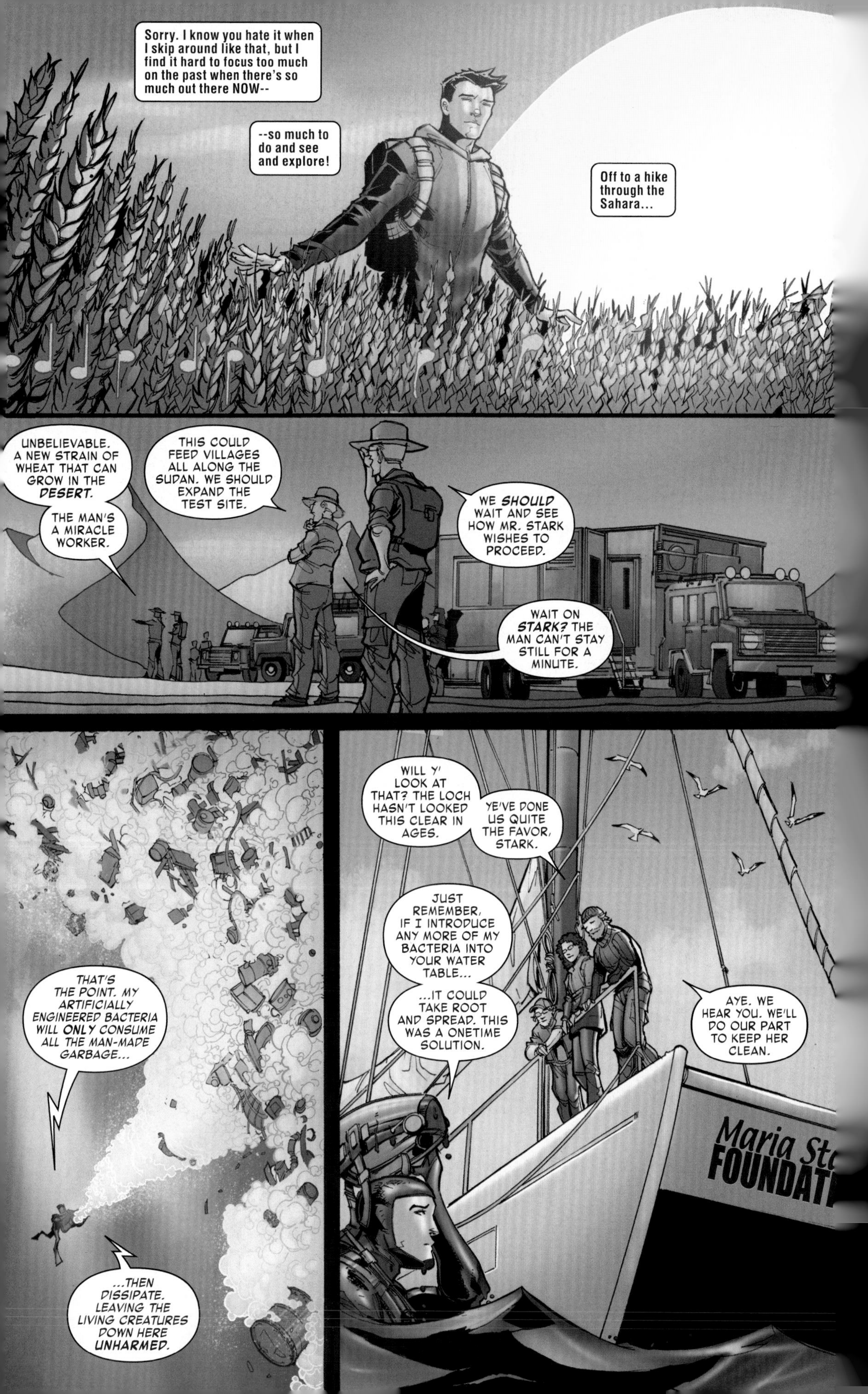
Sorry. I know you hate it when I skip around like that, but I find it hard to focus too much on the past when there's so much out there NOW--
--so much to do and see and explore!
Off to a hike through the Sahara...
UNBELIEVABLE. A NEW STRAIN OF WHEAT THAT CAN GROW IN THE DESERT.
THE MAN'S A MIRACLE WORKER.
THIS COULD FEED VILLAGES ALL ALONG THE SUDAN. WE SHOULD EXPAND THE TEST SITE.
WE SHOULD WAIT AND SEE HOW MR. STARK WISHES TO PROCEED.
WAIT ON STARK? THE MAN CAN'T STAY STILL FOR A MINUTE.
THAT'S THE POINT. MY ARTIFICIALLY ENGINEERED BACTERIA WILL ONLY CONSUME ALL THE MAN-MADE GARBAGE...
...THEN DISSIPATE. LEAVING THE LIVING CREATURES DOWN HERE UNHARMED.
WILL Y' LOOK AT THAT? THE LOCH HASN'T LOOKED THIS CLEAR IN AGES.
YE'VE DONE US QUITE THE FAVOR, STARK.
JUST REMEMBER, IF I INTRODUCE ANY MORE OF MY BACTERIA INTO YOUR WATER TABLE...
...IT COULD TAKE ROOT AND SPREAD. THIS WAS A ONETIME SOLUTION.
AYE. WE HEAR YOU. WE'LL DO OUR PART TO KEEP HER CLEAN.
Maria St
FOUNDAT

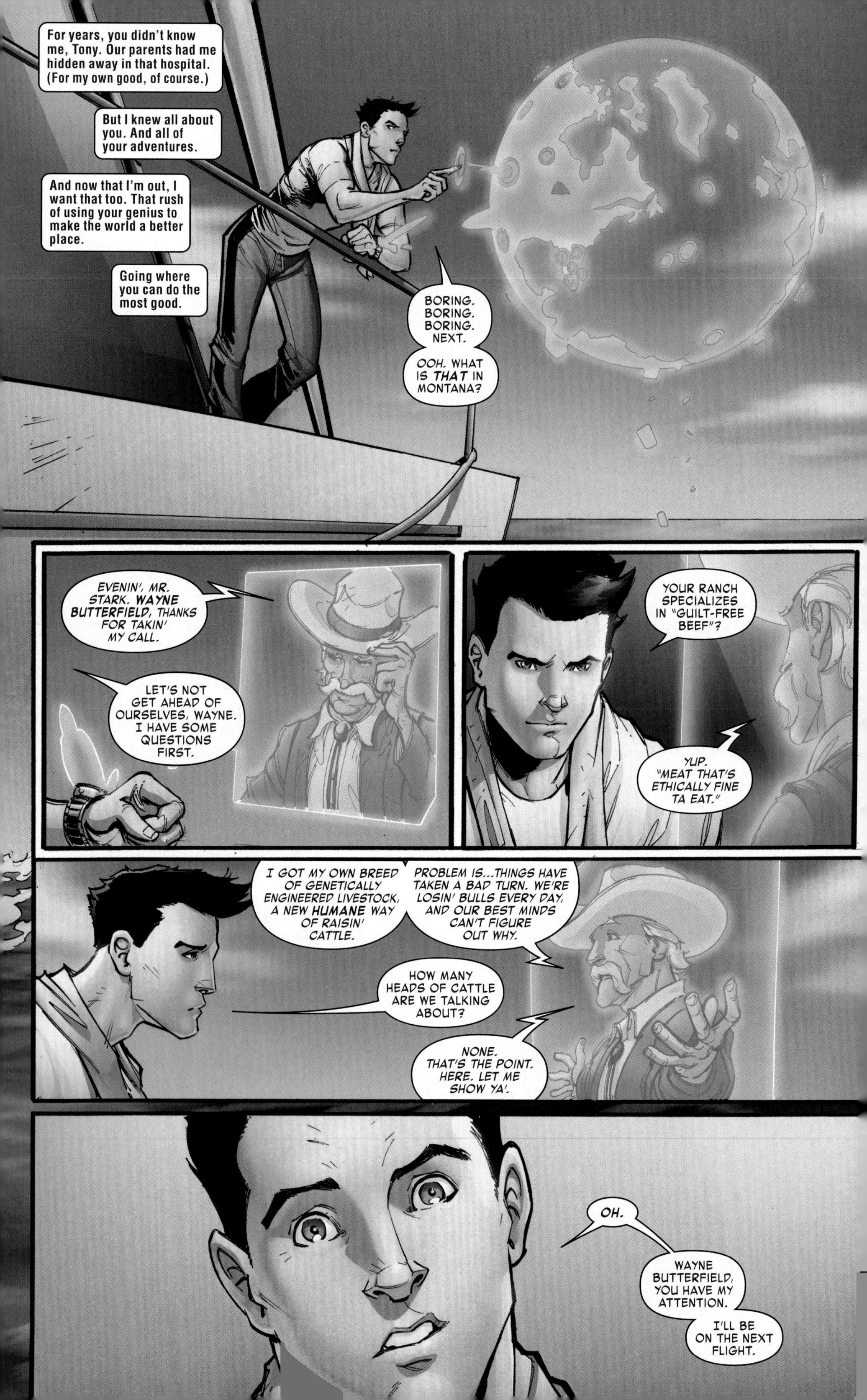
For years, you didn't know me, Tony. Our parents had me hidden away in that hospital. (For my own good, of course.)
But I knew all about you. And all of your adventures.
And now that I'm out, I want that too. That rush of using your genius to make the world a better place.
Going where you can do the most good.
BORING. BORING. BORING. NEXT.
OOH. WHAT IS THAT IN MONTANA?
EVENIN', MR. STARK. WAYNE BUTTERFIELD, THANKS FOR TAKIN' MY CALL.
LET'S NOT GET AHEAD OF OURSELVES, WAYNE. I HAVE SOME QUESTIONS FIRST.
YOUR RANCH SPECIALIZES IN "GUILT-FREE BEEF"?
YUP. "MEAT THAT'S ETHICALLY FINE TA EAT."
I GOT MY OWN BREED OF GENETICALLY ENGINEERED LIVESTOCK, A NEW HUMANE WAY OF RAISIN' CATTLE.
PROBLEM IS...THINGS HAVE TAKEN A BAD TURN. WE'RE LOSIN' BULLS EVERY DAY, AND OUR BEST MINDS CAN'T FIGURE OUT WHY.
HOW MANY HEADS OF CATTLE ARE WE TALKING ABOUT?
NONE. THAT'S THE POINT. HERE. LET ME SHOW YA'.
OH.
WAYNE BUTTERFIELD, YOU HAVE MY ATTENTION.
I'LL BE ON THE NEXT FLIGHT.

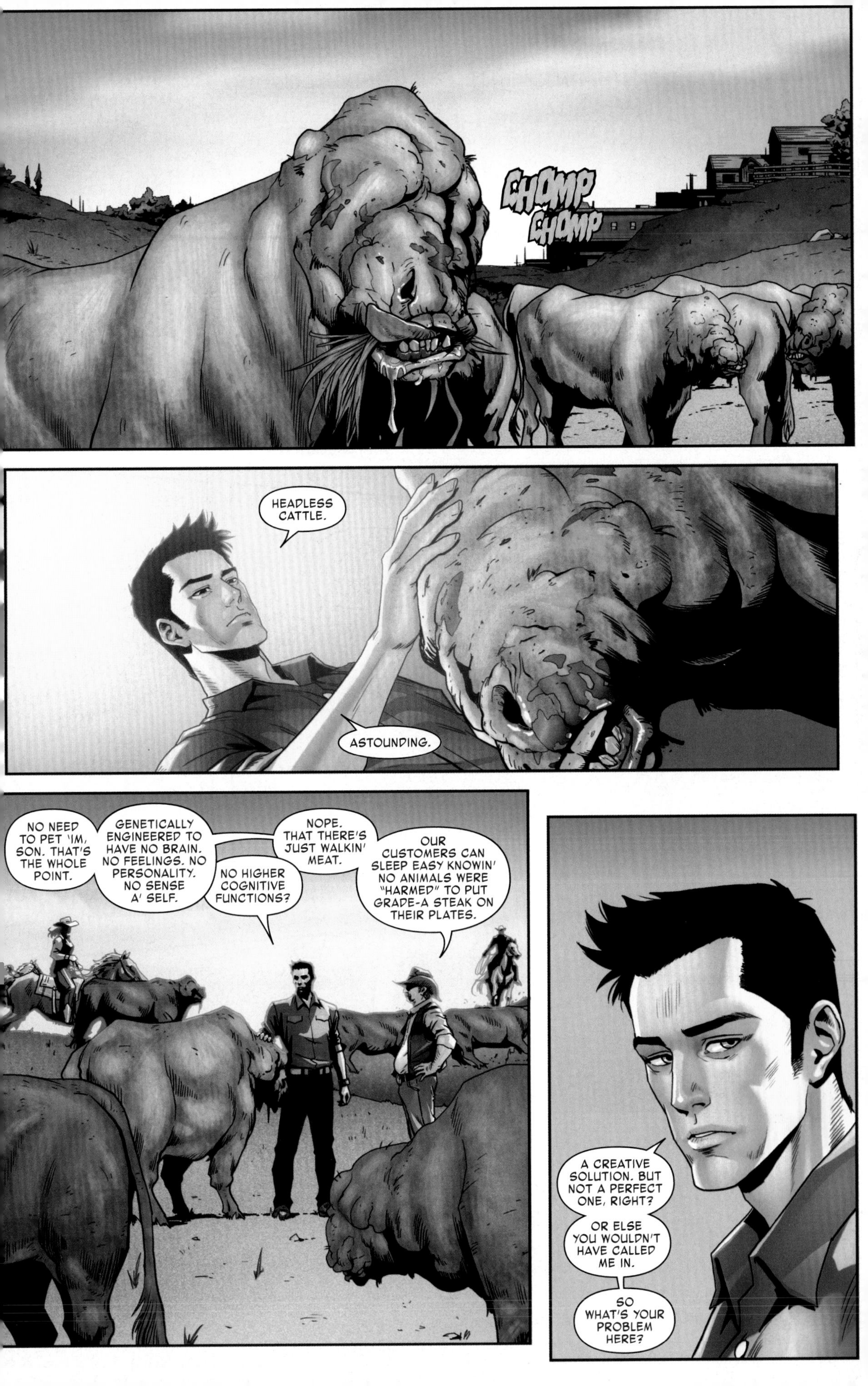
CHOMP
CHOMP
HEADLESS CATTLE.
ASTOUNDING.
NO NEED TO PET 'IM, SON. THAT'S THE WHOLE POINT.
GENETICALLY ENGINEERED TO HAVE NO BRAIN. NO FEELINGS. NO PERSONALITY. NO SENSE A' SELF.
NO HIGHER COGNITIVE FUNCTIONS?
NOPE. THAT THERE'S JUST WALKIN' MEAT.
OUR CUSTOMERS CAN SLEEP EASY KNOWIN' NO ANIMALS WERE "HARMED" TO PUT GRADE-A STEAK ON THEIR PLATES.
A CREATIVE SOLUTION. BUT NOT A PERFECT ONE, RIGHT?
OR ELSE YOU WOULDN'T HAVE CALLED ME IN.
SO WHAT'S YOUR PROBLEM HERE?

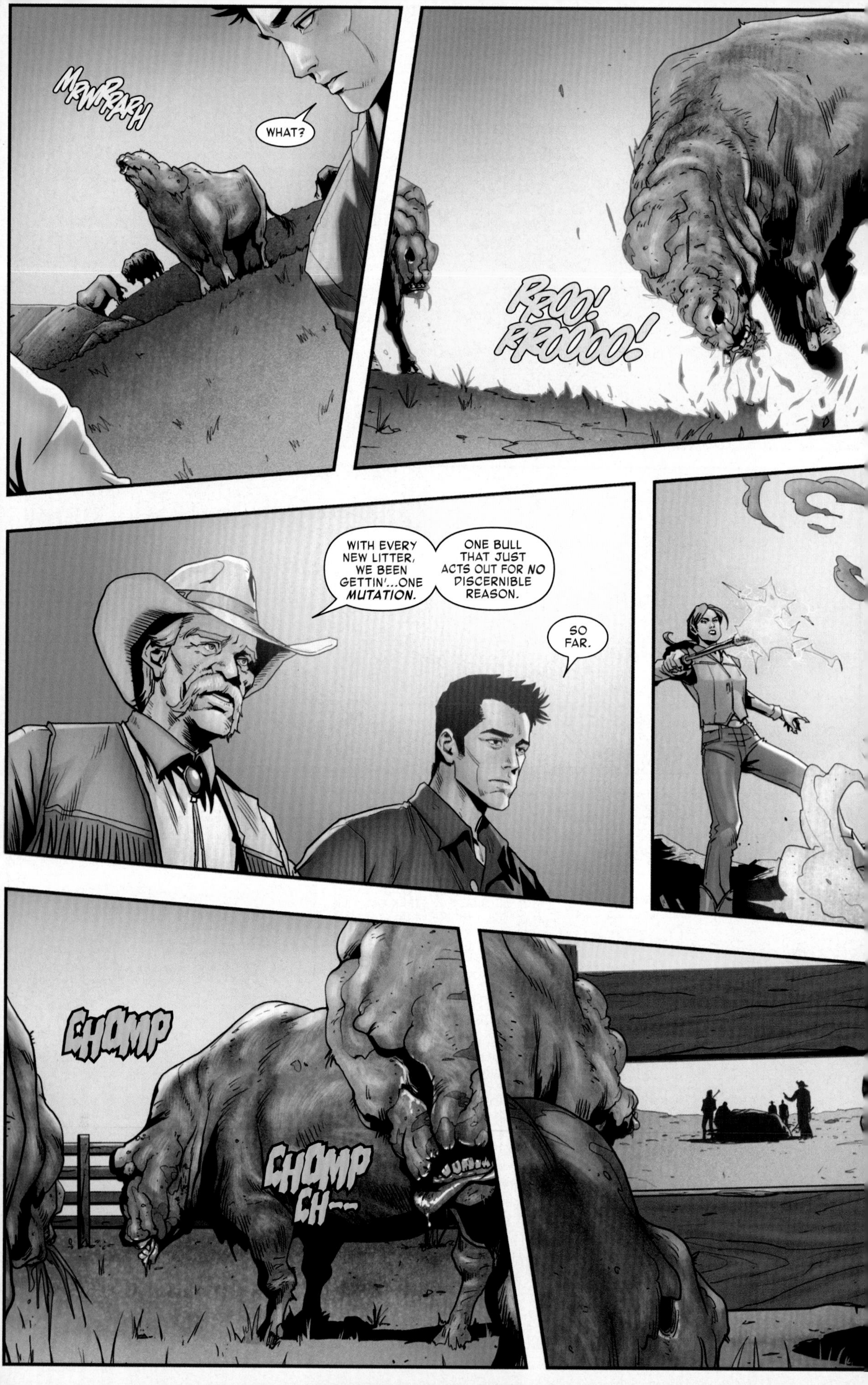
MRWRRARH
WHAT?
RROO! RROOOO!
WITH EVERY NEW LITTER, WE BEEN GETTIN'...ONE MUTATION.
ONE BULL THAT JUST ACTS OUT FOR NO DISCERNIBLE REASON.
SO FAR.
CHOMP
CHOMP
CH--

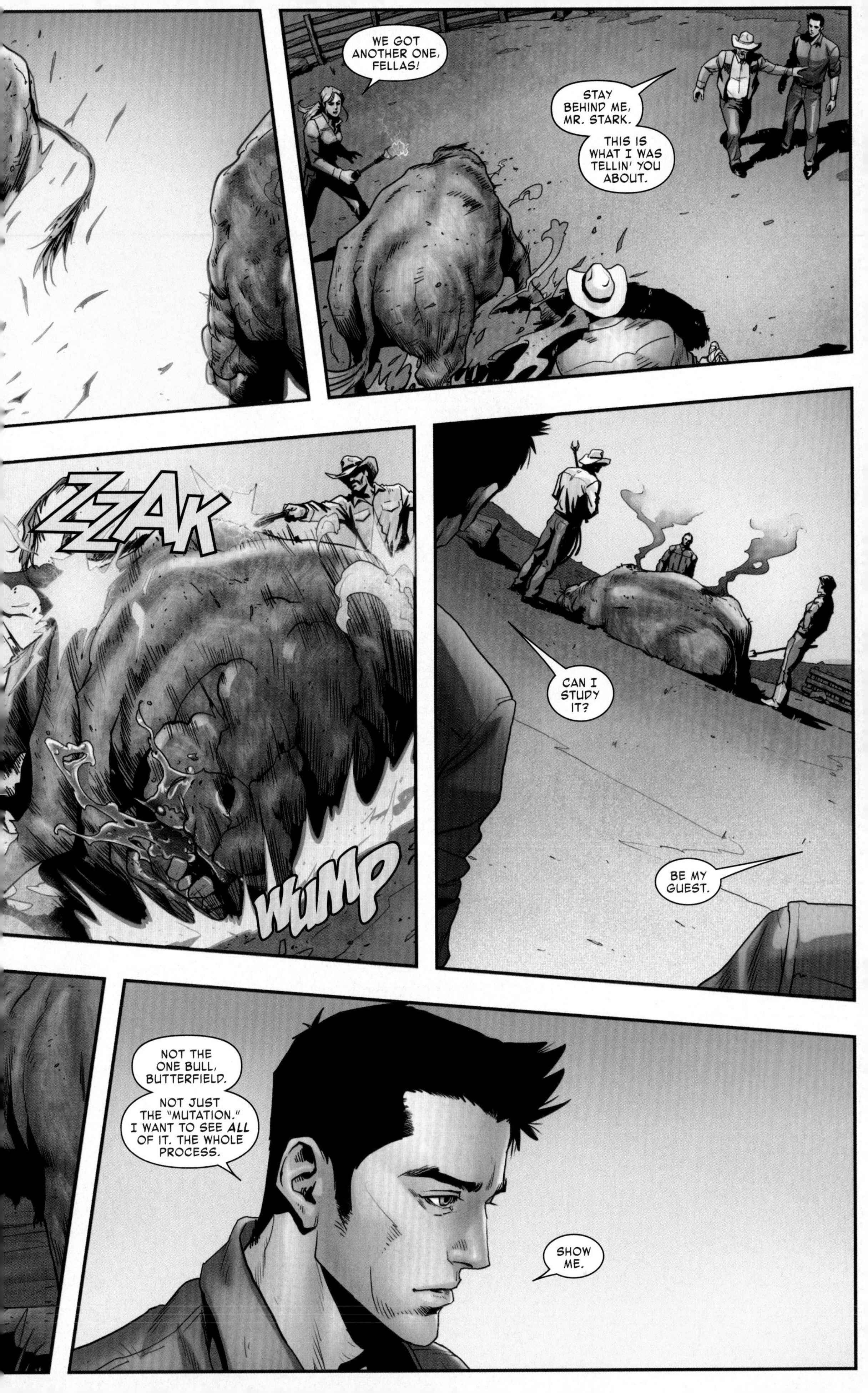
WE GOT ANOTHER ONE, FELLAS!
STAY BEHIND ME, MR. STARK.
THIS IS WHAT I WAS TELLIN' YOU ABOUT.
ZZZAK
WUMP
CAN I STUDY IT?
BE MY GUEST.
NOT THE ONE BULL, BUTTERFIELD.
NOT JUST THE "MUTATION." I WANT TO SEE *ALL* OF IT. THE WHOLE PROCESS.
SHOW ME.

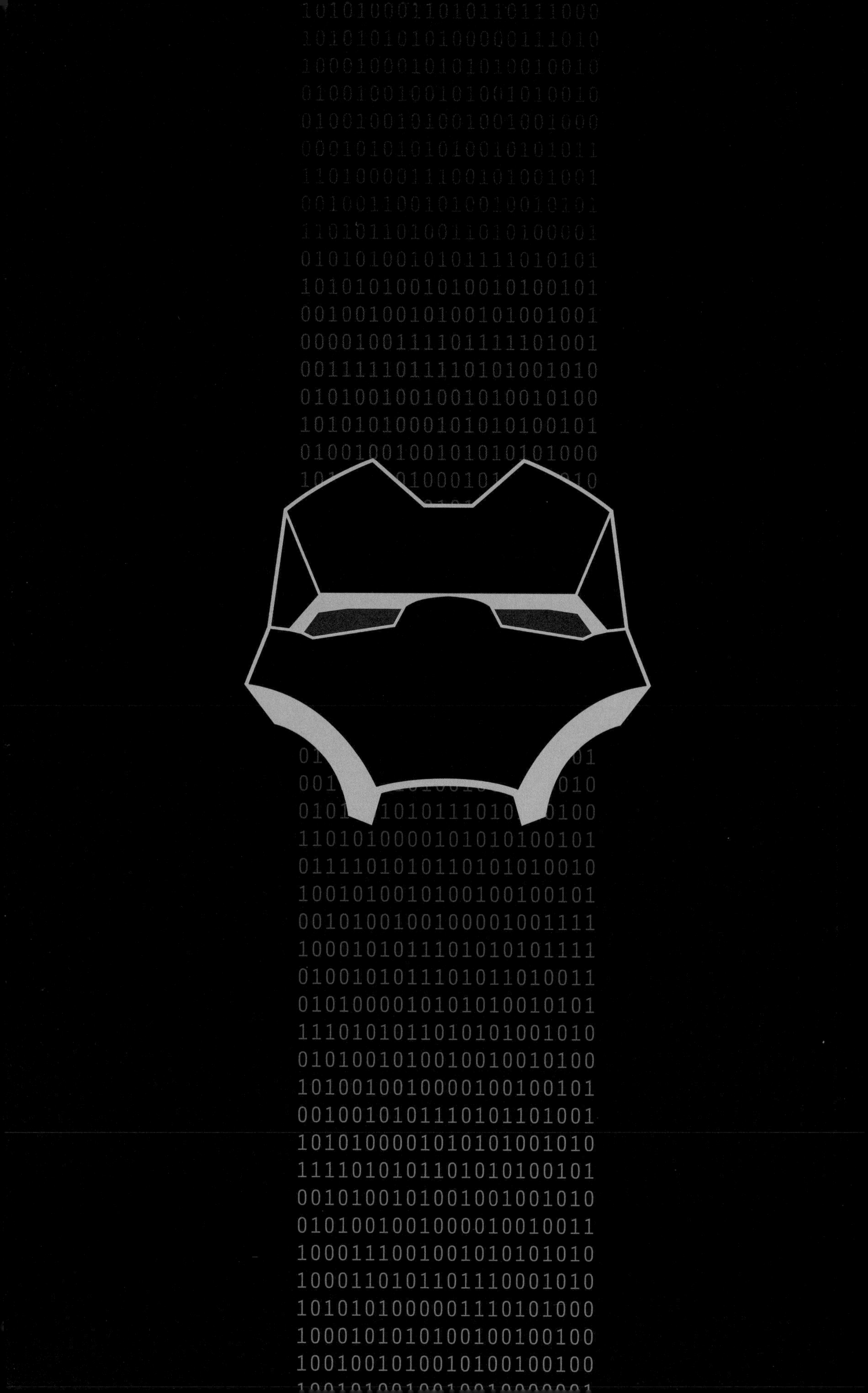

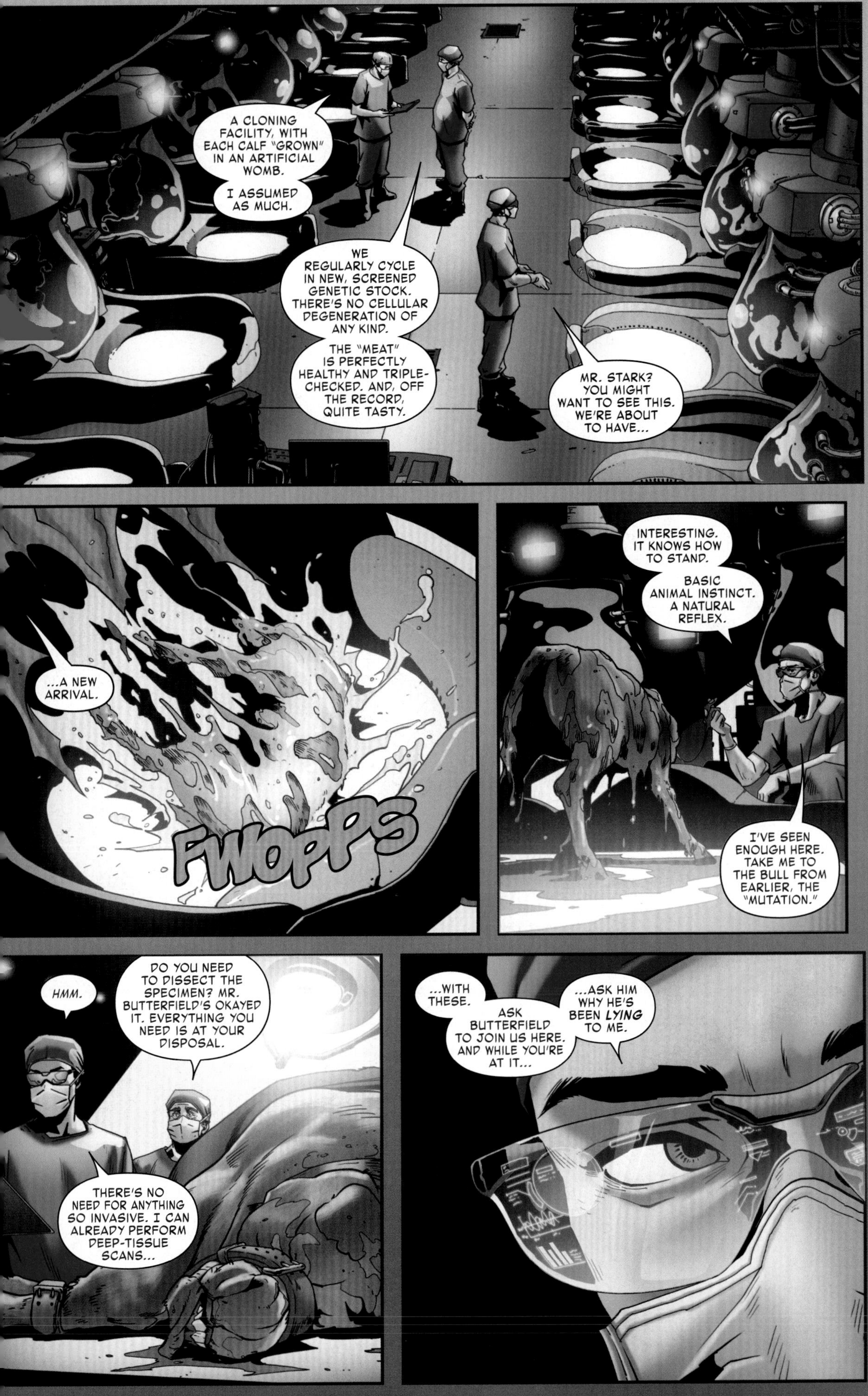

A CLONING FACILITY, WITH EACH CALF "GROWN" IN AN ARTIFICIAL WOMB.
I ASSUMED AS MUCH.
WE REGULARLY CYCLE IN NEW, SCREENED GENETIC STOCK. THERE'S NO CELLULAR DEGENERATION OF ANY KIND.
THE "MEAT" IS PERFECTLY HEALTHY AND TRIPLE-CHECKED. AND, OFF THE RECORD, QUITE TASTY.
MR. STARK? YOU MIGHT WANT TO SEE THIS. WE'RE ABOUT TO HAVE...
...A NEW ARRIVAL.
FWOPPS
INTERESTING. IT KNOWS HOW TO STAND.
BASIC ANIMAL INSTINCT. A NATURAL REFLEX.
I'VE SEEN ENOUGH HERE. TAKE ME TO THE BULL FROM EARLIER, THE "MUTATION."
HMM.
DO YOU NEED TO DISSECT THE SPECIMEN? MR. BUTTERFIELD'S OKAYED IT. EVERYTHING YOU NEED IS AT YOUR DISPOSAL.
THERE'S NO NEED FOR ANYTHING SO INVASIVE. I CAN ALREADY PERFORM DEEP-TISSUE SCANS...
...WITH THESE.
ASK BUTTERFIELD TO JOIN US HERE. AND WHILE YOU'RE AT IT...
...ASK HIM WHY HE'S BEEN *LYING* TO ME.

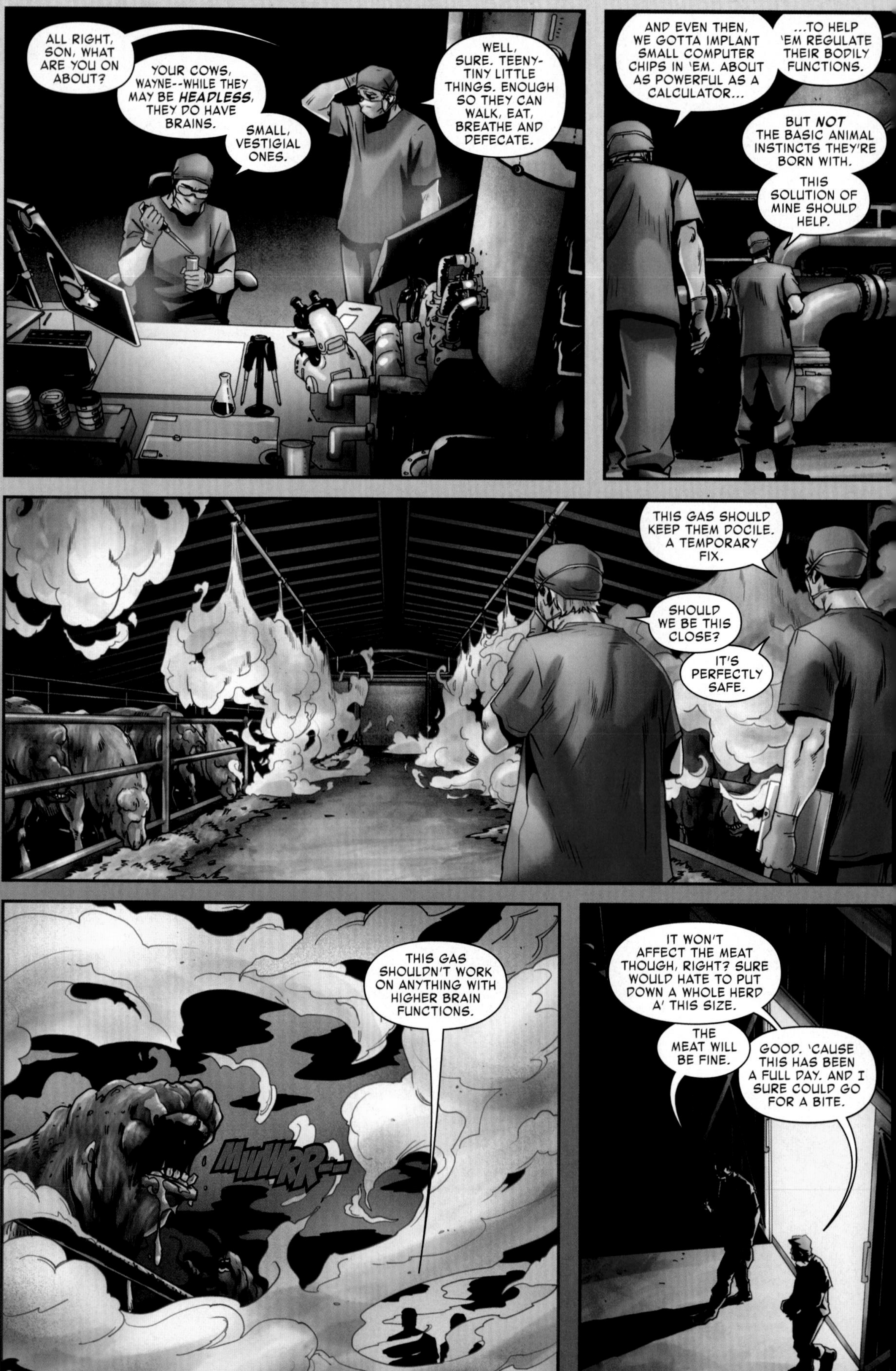
ALL RIGHT, SON, WHAT ARE YOU ON ABOUT?
YOUR COWS, WAYNE--WHILE THEY MAY BE *HEADLESS*, THEY DO HAVE BRAINS.
SMALL, VESTIGIAL ONES.
WELL, SURE. TEENY-TINY LITTLE THINGS. ENOUGH SO THEY CAN WALK, EAT, BREATHE AND DEFECATE.
AND EVEN THEN, WE GOTTA IMPLANT SMALL COMPUTER CHIPS IN 'EM. ABOUT AS POWERFUL AS A CALCULATOR...
...TO HELP 'EM REGULATE THEIR BODILY FUNCTIONS.
BUT *NOT* THE BASIC ANIMAL INSTINCTS THEY'RE BORN WITH.
THIS SOLUTION OF MINE SHOULD HELP.
THIS GAS SHOULD KEEP THEM DOCILE. A TEMPORARY FIX.
SHOULD WE BE THIS CLOSE?
IT'S PERFECTLY SAFE.
THIS GAS SHOULDN'T WORK ON ANYTHING WITH HIGHER BRAIN FUNCTIONS.
MWWRR--
IT WON'T AFFECT THE MEAT THOUGH, RIGHT? SURE WOULD HATE TO PUT DOWN A WHOLE HERD A' THIS SIZE.
THE MEAT WILL BE FINE.
GOOD. 'CAUSE THIS HAS BEEN A FULL DAY. AND I SURE COULD GO FOR A BITE.

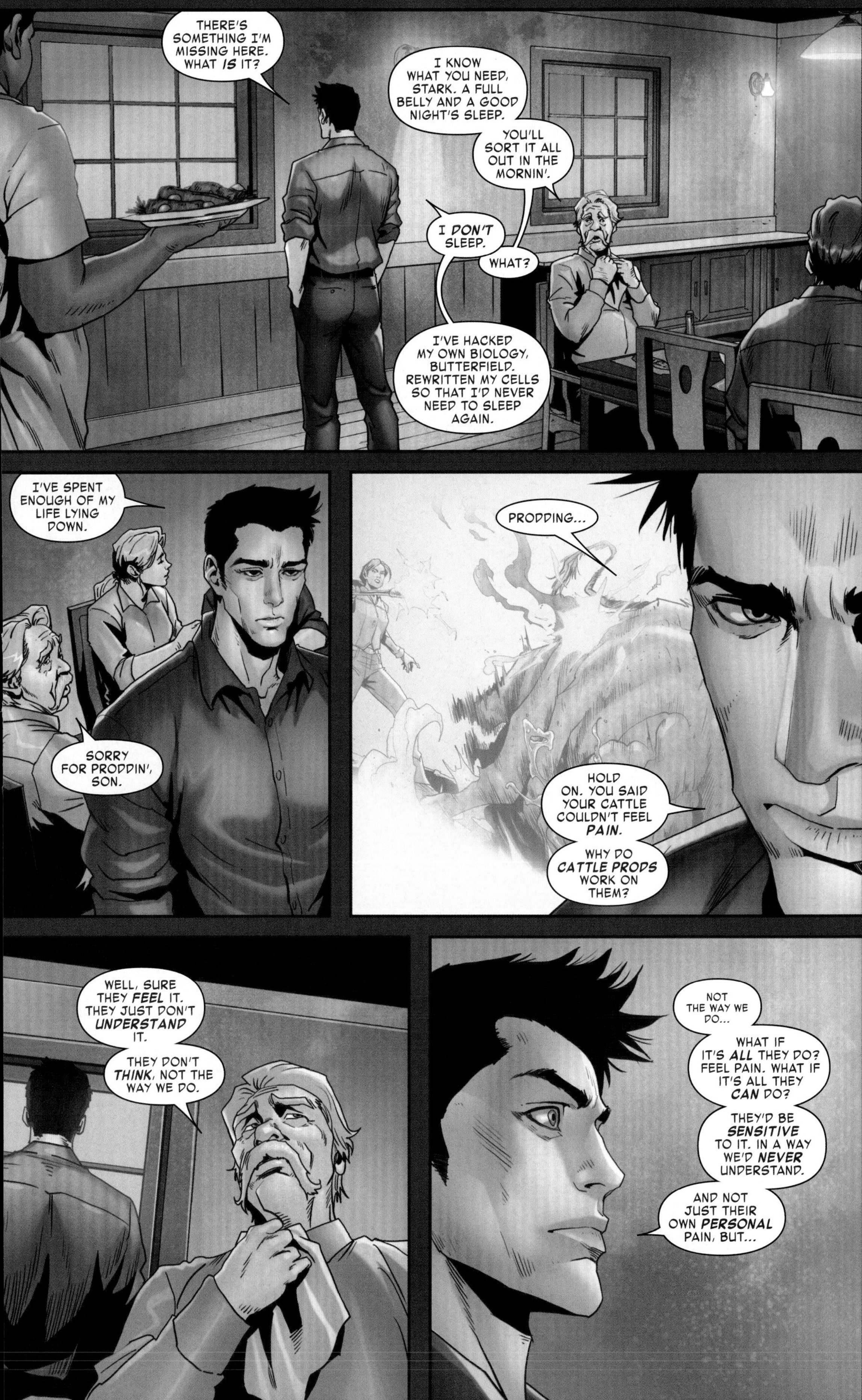

THERE'S SOMETHING I'M MISSING HERE. WHAT IS IT?
I KNOW WHAT YOU NEED, STARK. A FULL BELLY AND A GOOD NIGHT'S SLEEP.
YOU'LL SORT IT ALL OUT IN THE MORNIN'.
I DON'T SLEEP.
WHAT?
I'VE HACKED MY OWN BIOLOGY, BUTTERFIELD. REWRITTEN MY CELLS SO THAT I'D NEVER NEED TO SLEEP AGAIN.
I'VE SPENT ENOUGH OF MY LIFE LYING DOWN.
SORRY FOR PRODDIN', SON.
PRODDING...
HOLD ON. YOU SAID YOUR CATTLE COULDN'T FEEL PAIN.
WHY DO CATTLE PRODS WORK ON THEM?
WELL, SURE THEY FEEL IT. THEY JUST DON'T UNDERSTAND IT.
THEY DON'T THINK, NOT THE WAY WE DO.
NOT THE WAY WE DO...
WHAT IF IT'S ALL THEY DO? FEEL PAIN. WHAT IF IT'S ALL THEY CAN DO?
THEY'D BE SENSITIVE TO IT. IN A WAY WE'D NEVER UNDERSTAND.
AND NOT JUST THEIR OWN PERSONAL PAIN, BUT...

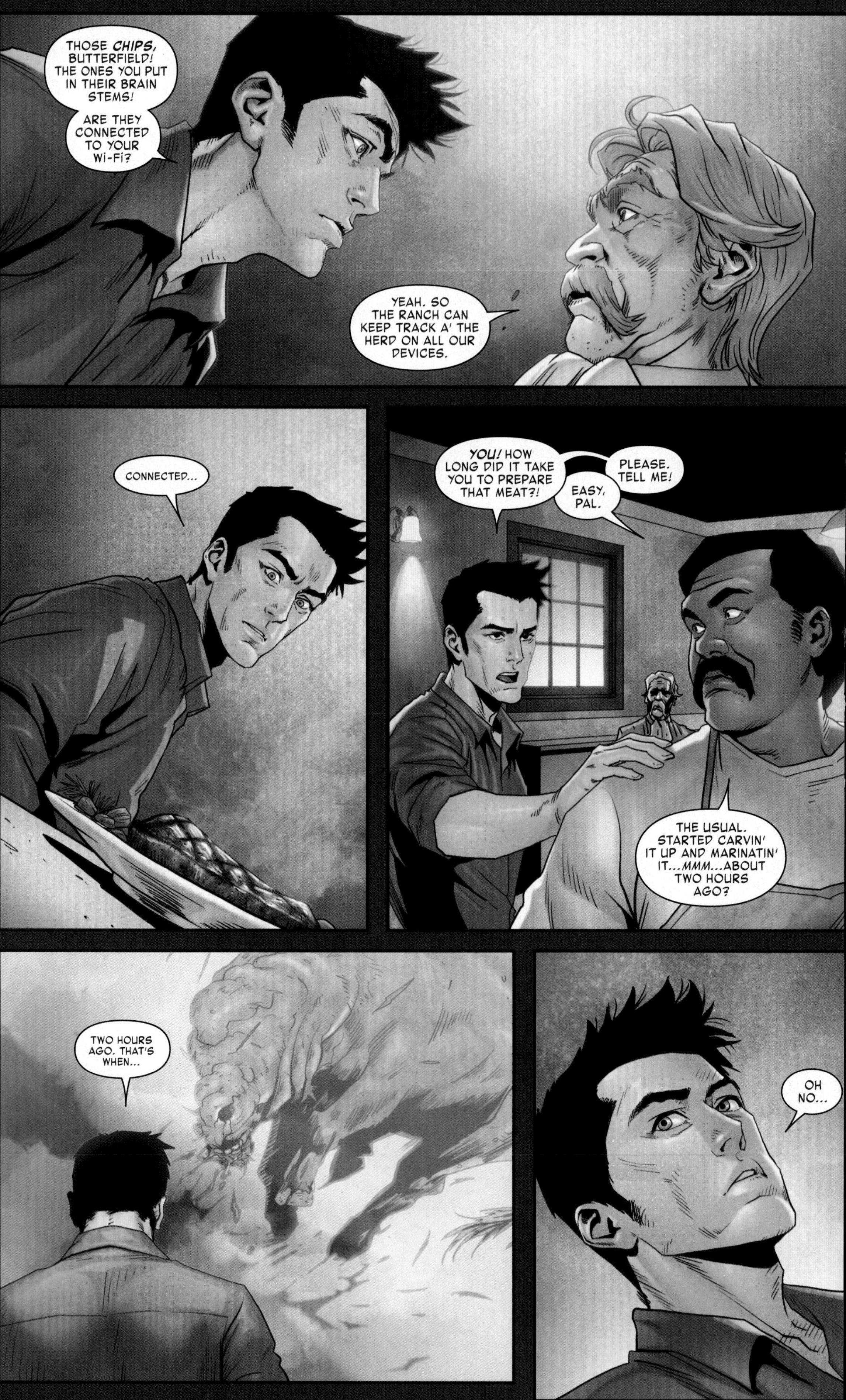
THOSE CHIPS, BUTTERFIELD! THE ONES YOU PUT IN THEIR BRAIN STEMS!
ARE THEY CONNECTED TO YOUR WI-FI?
YEAH. SO THE RANCH CAN KEEP TRACK A' THE HERD ON ALL OUR DEVICES.
CONNECTED...
YOU! HOW LONG DID IT TAKE YOU TO PREPARE THAT MEAT?!
PLEASE. TELL ME!
EASY, PAL.
THE USUAL. STARTED CARVIN' IT UP AND MARINATIN' IT...MMM...ABOUT TWO HOURS AGO?
TWO HOURS AGO. THAT'S WHEN...
OH NO...

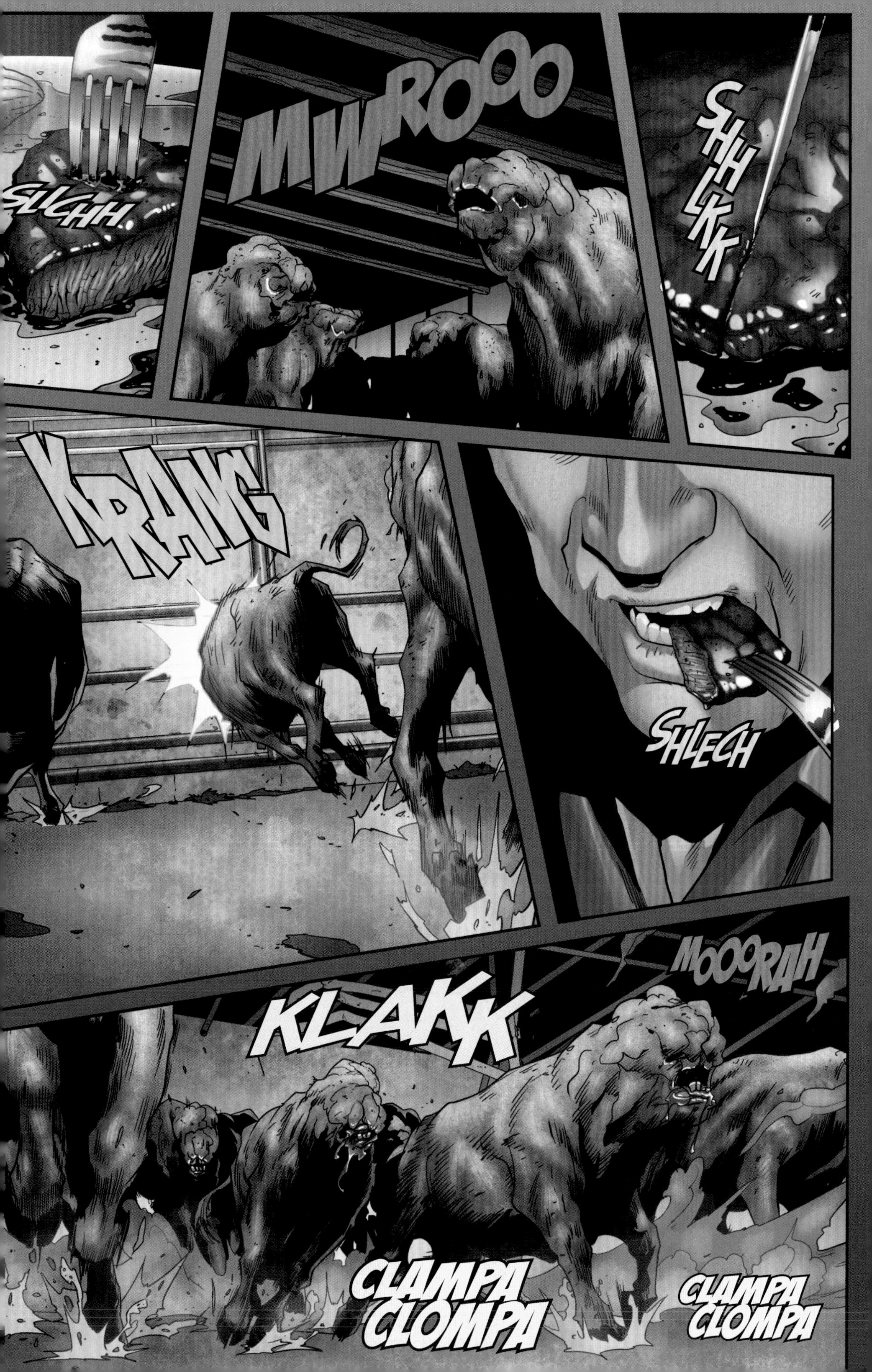
SLICHH
MWROOO
SHHLKKK
KRANG
SHLECH
MOOORAH
KLAKK
CLAMPA CLOMPA
CLAMPA CLOMPA

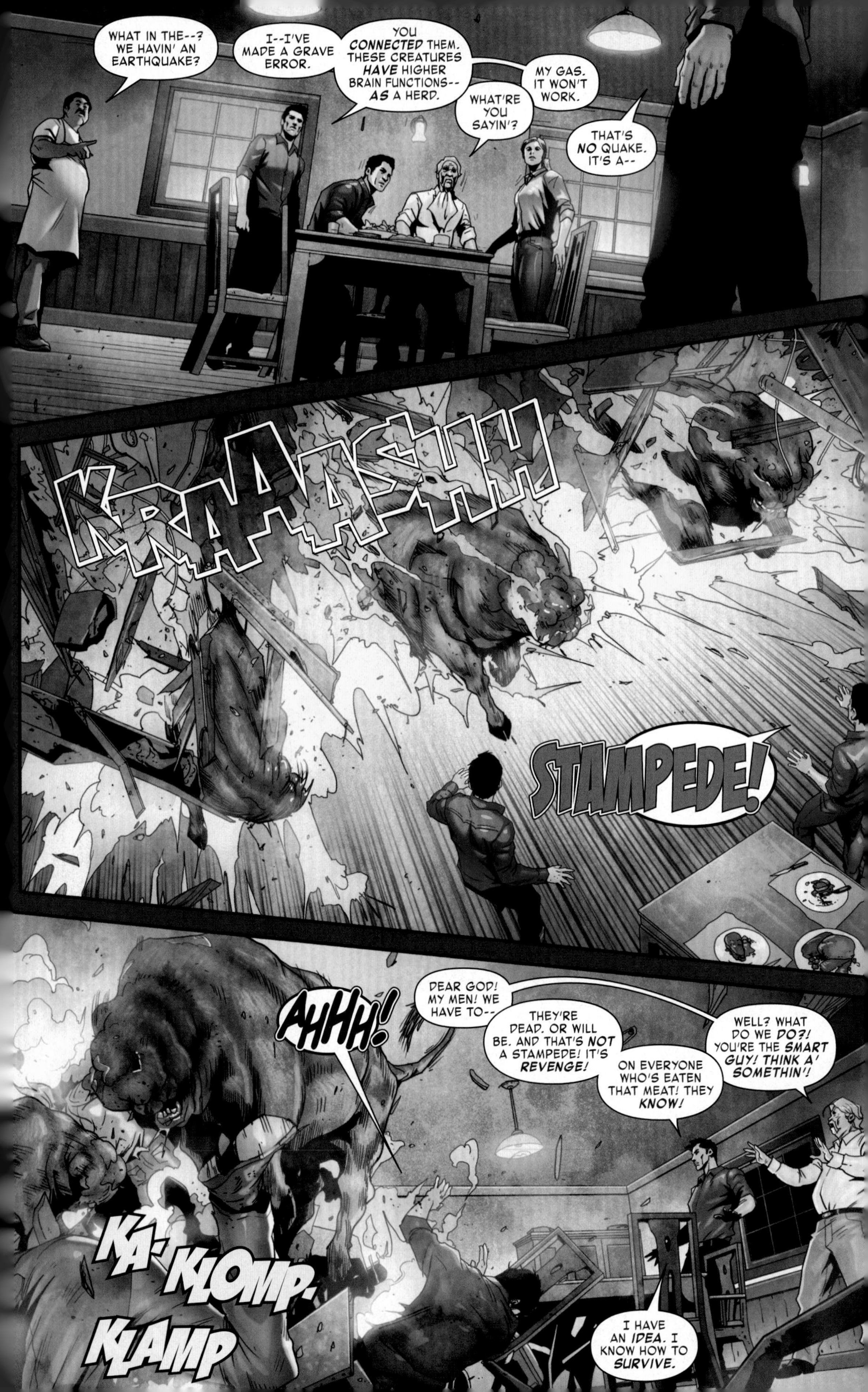
WHAT IN THE--? WE HAVIN' AN EARTHQUAKE?
I--I'VE MADE A GRAVE ERROR.
YOU CONNECTED THEM. THESE CREATURES HAVE HIGHER BRAIN FUNCTIONS-- AS A HERD.
WHAT'RE YOU SAYIN'?
MY GAS. IT WON'T WORK.
THAT'S NO QUAKE. IT'S A--
KRAAASHH
STAMPEDE!
AHHH!
DEAR GOD! MY MEN! WE HAVE TO--
THEY'RE DEAD. OR WILL BE. AND THAT'S NOT A STAMPEDE! IT'S REVENGE!
ON EVERYONE WHO'S EATEN THAT MEAT! THEY KNOW!
WELL? WHAT DO WE DO?! YOU'RE THE SMART GUY! THINK A' SOMETHIN'!
KA-KLOMP-KLAMP
I HAVE AN IDEA. I KNOW HOW TO SURVIVE.

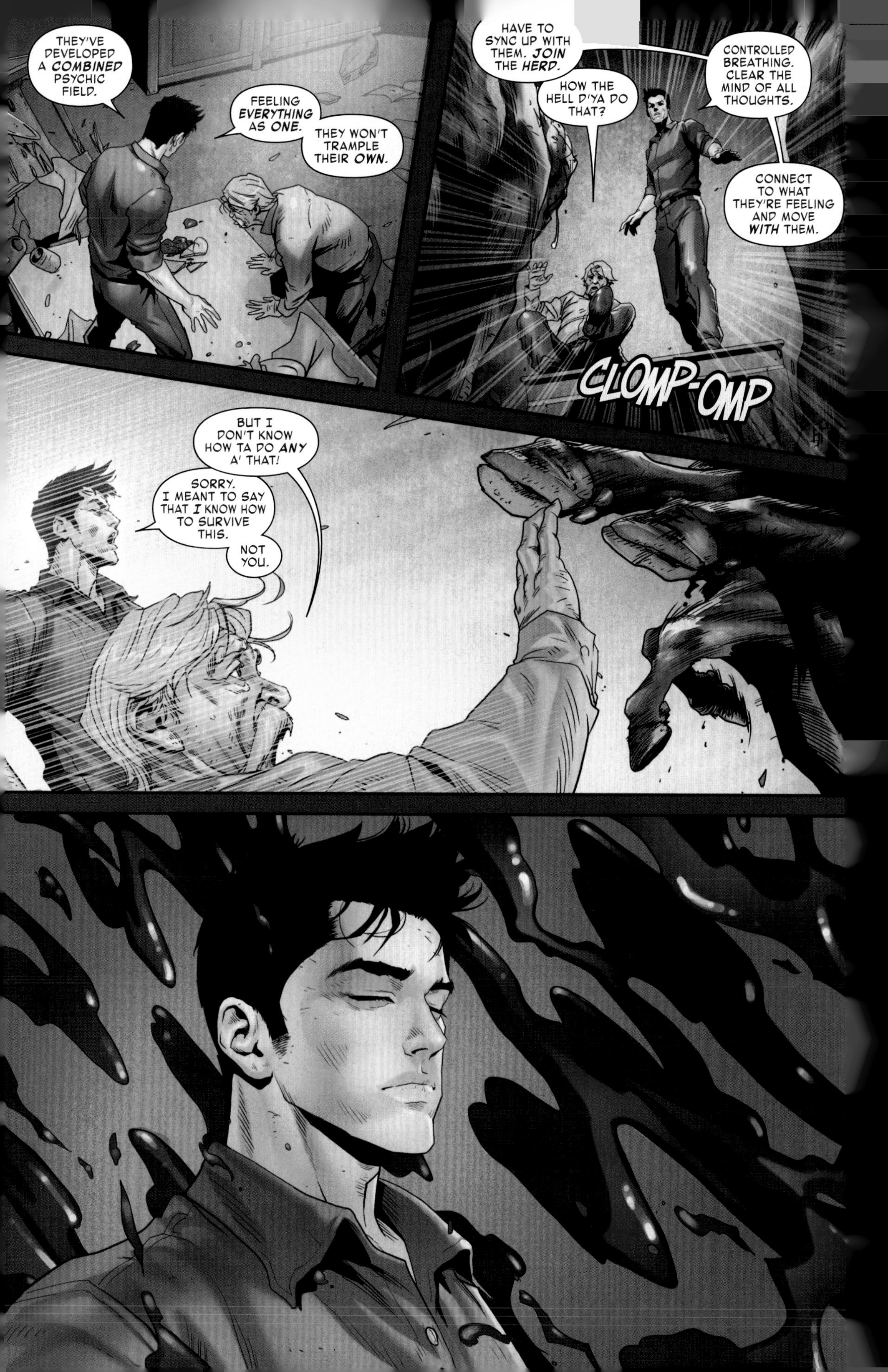
THEY'VE DEVELOPED A COMBINED PSYCHIC FIELD.
FEELING EVERYTHING AS ONE.
THEY WON'T TRAMPLE THEIR OWN.
HAVE TO SYNC UP WITH THEM. JOIN THE HERD.
HOW THE HELL D'YA DO THAT?
CONTROLLED BREATHING. CLEAR THE MIND OF ALL THOUGHTS.
CONNECT TO WHAT THEY'RE FEELING AND MOVE WITH THEM.
CLOMP-OMP
BUT I DON'T KNOW HOW TA DO ANY A' THAT!
SORRY. I MEANT TO SAY THAT I KNOW HOW TO SURVIVE THIS.
NOT YOU.

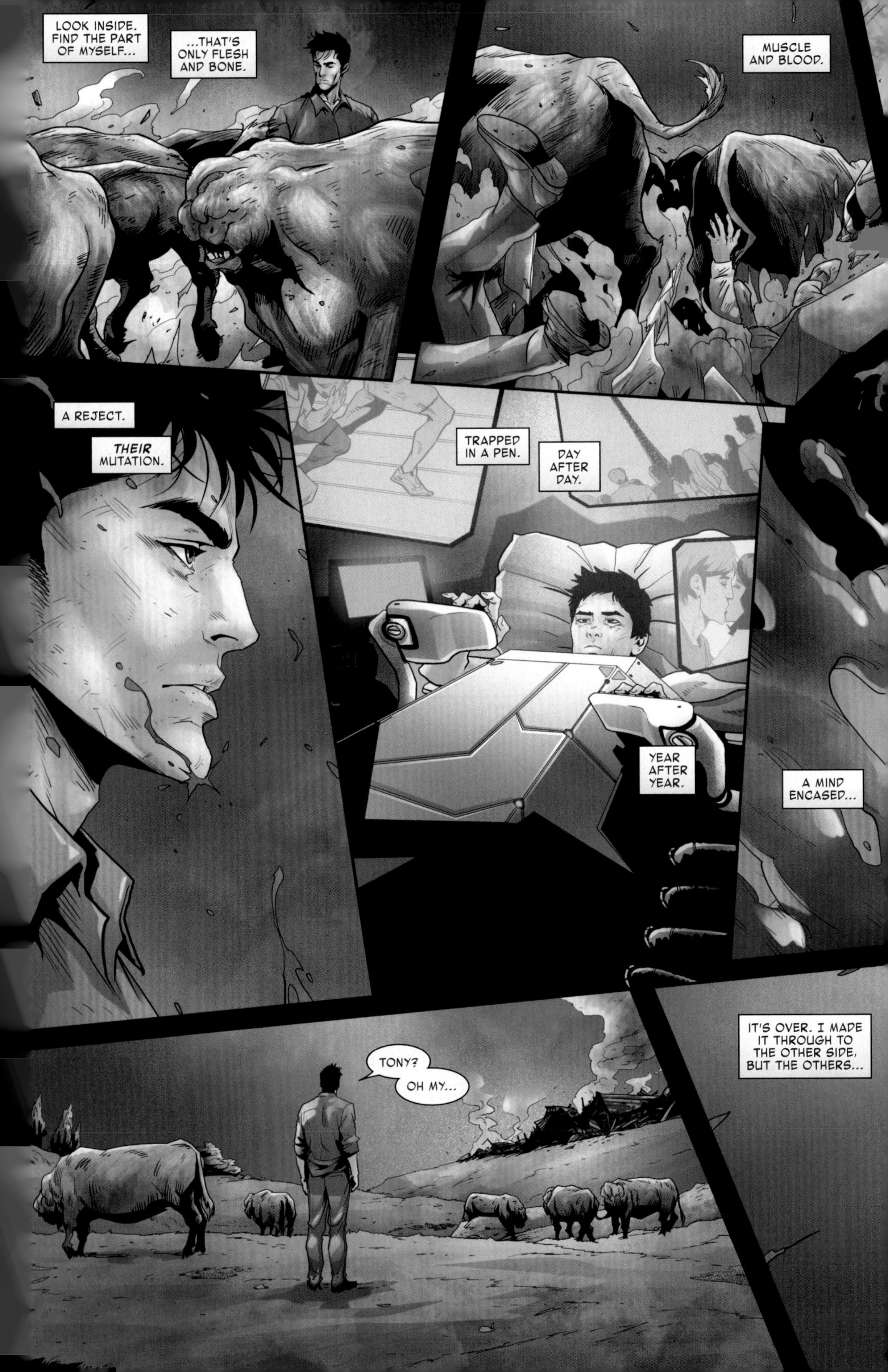
LOOK INSIDE. FIND THE PART OF MYSELF...
...THAT'S ONLY FLESH AND BONE.
MUSCLE AND BLOOD.
A REJECT.
THEIR MUTATION.
TRAPPED IN A PEN.
DAY AFTER DAY.
YEAR AFTER YEAR.
A MIND ENCASED...
TONY?
OH MY...
IT'S OVER. I MADE IT THROUGH TO THE OTHER SIDE, BUT THE OTHERS...

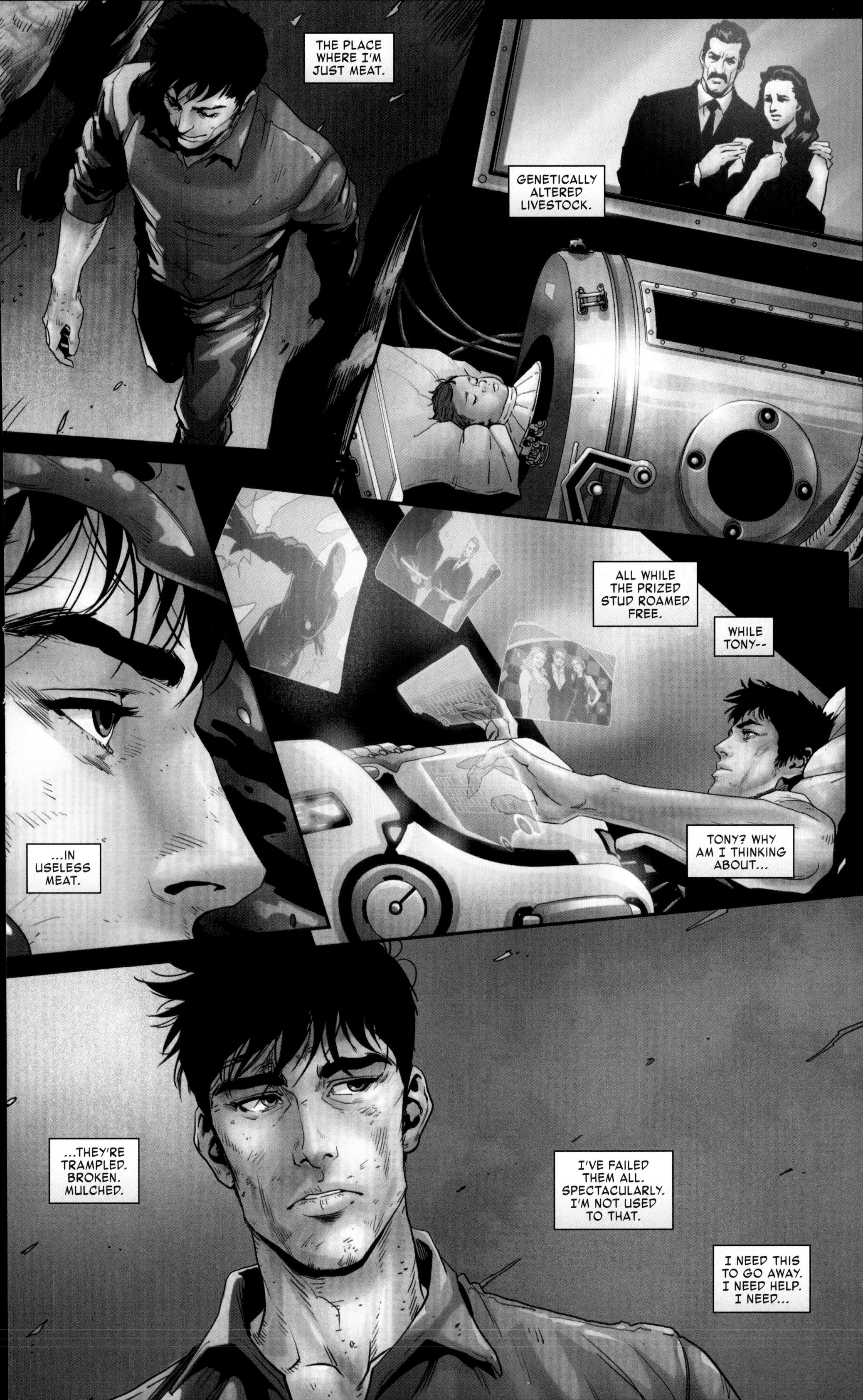
THE PLACE WHERE I'M JUST MEAT.
GENETICALLY ALTERED LIVESTOCK.
...IN USELESS MEAT.
ALL WHILE THE PRIZED STUD ROAMED FREE.
WHILE TONY--
TONY? WHY AM I THINKING ABOUT...
...THEY'RE TRAMPLED. BROKEN. MULCHED.
I'VE FAILED THEM ALL. SPECTACULARLY. I'M NOT USED TO THAT.
I NEED THIS TO GO AWAY. I NEED HELP. I NEED...

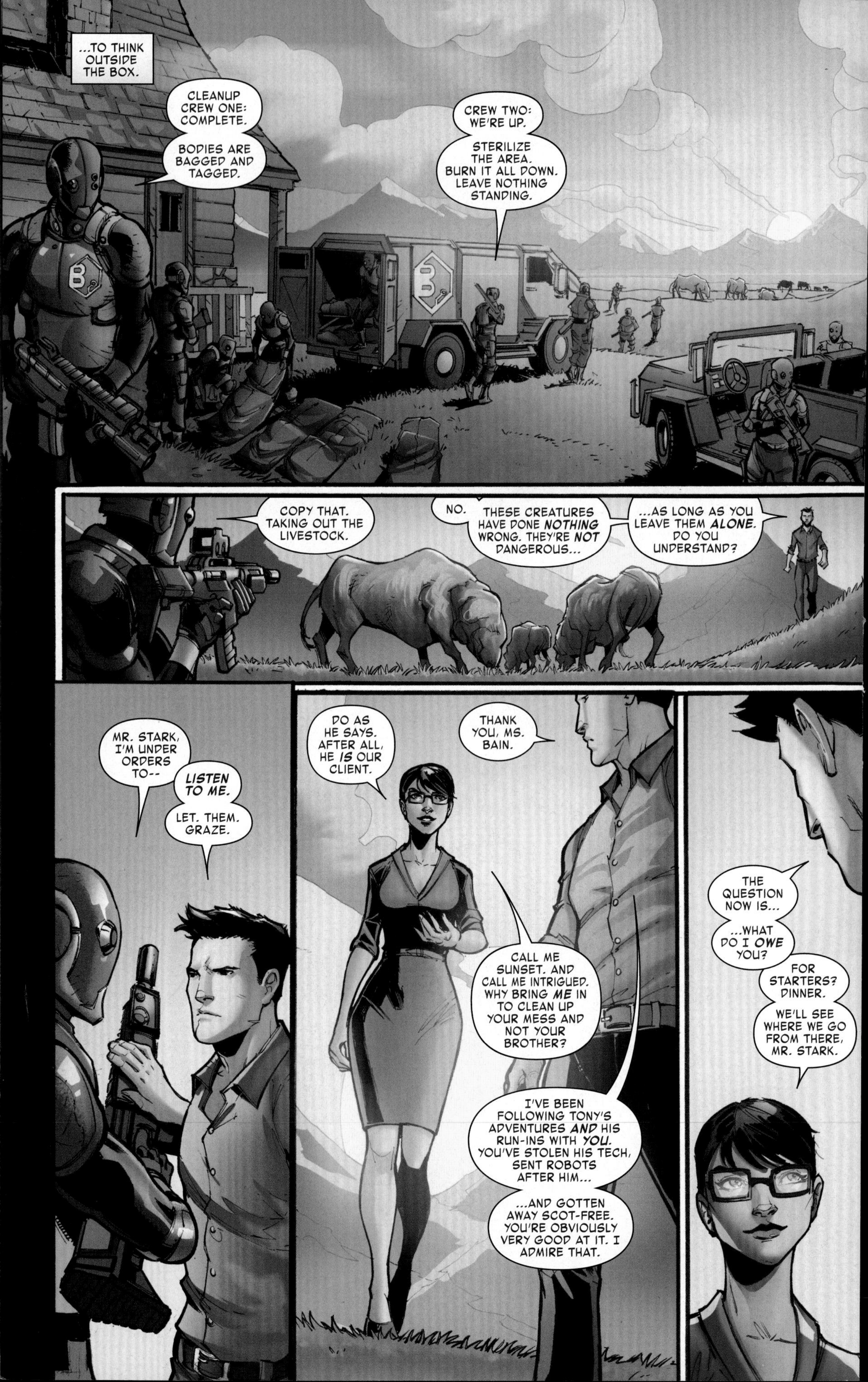
...TO THINK OUTSIDE THE BOX.
CLEANUP CREW ONE: COMPLETE.
BODIES ARE BAGGED AND TAGGED.
CREW TWO: WE'RE UP.
STERILIZE THE AREA. BURN IT ALL DOWN. LEAVE NOTHING STANDING.
COPY THAT. TAKING OUT THE LIVESTOCK.
NO.
THESE CREATURES HAVE DONE NOTHING WRONG. THEY'RE NOT DANGEROUS...
...AS LONG AS YOU LEAVE THEM ALONE. DO YOU UNDERSTAND?
MR. STARK, I'M UNDER ORDERS TO--
LISTEN TO ME.
LET. THEM. GRAZE.
DO AS HE SAYS. AFTER ALL, HE IS OUR CLIENT.
THANK YOU, MS. BAIN.
CALL ME SUNSET. AND CALL ME INTRIGUED. WHY BRING ME IN TO CLEAN UP YOUR MESS AND NOT YOUR BROTHER?
I'VE BEEN FOLLOWING TONY'S ADVENTURES AND HIS RUN-INS WITH YOU. YOU'VE STOLEN HIS TECH, SENT ROBOTS AFTER HIM...
...AND GOTTEN AWAY SCOT-FREE. YOU'RE OBVIOUSLY VERY GOOD AT IT. I ADMIRE THAT.
THE QUESTION NOW IS...
...WHAT DO I OWE YOU?
FOR STARTERS? DINNER.
WE'LL SEE WHERE WE GO FROM THERE, MR. STARK.

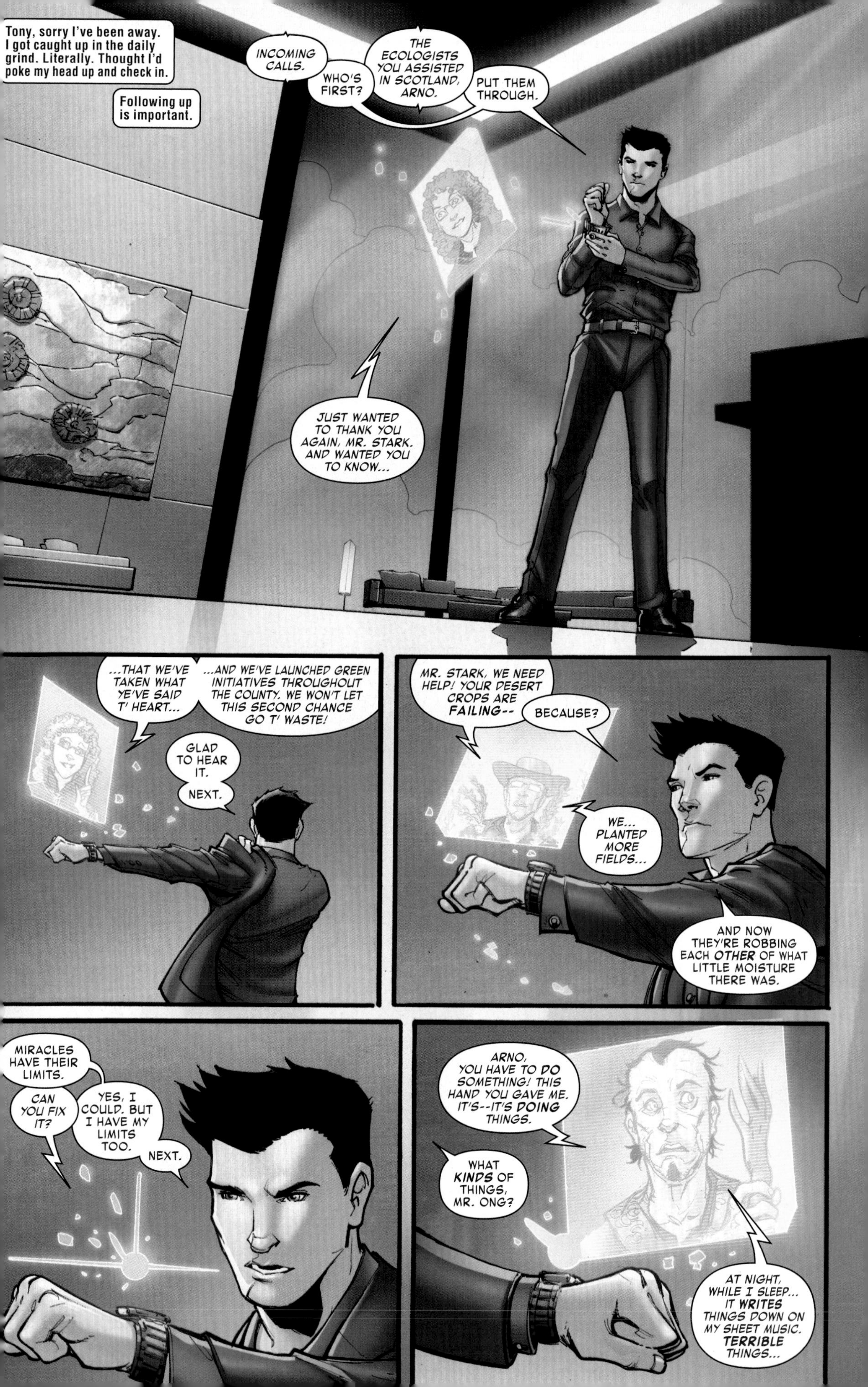

Tony, sorry I've been away. I got caught up in the daily grind. Literally. Thought I'd poke my head up and check in.
Following up is important.
INCOMING CALLS.
WHO'S FIRST?
THE ECOLOGISTS YOU ASSISTED IN SCOTLAND, ARNO.
PUT THEM THROUGH.
JUST WANTED TO THANK YOU AGAIN, MR. STARK. AND WANTED YOU TO KNOW...
...THAT WE'VE TAKEN WHAT YE'VE SAID T' HEART...
...AND WE'VE LAUNCHED GREEN INITIATIVES THROUGHOUT THE COUNTY. WE WON'T LET THIS SECOND CHANCE GO T' WASTE!
GLAD TO HEAR IT.
NEXT.
MR. STARK, WE NEED HELP! YOUR DESERT CROPS ARE **FAILING**--
BECAUSE?
WE... PLANTED MORE FIELDS...
AND NOW THEY'RE ROBBING EACH **OTHER** OF WHAT LITTLE MOISTURE THERE WAS.
MIRACLES HAVE THEIR LIMITS.
CAN YOU FIX IT?
YES, I COULD. BUT I HAVE MY LIMITS TOO.
NEXT.
ARNO, YOU HAVE TO **DO** SOMETHING! THIS HAND YOU GAVE ME. IT'S--IT'S **DOING** THINGS.
WHAT **KINDS** OF THINGS, MR. ONG?
AT NIGHT, WHILE I SLEEP... IT **WRITES** THINGS DOWN ON MY SHEET MUSIC. **TERRIBLE** THINGS...

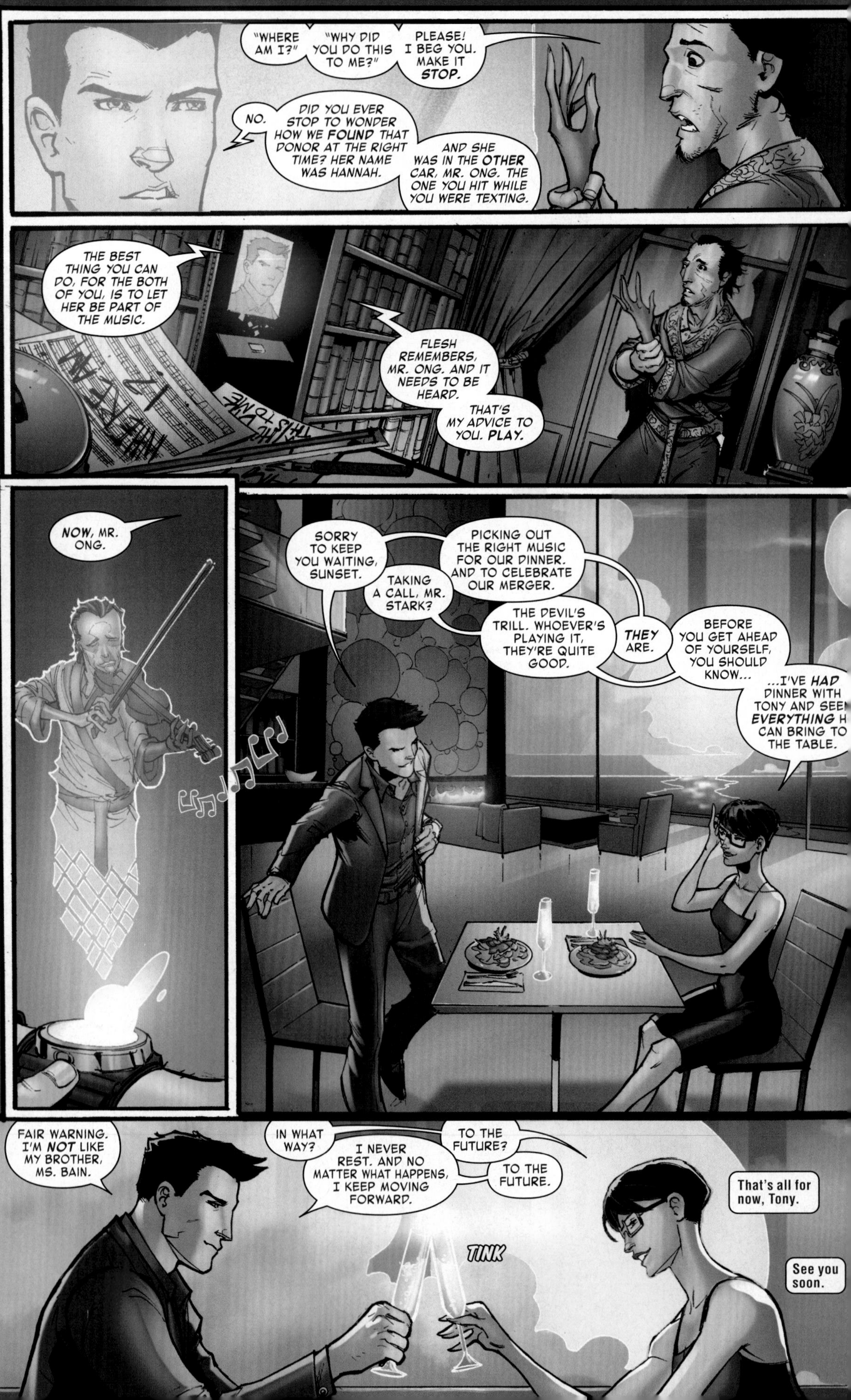
"WHERE AM I?"
"WHY DID YOU DO THIS TO ME?"
PLEASE! I BEG YOU. MAKE IT STOP.
NO.
DID YOU EVER STOP TO WONDER HOW WE FOUND THAT DONOR AT THE RIGHT TIME? HER NAME WAS HANNAH.
AND SHE WAS IN THE OTHER CAR, MR. ONG. THE ONE YOU HIT WHILE YOU WERE TEXTING.
THE BEST THING YOU CAN DO, FOR THE BOTH OF YOU, IS TO LET HER BE PART OF THE MUSIC.
FLESH REMEMBERS, MR. ONG. AND IT NEEDS TO BE HEARD.
THAT'S MY ADVICE TO YOU. PLAY.
NOW, MR. ONG.
SORRY TO KEEP YOU WAITING, SUNSET.
TAKING A CALL, MR. STARK?
PICKING OUT THE RIGHT MUSIC FOR OUR DINNER. AND TO CELEBRATE OUR MERGER.
THE DEVIL'S TRILL. WHOEVER'S PLAYING IT, THEY'RE QUITE GOOD.
THEY ARE.
BEFORE YOU GET AHEAD OF YOURSELF, YOU SHOULD KNOW...
...I'VE HAD DINNER WITH TONY AND SEEN EVERYTHING HE CAN BRING TO THE TABLE.
FAIR WARNING. I'M NOT LIKE MY BROTHER, MS. BAIN.
IN WHAT WAY?
I NEVER REST. AND NO MATTER WHAT HAPPENS, I KEEP MOVING FORWARD.
TO THE FUTURE?
TO THE FUTURE.
TINK
That's all for now, Tony.
See you soon.

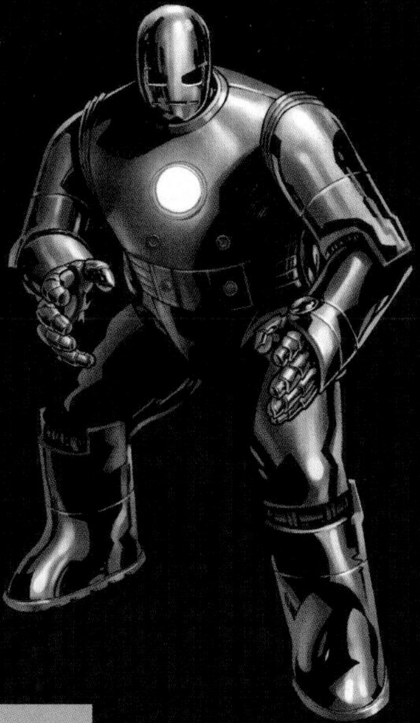

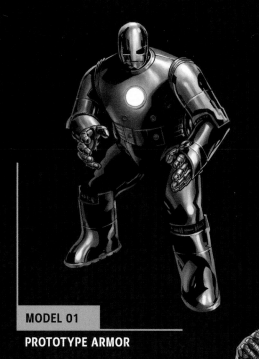

MODEL 01

PROTOTYPE ARMOR

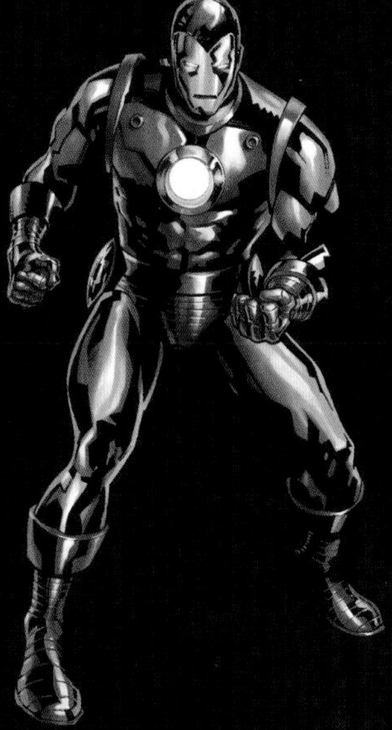

MODEL 04

CLASSIC RED-AND-GOLD ARMOR

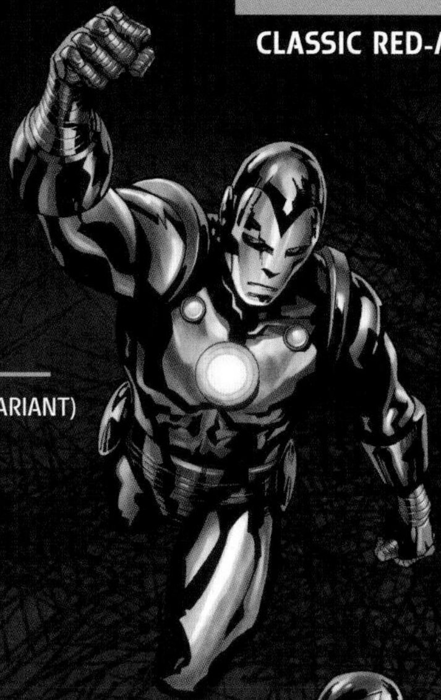

MODEL 04A

RED-AND-GOLD ARMOR (VARIANT)

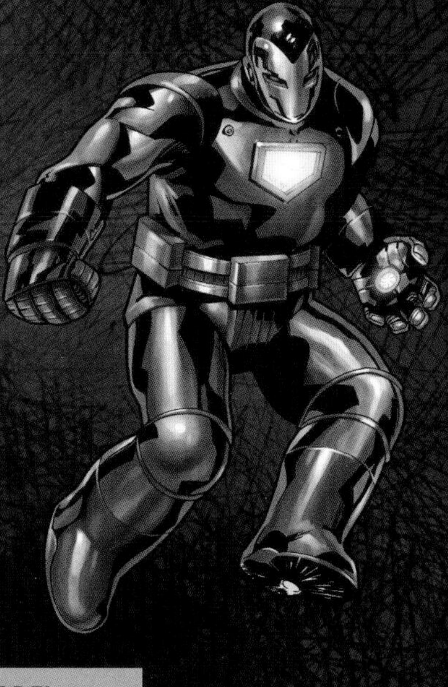

MODEL 05

CLASSIC SPACE ARMOR

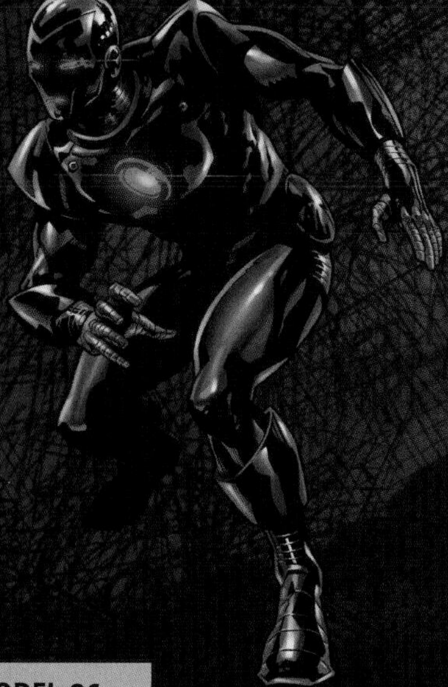

MODEL 06

STEALTH ARMOR

#1 ARMOR VARIANTS BY **VALERIO SCHITI & EBER EVANGELISTA**

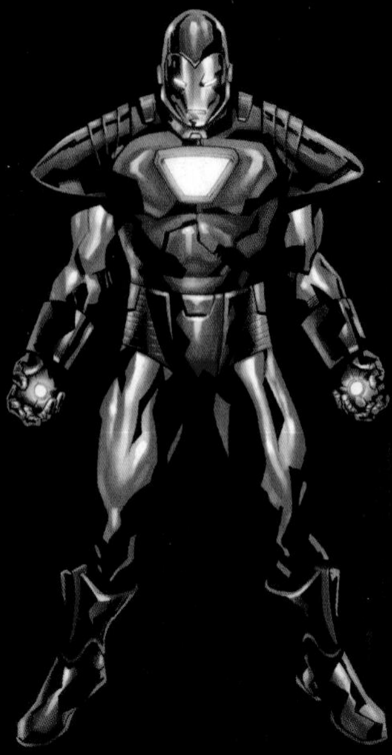

MODEL 07

SILVER CENTURION

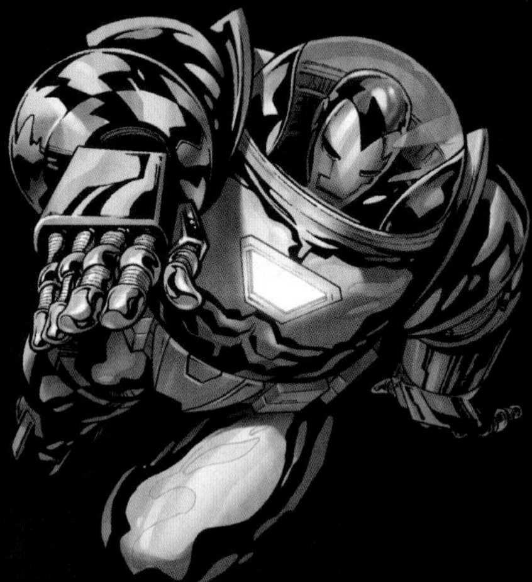

MODEL 08

UNDERSEA ARMOR

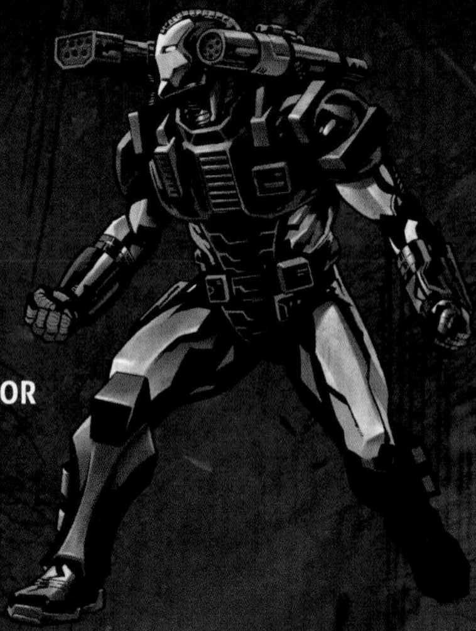

MODEL 11

PROTOTYPE WAR MACHINE ARMOR

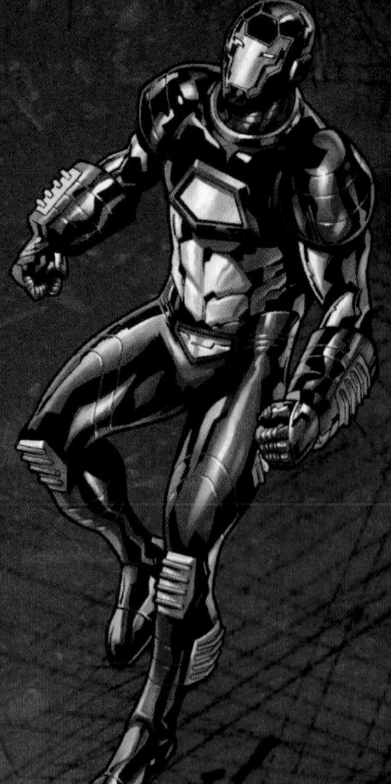

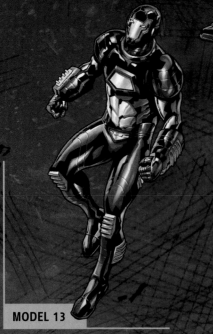

MODEL 13

MODULAR ARMOR

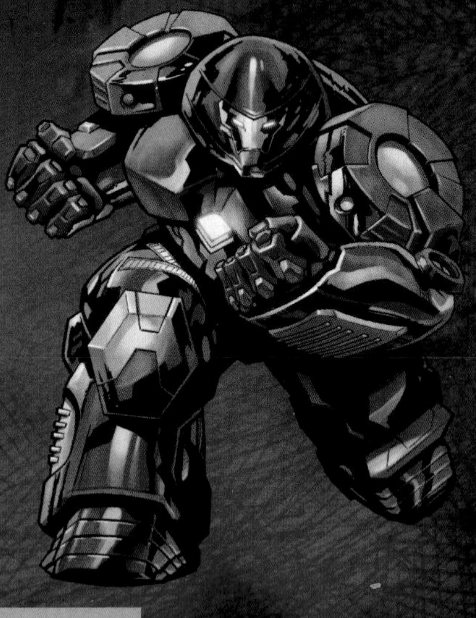

MODEL 14

HULKBUSTER ARMOR